Huntsville – Madison County Historical Society

The Huntsville Historical Bicentennial Review

Volume III

The Huntsville Historical
Bicentennial Review
Volume III

Madison County 1861-1865:
The War Years
Alabama at 200

Presented by the

Huntsville–Madison County
Historical Society

Dedication

Dedicated to the earliest settlers in Madison County, both known and unknown.

Cover photo by David Hitt
First Printing

President's Letter

There are, without question, cities that bear much more deeply the scars of the War Between the States, or that display those wounds much more prominently.

A visitor or newcomer to Huntsville might miss entirely any signs that the not-so-Recent Unpleasantness had touched the Rocket City at all. But look closely, and you see the evidence of the Union occupation of Huntsville and how it played out.

The story is written both in where that time left its mark - if you haven't, visit the third floor of the Depot museum and see where soldiers of both sides left their mark in a literal sense on the graffitied walls. And it's written in where it didn't' - an unusually large collection of antebellum homes for a Southern city captured by the Union bears testimony to our story being a little different than some.

But make no mistake, beneath the modern veneer of the today's Huntsville, there is a much smaller Alabama town that experienced occupation and came out of the war shaped by the experience.

One could argue that there is a tinge of irony to the fact that today's Huntsville is very much colored by the presence of the United States Army as well; almost a half century after that same army occupied Huntsville, the Redstone Arsenal made Huntsville what it is today.

This volume captures the largely forgotten history of those 19ths century occupations; a glimpse in to a Huntsville that is for many unknown.

David Hitt
President, HMCHS

TABLE OF CONTENTS

RECOLLECTIONS OF HUNTSVILLE DURING THE OCCUPATION OF 1862

By Bessie Russell

On April 13, 1862, Federal forces under the command of Brigadier General Ormsby McKnight Mitchel captured Huntsville and cut the important railway line of the Memphis and Charleston Railroad. For the visionary Mitchel, who had distinguished himself as an astronomer before the war, this accomplishment hopefully meant the quick capture of Chattanooga and East Tennessee. With that vast territory under Federal control Mitchel felt that Union armies could move in any direction they wished, threatening the Confederate rear in Virginia or marching southward into Georgia.

The Federal command did not accept this plan and left Mitchel in Huntsville as commander of the occupying army. This, of course, was not what he wanted and he chaffed bitterly over the assignment. Various accounts tell of the harsh manner with which he dealt with the populace. Probably he was venting his frustration with his superiors on the defenseless citizenry, who saw in him the epitome of Federal power and dominance, reaping dissolution in the wake of its control.

One such individual who witnessed General Mitchel's plight during this period was Miss Rowena Webster, who came to Huntsville from Beechwood, Tennessee, to escape from approaching Federal armies who had captured Fort Donelson in February, 1862. Her respite from the turmoil of war was short-lived, however, with the arrival of Mitchel's troops. In her later years Miss Webster recorded some of the highlights of the occupation. They offer an interesting insight into conditions in Huntsville at that time. The account, printed here in part, opens with the fall of Fort Donelson.

What is all the commotion? Church bells ringing! Soldiers moving rapidly to and fro! Women and children leaving the various churches on the Sabbath morning! People running here and there, seeking a place of safety - a place to flee! DONELSON HAS FALLEN - DONELSON HAS FALLEN! Who brings the news? Says one, and another, and another! No mistake, Oh, where is my father? Cries one, and where is my brother? And where is my husband? No tidings of any, as yet. Oh, this dreadful suspense! All may be either wounded or dead. Soldiers rushing to the Chattanooga Depot to join their command. Women and children fleeing to some place of refuge, crowding all of the trains that are leaving the City. Some going to one place and some to another. Many reaching the home of Mrs. Andrew Erwin of Beechwood, Tennessee. They find her doors wide open always to the Confederate soldiers, their sick and wounded, and her servants and provisions placed lavishly at their command, like Florence Nightingale who never wearied in her attentions - applying medicines and remedies for their relief.

What Tennessee soldier does not remember her kindness? Many, very many, under the sod, if able to speak would rise up and call her "Blessed." She was a noted monument among the living and will always be a precious memory to her many friends. While she was a rare exception, there were thousands of noble women who gave all they had to our Confederate soldiers for their comfort and relief. Grandly, nobly and beautifully did our women perform their part in this great sacrifice for their Sunny South. Many of the wounded arrived at Mrs. Erwin's home and were kindly nursed and cared for until they were ready to again join their command. Every attention was given them by the army physicians, some died and others soon restored. In the meantime, the Federals began to move in. The house was soon searched for soldiers and all of the provisions on hand used - nothing was ever left in their wake that they could possibly consume or destroy. Some officers of the Federal Army would protect our property, while the majority would encourage their soldiers to commit every depredation in their reach. Mrs. Erwin had many an altercation with them, but in a most ladylike way stood firmly to her principles.

It soon became necessary for the young ladies of the household to refugee to places south of the army. After having been in Huntsville a few days, the Federals came like a cyclone into the City. While I and my youngest niece (Miss Rosa Turner) were staying with friends (Mr. and Mrs. Matthews), Miss Turner was placed in school. I never received such a shock as when a servant girl at daylight proclaimed, "Miss Rowe, the turnpike is black with the Yankees - I can hear them a mile off." While I never was the least afraid of them, I was startled beyond measure. I looked out of the window and discovered that they had come to stay. Men, women and children were panic stricken, altho none ever showed the least fear of them. Every woman in the City was aiding Confederate Soldiers to escape, even disguising some of them in female attire. Soon they had all escaped. One of the first who was captured was a brother of General John H. Morgan. I said to the officer who held him captive, "I hope you will be kind to him." He replied, "I will." Soon Gen'l M[itchel], of Astronomy fame, Federal Commander, had possession of the City. A greater tyrant never lived in revolutionary times! An Ohio Regiment was encamped on Popes Hill, near us. They would pass every day to water their horses at the famous Big Spring of Huntsville. One of them chanced to see Miss Sallie Matthews and Miss Rosa Turner, playing with grace hoops wrapped with red, white and blue. The soldiers were quite amused until they saw a tiny Confederate Flag attached to my arm. Altho it was simply hanging on my arm, one ordinary soldier, without any authority, rushed in the yard, saying, "Miss, I want that flag." I replied, "You haven't the bravery to capture one on a battle field, but ask for a baby flag from a woman?" He replied, "If you don't give me that flag, I will put a case of smallpox in this house and one in the house opposite." I said, "Bring your smallpox case, I am not afraid of you, nor your smallpox," and

I immediately tore up the flag, placing it in my pocket, and threw the hoop into a reservoir at the foot of the hill, saying, "If you are a good diver, you can get that hoop." In the meantime, the Captain came up with his Company and saw me destroy the flag and put it into my pocket, saying, "You shall not have this flag." He informed the Officer, and the next day Mr. Matthews, his daughter Sallie, Rosa Turner and I were arrested. Mr. Sam Matthews ordered his carriage, saying we had to go into Camp by order of Gen'l M. I rebelled and said I would not go if they brought a regiment for me. Seeing that Mr. Matthews was in earnest, I was compelled to yield and remarked to him, "I am very indignant and vexed but if I have to go, I will try to be a lady, even among my enemies." On arriving at Camp several officers offered to assist us out of the carriage and escort us to the tent, but we all refused to accept their offer. Under the trees, in Gen'l Lowe's grove, the tents were arranged and the General's son received us with far more politeness than his father, saying the General would receive us in a few minutes. Not in the least excited, I waited my summons. Soon we sallied to the tent where the General was seated behind a table with a pile of "green backs" placed before him. The young school girls were a great deal frightened and kept on their veils. Mr. Matthews, being a stammering man, was very slow in his introductions, first introducing the girls. I awaited my presentation and my wrath began to stir at the thought of being held to account for such a trifle. I sneered, looked to the right and to the left, and was a long time taking my seat, trying to keep as calm as possible. When Gen'l M. began his questions, asking Miss Matthews if she had not insulted his soldiers, she replied, "I did not; one of them asked me for the little flag and I gave it to him." Then I said, "It was not larger than my hand." He said, "I don't care if it was mite, it was a flag." Then turning to me, he said, "Don't you know that you are in open rebellion?" I said, "I am a Rebel open and above board." Growling like a lion, he said, "No man, or woman, or child shall say that they are Rebels in my tent." I replied, still more firmly, "I am a Rebel." He then said, "Don't you know that I could send you to Fort La Fayette in five minutes." I replied, "that is very rapid traveling." I could see a lurking smile pass over his face, and he said, "Are you a lady"? I replied in a most indignant manner, "Who doubts it?" He then said, "You women, get to your homes." He was surely no gentleman but an arrant coward and a tyrant. He seemed particularly bent on insulting the women and children and went into the Army for gain. No worse order was ever given in the days of the French Revolution than that he issued to old Gen'l Turchin (a Dutchman) when he told him to march into the town of Athens, Alabama and to give the soldiers the liberty of the town for two hours. And they surely obeyed the order, in every sort of mischief and crime of which soldiers are guilty, without restraint. The people of Athens will never forget this outrage, as long as any inhabitant is left to tell the story. At the home of Judge C. they completely demolished the place, to punish the family - they pitched their tents as close to the house as they could get them and never removed them until they had orders to leave. All of the vehicles, carriages, buggies and everything of the kind were rolled miles away unless they destroyed them by chopping them up with axes or hatchets. One of their chief delights was to strew molasses and lard all over the carpets, break up the furniture and smash the mirrors, and to leave nothing that they could possibly destroy. Had not the Rebels, in their shrewdness, hid much of their provisions, they would have perished. This Ohio Regiment did the fighting of that command for they went out 1400 strong and only fifty survived, but this old General never went out with them - he was too busy buying and selling cotton and enriching himself.

One day, in Huntsville, Alabama, a rumor came that a Confederate General, with 10,000 Indian soldiers, was crossing the river a few miles off, which created a great panic among the Federal troops. Artillery, infantry and every available piece of armor was ordered out. Such clashing and clattering of arms through the streets we had not heard before. This gave the ladies a chance to exult and clap their hands for joy, hoping that the Yankees might have to retreat. It was soon found to be a false alarm and the citizens, and never did they have any peace while this branch of the army remained. We often kept the Yankees in hot water, reporting that Forrest, Morgan or some famous General was in the neighborhood, when we had no tidings from them. It was a mere ruse to defend ourselves from insult.

On one occasion Gen'l M. gave an order that the Rebel ladies might attend the burial of a nephew of Gen'l C. Whether it was a kind streak he took or whether it was to ascertain the feeling of the ladies we did not know, but believed it was the latter, and altho they were using all of the horses and carriages in the City, every lady in town robbed all of the gardens of flowers and each carried an immense bouquet and walked behind the hearse for a mile and a half to decorate, not only his grave, but all of the Rebel Soldiers' graves in the cemetery. Gen'l M. might have known that it was a good time to show their principles and they never lost an opportunity to exhibit them.

The first Yankee soldiers that I encountered, I was walking with my lovely friend, Mrs. William Mastin, Sr., and I shut my eyes as I passed. She remarked, "Miss Rowe, it is all lost on them for they will think that you are a blind woman."

Some of us went to an old Baptist Church, out of use, and found many soldiers there waiting to be exchanged. They were always a jolly, wholesome set and one of them remarked, "People cannot say that we don't stand by our church."

Shortly after the Battle of Shiloh, Major C. arrived limping on crutches. We had told him, when he left, not to come back wounded in the foot and limping on crutches. Miss Fannie Donegan had told him, if he was wounded to come to their house and we would nurse him. The Yankee Surgeon attended him and the surgeon remarked that "Huntsville was a lovely place, so full of flowers early in the Spring that it was like a fairyland." Maj. C. said, "Doctor, the flowers are nothing, the society is charming, so refined, so cultured." A short time after, many of our soldiers returned, wounded from this battle. One Sabbath about a dozen Yankee soldiers came to arrest Major C. We endeavored to conceal his crutches and disguised him, but they rushed into his room saying that by the authority of Gen'l M. they must arrest him. Maj. C. seemed calm, but the ladies, Miss Mary H. (to whom he was engaged at the time), Mrs. B., her mother, Miss Donegan and I, were very indignant and asked them if it took twelve of their men to arrest one of ours. We thought Maj. C was getting along very well with his wound but from imprudence he was threatened with lockjaw and his features were rigid and extremities cold. He threw a book at the head of a servant to awaken him, and sent him to wake Miss Fannie Donegan and myself. We went to him, kindled a fire, gave him a strong toddy, put a cloth of laudnum on his foot and heated it with our hands. He declared that we had saved his life. A short time after this, when he joined his command, he was married to Miss Mary H. at Brentwood, Tennessee, and returned to his command without his bride.

We had two soldiers concealed on the flat roof of Mr. Donegan's house - Mr. W. and Mr. R - we used to pass their food to them every day until they could steal a chance to escape from the Yankee soldiers. They finally made their escape and joined their command. One day a woman, in deep mourning and heavily veiled, was seen getting over the cemetery fence to decorate some Yankee graves, when a man's boots were seen and some of the Rebel ladies discovered that he was a Rebel spy who brought letters to them through the lines.

Miss Fannie Donegan and I had never seen the burial of an officer so, as one of the noted Yankee officers had died, we concluded to conceal ourselves in the dense shrubbery and watch the procession as it was passing the cemetery. The body was in an ambulance, draped with crape; his war horse was draped also; the officers were riding with reversed arms; many soldiers; a band was playing the dead march with muffled drums. It was a solemn sight to us. The cemetery was just a short distance from Mr. D's residence, near enough to hear the guns and cannons fire quite frequently, for he was Col of Artillery and was a great loss to them. On their return, after the procession was out of sight, three grave diggers came along; Miss Donegan asked the first one if they had buried an officer. He said "No, it was one of their men." I said, "that is not so, I know it was one of your officers." He passed on; a second one came by, she asked again if that was not one of their officers. This one said the same thing and denied it. I said, "I will ask the next one." The third one passed; I halted him and said, "What officer was that you have just buried"? He said he was not an officer. I said, "I know better, he was one, for I have noticed you have buried five or six of your men and did not make any parade over them - did not even fire a gun - now this man had all of the honors and flourishing of trumpets accorded to him, there is no use in denying the fact." He at last acknowledged that it was an important man they had lost.

Another day I was sitting on the front porch with Harvey Donegan and one or two more friends, when a number of Yankee officers passed along, escorting a daughter of Gen'l M. She was also dressed in a blue riding habit with a sword at her side, which seemed coarse to us Southern women. Harvey Donegan remarked in their hearing, "Miss Rowe, there are some beaux for you." I replied, loud enough for them to hear, "I hope never to be reduced to such as that - I keep better company."

Daily depredations were committed as long as the Federal soldiers were in our midst. Many say that this is the result of war, but I am sure they must have had many an officer who was merely vested with a little authority who took advantage of it and abused it by all the arbitrary acts they could show. Many had never commanded soldiers before, and showed even their own soldiers the greatest tyranny, but when their regular officers commanded they were born gentlemen, they were always polite and controlled their men and were willing to have wrongs redressed and grant favors, when not unreasonable. You may say that about one-third of the latter class controlled their army, while two-thirds were turned loose to do what they pleased. Most of the population of Huntsville were Confederates and would have died before they would have denied their principles. In the beginning, I admit, that we often tantalized the Yankees by walking along the streets and giving ourselves the titles of our noted Generals - but take it to yourselves, if you were about to be robbed of all your possessions and accumulation of wealth which was honestly gotten by our parents and your rightful inheritance, would you not have felt the same way, especially when the parents and grandparents of these Yankees had bought and sold slaves? They were once as much their property as ours!

MILITARY PERSPECTIVES ON THE INVASION OF HUNTSVILLE, ALABAMA, APRIL 11, 1862

The following letters were taken from The War of the Rebellion: A Compilation of the Official Records of the Union and Confederate Armies! Series 1, Volume X, part 1. Washington, D.C., Government Printing Office, 1884 and pertain to the takeover of North Alabama.

Reports of Brigadier General Ormsby M. Mitchel, Commander of the Third Division of the Army of the Ohio.

HEADQUARTERS,THIRD DIVISION
Huntsville, Ala., April 11, 1862

SIR: After a forced march of incredible difficulty, leaving Fayetteville yesterday at 12 m., my advanced guard, consisting of Turchin's brigade, Kennett's cavalry, and Simonson's battery, entered Huntsville this morning at 6 o'clock.

The city was taken completely by surprise, no one having considered the march practicable in the time. We have captured about 200 prisoners, 15 locomotives, a large amount of passenger,box, and platform cars, the telegraphic apparatus and offices, and two Southern mails. We have at length succeeded in cutting the great artery of railway intercommunication between the Southern States.

Very respectfully, your obedient servant,

O. M. MITCHEL,
Brigadier-General, Commanding

Capt. J. B. FRY,
Assistant Adjutant-General

HEADQUARTERS THIRD DIVISION,
Huntsville, April 11, 1862.

The work so happily commenced on yesterday has been completed to-day upon a train of cars captured from the enemy at Huntsville. A heavy force of the Ninth Brigade, under command of Sill, was ordered to drive the enemy from Stevenson in the east, while an equal force from the Eighth Brigade, upon captured cars, was directed to seize Decatur upon the west. Both expeditions proved eminently successful. I accompanied the most difficult one to Stevenson in person, from which place 2,000 of the enemy fled as usual at our approach without firing a gun, leaving behind five locomotives and a large amount of rollingstock.

To prevent the enemy from penetrating toward Nashville, I ordered the destruction of a small bridge between Stevenson and Bridgeport, which we can replace, if necessary, in a single day. The expedition from the Eighth Brigade, under the immediate command of Colonel Turchin, proved eminently successful. To arrest his advance the enemy fired a bridge on the farther side of the Tennessee River, but our troops reached it in time to extinguish the flames. A small force of the enemy fled from the town, leaving their tents standing and their camp equipage behind them.

Thus in a single day we have taken and now hold a hundred miles of the great railway line of the rebel Confederacy. We have nothing more to do in this region, having fully accomplished all that was ordered. We have saved the great bridge across the Tennessee, and are ready to strike the enemy, if so directed, upon his right flank and rear at Corinth.
Respectfully,

O. M. MITCHEL,
Brigadier-General.

General BUELL.

The Eighth Brigade left Murfreesborough, Tenn., on April 5, at 6 a.m., and marched to Huntsville, Ala., arriving there at 7:30 a.m., on the 11th.

At 6 p.m., April 11, the Twenty-fourth Illinois were moved on cars for Decatur, arriving opposite Decatur on the morning of the 12th, driving the enemy's troops from the fortifications at Decatur, and saving the bridge over the Tennessee River that the rebels had fired on their retreat, occupying the town on the 13th. The rest of the brigade were moved by cars to Decatur, arriving there the same day at 8p.m.

April 15, the brigade, except guard for baggage train, was moved to Tuscumbia, Ala., arriving there April 16, at 11 p.m.

At 12 noon, April 24, the brigade fell back from Tuscumbia to Decatur, arriving there at 8 p.m. April 26.

April 26 and 27, the brigade, except the Eighteenth Ohio, fell back to Huntsville, Ala., the Eighteenth Ohio going to Athens.

The Ninth Brigade left Murfreesborough, Tenn., April 4, and marched thence, via Shelbyville and Fayetteville, to Camp Taylor, Huntsville, Ala., arriving April 11; since which time the brigade has been divided and sent in different directions on the line of the railroad. The Eighteenth Wisconsin Regiment now being at Bellefonte, the Second Ohio on provost duty at Huntsville, the Twenty-first Ohio at Athens, and two companies of the Thirty-third Ohio now in camp, the balance guarding the water-tanks, bridges, &c., on the Memphis and Charleston Railroad.

The Seventeenth Brigade left Murfreesborough April 3, arriving at Shelbyville April 4, and left for Fayetteville April 8, remained at that point until the 14th, and received orders to proceed to Huntsville, Ala. The brigade, with the exception of the Forty-second Indiana, which was left at Shelbyville, marched into camp on the 15th; remained there until the 18th; proceeded to Decatur with the Tenth and Third Ohio Regiments, and remained until Sunday, the 27th, and, after destroying the bridge over the Tennessee River by fire, proceeded by railroad to Stevenson, Ala., and marched from there to Bridgeport, at which place it remained up to May. The Fifteenth Kentucky Volunteers was left at Fayetteville, as provost-guard, from April 9 to May 1.

Note: Because of his successful operations in the Tennessee Valley, Mitchel was promoted to the rank of Major General. After complaints were lodged against him because of the conduct of his troops and his handling of the cotton trade within the occupied area under his command, he was transferred to the Command of the Department of South Carolina and the Tenth Army Corps with headquarters at Hilton Head, South Carolina. Before he could organize the work to be done there, he was stricken with yellow fever and died at Beaufort on October 30, 1862.

Report by Confederate Major-General E. Kirby Smith, Commander of the Department of East Tennessee, Headquarters at Knoxville, Tennessee.

HEADQUARTERS DEPARTMENT OF EAST TENNESSEE,
Knoxville, Tenn., April 13, 1862.

MAJOR: On the 11th General Mitchel, with a Federal force, well ascertained to be about 8,000, with four batteries, entered Huntsville, capturing twenty-one engines and three trains of cars. They came from Murfreesborough via Shelbyville and Fayetteville, and were followed by two additional regiments, making a force between 8,000 and 10,000 strong. Pushing their trains on beyond Stevenson, they destroyed the bridge over Widden's Creek, 4 miles west of Bridgeport, and secured their flank against any movement by rail from Chattanooga. I have two regiments at Bridgeport and two at Chattanooga, under the command of General Leadbetter; one of the latter, the Forty-third Georgia is awaiting the arrival of arms from Richmond.

General Maxey, with three regiments and a battalion, passed through Huntsville the day previous to its occupation by the enemy. The three armed regiments between Bridgeport and Chattanooga were to have completed the re-enforcements intended for General Beauregard. My own command not being large enough for offensive movements, and feeling that on the fate of the army at Corinth hung the fate of East Tennessee, I felt justified in ordering this force to General Beauregard even before being called upon by him for re-enforcements.

General Beauregard telegraphs that six regiments from Pemberton's command are enroute for Chattanooga. He suggests a movement from that point, taking the enemy in reverse at Huntsville. I could add four regiments, making a force of between 5,000 and 6,000 effective men, but the destruction of the road west from Bridgeport renders the operation of artillery on that line now impracticable. A demonstration of 5,000 infantry toward Huntsville might alarm Mitchel, but no decisive results could be reasonably anticipated. The advance of a force from Kingston by Sparta on Nashville is the strategic move, offering the greatest results and the most practicable in operation. I so telegraphed General Beauregard, notifying him of the destruction of the bridges on the Memphis road, and giving him an opportunity to countermand the order to the South Carolina regiments and to direct them to re-enforce him by [the] Montgomery and the Mobile and Ohio road.

The Eufaula Artillery, which was ordered here with its battery, is still without guns. The pieces, with ammunition, should be sent from Richmond as soon as practicable.

I am, sir, respectfully, your obedient servant,

E. KIRBY SMITH,
Major-General, Commanding.

Maj. T. A. WASHINGTON, A.A.G., Richmond, Va.

Editor's Note: At the time he recorded this report, Major-General E. Kirby Smith was Commander of the Army of the Department of East Tennessee. He was later promoted to Lieutenant General and succeeded General T. H. Holmes to the command of the Department of the Trans Mississippi, which comprised all of the Confederate forces west of the Mississippi. In May of 1865, he surrendered his forces at Baton Rouge, Louisiana. After the war, he returned to his chosen profession of teaching, and served as professor of mathematics at the University of the South in Sewanee, Tennessee, until his death in 1893.

A JOURNALIST'S PERSPECTIVE ON THE INVASION OF HUNTSVILLE

John Withers Clay, editor of *The Huntsville Democrat* gave the following account of the invasion of Huntsville in a letter to his brother, Clement Claiborne Clay, who was serving at the time as a senator in the Confederate Congress in Richmond, Virginia. After he fled from Huntsville, he joined another brother, Hugh Lawson Clay, at Knoxville, Tennessee, where he secured a position as agent to make contracts for saltpeter for the Confederate government. Lieutenant Colonel Hugh Lawson Clay was serving as assistant adjutant general to Major General E. Kirby Smith.

Knoxville, Tnn., May 15, 1862
Hon. C. C. Clay, Jr.,
At Large.

My dear brother: I should have written to you, ere this, to relieve your mind as to my status & locus, but did not know how to direct my letter & brother Lawson was unable to inform me. I was, probably, the first man who left Huntsville after the Federals came in. You may be astonished that I should not have been fully apprised of their advance & did not leave sooner, but you would not have been, probably, if you had been there. For weeks, we had had rumors of the approach of the enemy - that they were in such & such numbers at Pulaski, at Elkton, at Madison X Roads, at Fayetteville, at Winchester &c. - would be in Huntsville on a certain day, at a certain hour - & facts had as often contradicted rumors. So, we only illustrated the old fable of the shepherd's boy & the wolf, when the enemy did come. On the 10th of April, the reported arrival of the enemy at Fayetteville en route to Huntsville assumed more plausibility than previous reports. At dark, several citizens from the neighborhood of Fayetteville reached Huntsville & reported that they saw several regiments of them marching on the Shelbyville Road, within a few miles of Fayetteville, in the afternoon of the 9th. We took for granted that the bridge across Elk would be burnt & the necessity of rebuilding it & the bad condition of the roads would retard their progress, if they really intended coming to Huntsville & were not merely making a diversion in our direction, with a view of going by a different route to Savannah, Tenn., from that pursued by the rest of Buell's Army, for greater convenience of supplies. About 11 o'clock the night of the 10th a courier arrived from Meridianville, stating that the enemy had encamped two miles North of that place. I was at home, having just returned from a visit to Bishop & Mrs. Lay, who had arrived at Mrs. Rice's, the day before; & was summoned to the door by one of the hands in my Office knocking at it, having come to report to me the news. I went up town & found a number of persons - among them John Bell & Sam Morgan, of Nashville, Joe Bradley & Zeb Davis, who were desiring to get away before the enemy arrived - all consulting as to the probable truth of the courier's report. It was, finally, concluded that Bob. Brickell, Joe Bradley, Jr. & Blanton (page torn] should ride toward Meridianville & ascertain the truth of the report. Bell & the others went home to their beds. I went to my Office & before day, with the aid of my Office hands, Guilford, Charles & Campbell, stowed about 3/4th of my type & material in the cuddy in the Attic of your Office building, put my job press (the one with a wheel) in Dr. Wilkinson's basement, carried my two desks to my residence & packed my Office books & accts in my trunk, with my clothes, intending to take my trunk with me to Guntersville; where, also, I proposed moving my newspaper press & enough type to continue the publication of my paper. I had obtained from Dr. Burritt the loan of Guilford & his buggy & horse, to take me to Whitesburg, & had hired John Robinson's wagon, to be ready at a moment's notice, to carry down my press, type, paper, ink &c. About 4 A.M., April 11, I went down home to make arrangements there for leaving

& ordered breakfast, intending to leave directly after it. About 5 I returned to my Office, expecting to find the newspaper press taken down & type put up ready for shipment, but, on the contrary, found my foreman, Cauthers, had dismissed my hands without taking down the press &c. He excused himself on the ground that it could all be done in an hour, & our scouts would certainly give us that much notice of the enemy's approach - & if the enemy did not come, the setting-up of the press would be a very hard job, which he wished to avoid, if possible. Every one seemed so incredulous of the enemy's approach & so unconcerned that I yielded to the general fatuity - but concluded I would go over to Mr. Fackler's, where Sam Morgan & his two nephews (brothers of Capt. John, wounded at Shiloh) were staying & learn what news a courier from Winchester had brought him. Arriving there, I found all apparently wrapt in sleep & so quiet that I concluded not to arouse them, & returned homeward & just as I turned Pope Walker's corner, I saw great commotion among a number of slaves on the Street as far down as Mr. Erskine's corner - & several running toward me. I accosted the first & he exclaimed - "Dey done come, sir, deys done come!" "Who?"

William McDowell Home, 517 Adams Street

"De Yankees, sir!" "How do you know?" "I seed 'em myself. Dey at the telegraph Office & all over de Square." "Did they have on blue coats?" "Yes, sir." "Well, then, I reckon they are the Yankees" - and I walked quietly back to Fackler's & rang the doorbell violently. Sally Pynchon (nee Fackler) thrust her head & nearly half her body out of an upper window & asked excitedly, "Who's that?" "Mr. Clay - the Yankees are on the Square & have the telegraph office." "Lord have mercy upon us!" - & back she dropped. I went into the Street &, seeing Mr. McDowell's Alfred running home, almost breathless & eyes looking as though they wd pop out of the sockets, I told him to run back & tell Guilford to meet me at Coltart's with [page torn] & then go & tell my wife that I was off. "Lord, let me go & tell my master, first, sir!" "Well, go and tell him, first." I waited for him to return & started Bob Fearn's Elliott on the same errands, to ensure their delivery, & walked out toward Coltart's. After crossing Dry Creek, I saw four men riding

Fackler House, 518 Adams Street

rapidly down the parallel street toward Coltart's - & thinking they might be Yankees, I stepped into a deep ditch & walked in it till they disappeared & then took the open road for

Coltart's. Getting there, I saw Mrs. C., told her the Yankees had the telegraph office & enquired who those men were, dismounted at her well. She reckoned they were the Yankees & I had better run. I ran about 100 yards, having Coltart's house between me & the enemy, & then quietly walked over to North Ala. College, & after waiting awhile there, went into the mountain & soon found myself at old Jimmy Hall's place, between old Andy Drake's place & town, & occupied by a Mr. Crenshaw. I ate breakfast there &, while sitting by the fire after breakfast, in popped A. R. Wiggs ("Hal") each of us greatly surprised. He knew nothing of the enemy's arrival until after usual breakfast time at Mrs. Fleming's - & then had out his horse & was about leaving when a detachmt of the

George P. Beirne's home, 300 Williams Street

enemy appeared. He ordered his horse to be put up &, lighting his pipe, walked carelessly along up the Street to the Masonic Hall & down Adams St., dodging into Trotman's to avoid another detachmt of the enemy & made his way through the fields into the mountain. Sam Morgan & one nephew escaped the other was captured & put on parole. Col.

Jno. G. Coltart, slighted [sic] wounded in the heel at Shiloh, & Lieut. Col. Russell, with his left arm broken by a minie ball, were at Old Sammy Coltart's, but left the night before. Old Sammy had ridden to town to see Robert about sending John's clothes &, on the appearance of the Yankees, rode hurriedly homeward. This caused him to be pursued & captured &, 'tis said, he was made to take the oath of allegiance, but, it may be, he was only put on his parole. Joe Bradley was aroused from sleep by servants, & then wife & children, clamoring for him to run, for the Yankees were all over the Streets about his house. He succeeded in getting out of town about 12 o'clock M., by slipping from lot to lot. He got to George Beirne's & the Feds. appearing in the lane between Beirne's & Bob Fearn's, the Beirne girls locked him in the cellar.

Getting to Fackler's, a horse was brought to him, & he attempted to get off but his heart failed him & he returned. Again he started & Feds on horseback appeared about Pope Walker's corner.

He had no alternative but to assume a bold front & move toward them they turned off & he went by Lawrence Watkin's to California St. & thence through the fields to the mountain & over the Tenn. River to Buck's. As he passed Jim Ward's, Jim's children halloed "Run, Mr. Bradley, run! the Yankees'll catch you." He implored them to keep quiet & got off. I met with no refugees but Wiggs in the mountain, but numbers, who were or had been soldiers, found their way out, that day & for several days after. Old Jno. Bell & Zeb Davis made their way on foot, through the Grove, &, in a round about way through mud & water, to Whitesburg & over to Buck's. 'Tis said, that Bob Brickell & his party sent out as scouts, met the enemy's advance on the brow of a hill unexpectedly, & Bob accosted them "Gentlemen, you are riding rather late." "Yes & so are you. Where are you going?" Blanton replied "We're looking for a fellow that stole a buggy & horse in town & came out this way." "And we are looking for some fellows that stole some States out of the Union, & we think we've found some of them. Turn back with us." So, our scouts were brought back as prisoners & were released on parole not to leave the town. It is most astonishing that 13 or 14 locomotives & a number of cars should have been kept at the Huntsville Depot, with the assurance that the enemy might be expected any day & that the passenger train from the West, with wounded soldiers & others should have been allowed to come to the Depot without warning, as is said to be the fact. Coincident with these facts are the further facts that the R. R. Superintendent of Transportation at Huntsville, Hooper, is a Pennsylvanian, & the telegraph operators are Yankees. They may be all right, but the coincidences are unfortunate. 'Tis said that when the train was approaching Huntsville, efforts were made by persons, down towards Pinhook, to warn it to go back, the Federals having arrived two hours before, but the conductor & engineer did not heed perhaps, did not understand, the warning & when the train reached the Depot, the engineer, seeing the Feds, attempted to back, but had only 8 lbs. of steam on, & besides, was threatened with sundry Federal guns in dangerous proximity, which, doubtless, exercised some control over his will. Four locomotives were fired up at the Machine Shop & started off Eastward, & the Feds rushed to arrest their progress. A man was ordered to throw a rail on the track, to throw the locomotives off, but Pres. Yeatman, the conductor on the locomotive in front with the engineer, presented a five-shooter at the man & he allowed them to pass, &, 'tis said, they opened every valve & put on all steam & sped, with lightning rapidity almost, heedless of the cannon shot sent after them & striking the single box-car attached. The first locomotive got to Stevenson & prevented the Chattanooga train with a regiment of soldiers 23 Ala. Frank Beck, Colonel or 20 Ala., J. W. Garrott, Col. from going down. The other locomotives were captured. Wiggs & I remained at Crenshaw's till 1 or 2 o'clock Saturday, April 12 a day & a half eating & sleeping there, but spending most of our time roaming about the mountain, watching the Feds mostly Dutch, walking or riding about the fields between us & town.

With long range guns, we might have picked some of them off. I got Crenshaw to go to town, on the morning of my arrival at his house, & carry a note to my wife, telling her my whereabouts, & encouraging her with words of advice & comfort, without, however, putting any names in the note & bidding wife, children, mother, &c. farewell. She was thoughtful enough to send me a heavy pair of pants, which was all the extra clothing, except my great coat, that I had & all I could get, except by borrowing, until I reached Chattanooga, & then I could get nothing but a coarse domestic shirt, with coarse linenor Marseilles, bosom, such as formerly sold for $1.25, for which I paid $2.50 & I had to borrow an undershirt from bro. L. & he had to send by telegraph to Lynchburg for it to be sent by Express, there being no such shirts here. My wife sent me word by Crenshaw that two Feds. had called at my house for breakfast, that morning, she gave it to them & they left, thanking her for it & their conduct was unexceptionable. Bob Coltart, as mayor was called on by Gen. Mitchel to provide breakfast, in two hours, for 5,000 soldiers (as we were told by several) otherwise, it would be taken from private houses & Bob, accordingly (& properly, I think to prevent private pillage) bought at City expense $500 worth of bacon, beef, flour, meal &c., for the Vandals & had them cooked by distribution, I understood. Mrs. Pope Walker, who was staying at Gov. Chapman's, was riding on the turnpike to town, on the 11th, (probably fearing to remain in the country) & soldiers jumped upon the box with the driver & behind the carriage, & so frightened her, that she asked them to let her get out. They permitted her to do so & then jumped in the carriage & rode off to town, leaving her on the pike. They went to Jos. B. Robinson's, pressed his horses & wagons & carried off all his provender, & killed all his poultry. Some of them rode into town with dead turkies swinging to their saddle bows. They went to Mr. Fackler's & asked Mrs. F. where her son, Willie, was. "Thank God, he's in the Southern Army at Corinth." "And where's your son, Calvin," "Thank God, he's there too." They arrested Fackler for

Thomas White Home, 315 White Street

aiding "rebel soldiers" to escape, & asked him if he had not done so. He said he had & wd. do so again. They called for breakfast at Tom White's. It was furnished. Some remark was made about the rye coffee. Mrs. W. told them she gave them what she had for herself. They told her she wd soon be able to get coffee at 15c & went away, returning with 5 lbs. for her. They asked her if she was not Mrs. Thos. W. White. She said "Yes, but how did you learn my husband's name?" "Oh, we have a little bird about our camp that tells us these things. Where are your sons, Willie & Sandy?" "They are in the Confederate Army in Virginia, & I wish I had 36 more there." As some of the Federal cavalry rode by Tom Burton's (living where Lawrie lived) his wife (nee Bel Brandon) ran out, waived a Confederate flag & shouted "Hurra for Jeff. Davis & the Southern Confederacy!" They merely tipped her the military salute & passed on. It was very hazardous conduct, however brave, for, besides subjecting herself to danger of insult, her brother who distinguished himself for bravery in Tracys Co. at Manassas & was wounded at Shiloh was then confined with his wound, in the arm or shoulder, I believe, at her house. Her Uncle, Jere Clemens, &, also, Nick Davis, I am informed, remain in Huntsville, & drink & get drunk with the "flop-eared Dutch" &, I'm told, Nick got badly bruised in a drunken brawl with one of them. To drop the relation of perhaps, tedious details, on the day after our flight, Wiggs & I sent Crenshaw into town he sending a note to Mrs. Fleming for his horse, accoutred & saddle-bags with his clothes & I sending a note to my wife for clothes. Crenshaw went afoot, but took his little son on a mule with a bag of peas & getting Wigg's saddle bags, placed them in the pea bag, on the mule, & mounting Wigg's horse, he & his son rode across the Square, where, meeting with Billy McCoy, Billy, in his oracular way, told him the enemy were going to extend their pickets 4 miles into the country & he had better hasten out of town, or he might not be able to get out at all. That very circumstance wd. have placed Crenshaw's house within the Federal lines & then have facilitated his ingress & egress to & from town, but he did not understand it so, & hastened out, & sent my note to my wife by McCoy, & I failed to get my clothes & an answer. I have heard nothing directly from my family or any of our kin since, although I have seen several persons who left Huntsville within 8 or 10 days after; & I have been unable to find any one going to Huntsville, who could bear a letter from me. Wiggs & I left Crenshaw's about 1 or 2 o'cl'k, Apl. 12 he riding half way, I, the other half, to Jack Esslinger's in the Little cove. There I borrowed a mule, saddle & bridle, & we rode over to Mr. Bill Robinson's plantation, stayed there that night & went, next day, to Col. Fleming's, where we found the Col., the two Christians, John Young, & a Judge Everett, a Kentuckian, but a refugee from Cincinnati. In the evening late, Erskine Russell & Ned Mastin arrived & told us, the enemy's cavalry were to be over at Vienna, the next day & then Wiggs, Harry Christian, & I mounted our steeds & crossed Paint Rock, that night, put up at farm-houses at 1 o'clock &, in the morning, crossed the Tennessee to Guntersville, where we (Wiggs & I) stayed till the 19th, cut off from mail communications & hearing nothing except from rumor. I, then, left on the steamer Paint Rock for Chattanooga or rather Bridgeport a detachmt. of soldiers having been sent down to take the boat up. I heard there were 3,000 Confederate troops at Bridgeport & the 5 to 7,000 Feds. extended from Stevenson to Tuscumbia, the most of them having crossed the River at Decatur, leaving only 5 or 600 at Huntsville & I wanted the Confederates to reoccupy Huntsville. But Frank Beck had parts of two regiments, about 700 effective men only besides a Company of artillery. So I went to Chattanooga, to see Leadbetter, & found that he had only part of another regimt. He & Reynolds, both, requested me to come to Knoxville to represent the state of affairs & seek the sending of 2 or 3 regimts to them, with orders to proceed to Huntsville; but Genl. Smith couldn't spare the forces from E. Tenn. & the Cumberland Gap & so my mission was fruitless, unless it resulted in Genl. Lee ordering the 30th Ala., Col. Shelby, Lieut Col. Saul Bradford & 31st Ala. Col. Hundley Lieut. Col. Tom Arrington to this place. These regmts have arrived. They bring rumors of depredations of the enemy about Huntsville among others that they have taken 100 of Pope Walker's slaves, 30 of Chapman's mules & some of your slaves, besides committing other depredations on other personal property of yours what not stated & some on Father's property, what not stated & that they had gone to Ben. Patteson's, broken his doors & windows, piano, furniture &c. &c. (eased themselves in his house) & taken horses, provender & everything they could make use of. Brother L. thinks they have mistaken your name for his & it was not your property but his, because of its proximity to Patteson's. I think accounts are exaggerated if there be any truth in them for I saw Sam. Moore (Judge) here, week before last, from Jackson Co. & he had seen Dr. Jordan, who told him of the depredations in part at Patteson's, but nothing of the seizing of Walker's slaves or Chapman's mules, or interruption of your or Father's property, whilst he did tell that Chapman was held in custody as a hostage for the good behaviour of the people of Jackson. [page torn] ...Sam Moore came up to get ammunition for troops organizing in Jackson 250 were already armed & ready to operate against the Federal incursions. He expected to be able to get 1000 men there & in Madison, Marshall &c. he said. Lieut. Col. Pettus told Moore that he had married a niece of Gov. Chapman & liked the old fellow very well, but hoped he wdn't let Chapman's arrest interfere with the killing of a single Yankee. Pettus says, he wants to be Provost Marshal of Huntsville, when recovered, just to have the pleasure of hanging George Lane.

Judge George W. Lane's home, 511 Adams Street,a strong Union supporter throughout the war

By the way I had liked to have forgotten totell you that Lane sits in the ProvostMarshal's office & approves or disapproves applications for passports giving them as to proper persons to be trusted &, 'tis said, he said that he had been requested (by Mitchel, I suppose) to accept the office of Provost Marshal, & I am told that Sam Browne (acting as State Agent for distributing clothes to Sheffield's Regt. at Gadsden) says Bob. Smith (Jack Fariss's son-in- law) told him a petition (or recommendation) for Judge Lane's appointmt. had been circulated & recd. a number of signatures among others, Smiths. Before leaving Guntersville I learned that two of B. S.

Clapp's (of Marshall Co) sons got passports from Huntsville on the recommendation of D. B. Turner, Ben. Jolly & W. B. Figures. I asked Wiggs how far he tho't my recommendation wd. have carried them. He promptly replied, "To jail." He said he'd bet Figures wd. make money out of the Federal's visit to Huntsville & I think it likely. I have not heard whether he publishes the *Advocate* or not, but, if I mistake not, the passports I saw given by the Pro. Mars. at H'v'lle, were printed at his Office. I took Celeste, Comer & Amelia to Atlanta on the 1st May, bro. L. having started, that day, to Cumberland Gap with Genl Smith, the enemy having approached the Gap several thousand in number [page torn] ...Smith & Staff, with Genl Barton's command, some 2 or 3000 strong crossed at Woodson's Gap between the other two intending to attack those at Big Creek in the rear, by surprise while Genl. Stevenson, at Cumberland Gap advanced toward Cumberland Fort with some 2 or 3000 more. Gen. Smith's project failed on acct. of the heavy rain & darkness so dark they could only follow one another over the mountain by the front men giving a low whistle, which was imitated by all the rest successively to the rear. After passing over the mountain, they lay on the ground without tents (except a fly) each officer holding his own horse &, after day, returned. Gen. Stevenson succeeded in driving the enemy's pickets over the river, capturing one & some wagons loaded with telegraph wire & poles, intended to be put up as far as the Cumberland Gap. He destroyed what he captured, except the teams & returned. The expedition has caused the enemy to retire to London, Ky., spies report. Celeste has had ulcerated sore throat, Jno. Comer telegraphs & night before last, she telegraphed to bro. L. "Comer exceedingly ill, come and comfort me." She had previously written that Comer had the scarlet fever. Of course, bro. L. was greatly distressed & left, yesterday morning, for Macon. For want of something better to do, I am engaged as Agent to make contracts for saltpetre for the Confederate Govmt. at $100 per month, with the understanding that I am to be released as soon as the way is open for my return to

Huntsville. I was appointed by Lieut. R. H. Temple, Supt. of 7th Nitre District, which embraces most of the counties of E. Tenn. For the present & probably all the time, Knoxville will be my place of business & my occupation filling up contracts, writing letters & explaining matters to those desirous of engaging in the manufacture. I have much more to say, but have probably wearied you & must close. Best love to Sister, Cousin Tom & other kin. May God bless us all, rid our country ... [page torn]

SOURCE: The original of this letter is housed in University, the Clay Collection, Manuscript Department, William R. Perkins Library, Duke Durham, North Carolina.

Editor's note: J. Withers Clay, whose Huntsville residence was at the corner of Gates and Henry Streets, pursued an adventurous career as a journalist despite the trials and tribulations of wartimes. In order to support a rather large family, he struggled to continue the publication of his newspaper. In October of 1862, he returned to Huntsville and began publication of *The Huntsville Confederate*. In May 1863, he decided to publish *The Daily Confederate,* but with the second occupation of Huntsville in July 1863, he was forced to suspend this operation. After sending his presses to Chattanooga, he published there until August when, under pressure of Union forces, he had to move to Marietta and thence to Dalton, Georgia (often only one-step ahead of General Sherman's march) until he finally had to suspend publication for the remainder of the war. As an ardent Democrat, he continued the weekly publication of his paper until his death in 1896. After suffering a stroke in 1884, his two daughters, Susanne and Virginia, assumed major responsibility for *The Huntsville Democrat* and conducted its affairs until its demise in 1919.

CONFEDERATE ACTIVITIES IN AND AROUND HUNTSVILLE, ALABAMA

From the papers of the late
Rev. James Monroe Mason, D. D.

It is probable that no complete history of the operations of the Confederate Cavalry in connection with the Army of Tennessee will ever be written. The area of country over which they were scattered, extending from the Alleghany Mountains to the Mississippi River; the nature of the service in which they were engaged, requiring them to act whether upon the raid, the scout or the vidette post, not as a compact body but in small detachments; and the fact that the nature of the country prevented their being used upon the great historic battlefields, all conspire to render the task of the historian who shall make the attempt, extremely difficult. Yet no soldier who following the fortunes of Forrest or of Wheeler should be willing to admit that the services rendered by this branch of the Army were less important, the hardships endured less severe, the dangers encountered less deadly, or the casualties fewer than in any other branch. Doubtless, there were many cavalry regiments the list of whose killed and wounded, in the incessant skirmishes, was as great as that of the most famous infantry regiments that ever stormed a battery or crossed bayonets with the foe. While no historian may ever succeed in so grouping all these as to present a fitting companion picture to the great infantry and artillery battles, yet much may be done in the way of personal reminiscence to rescue the memory of our Cavalry service from undeserved oblivion. And if a connected history is ever written its material can be gathered in no other way. It is with a view to accomplishing something in this direction that I have undertaken my present task. Being only a soldier in the ranks, I shall attempt to recite only that which I saw and participated in from June 20th, 1862 to May 9th, 1865, the former being the date of my enlistment and the latter of my discharge by parole at the surrender of Forrest.

In April 1862 the writer was a schoolboy in Huntsville, Alabama. On the morning of the 11th of that month Huntsville was occupied by the Federal Army under Gen. O. M. Mitchel. The school was disbanded, and the building seized for military uses.

Soon after this event I undertook in company with a schoolmate to pass through the lines of the enemy and make my way to Southern Alabama. Being under military age, we had no trouble in getting permission to go for a few days to visit friends in the country but having spent more than the specified time in a vain attempt to evade the enemy's pickets and cross the Tennessee River, we were afraid to return home. We communicated our fears to the friend at whose house we were staying, and he informed us of a small band of Confederate cavalry that was being organized in the mountains of Madison and Jackson counties, and advised us to place ourselves under their protection.

At this time there were many Confederate soldiers lurking in this section. A company of the 7th Alabama Infantry whose term of service had expired, reached their homes only a few days before the arrival of the Federal Army and were hiding about to avoid arrest. There were several from other commands who were at home on furlough or on account of wounds or sickness, and many persons of military age, who had not yet joined the army, were also compelled to conceal themselves in order to avoid imprisonment. Gen. Bragg who was then maturing his plans for the march into Kentucky, gave to Frank Gurley of Forrest's Regiment a commission as a Captain of Cavalry, and ordered him to organize these men into a cavalry company, and operate in rear of the enemy. When we reached his camp he had collected only about one dozen men. This number was rapidly increased to new recruits, and within a week or ten days it had swelled to fifty or sixty.

Though not members of this band my friend and I being under their protection while awaiting an opportunity to go south, were compelled to move with them from place to place. At length seeing no opportunity of carrying out our original purpose, we, on the 20th of June entered our names on the Company's roll, being respectively 16 and 15 years of age.

The service assigned to this company was both difficult and dangerous. The Tennessee River, with an average width of about eight hundred yards, turns to the Southwest below Chattanooga and entering Alabama near Bridgeport purses this course to Guntersville, about fifty miles, thence turning again to the Northwest, it passes out of Alabama at the Northwestern corner of the State. The northern bank of this river was in the possession of the enemy and was closely picketed. In the four counties of Alabama lying north of this bend there was a large Federal Army, numbering perhaps twenty thousand, who occupied every town and hamlet of importance, and a due portion of the force was cavalry, engaged continually in scouting. This was the field of our operations. Our dangers were increased by the presence of a few unauthorized bands of Guerillas in the same region, whose operations gave the enemy presumptive evidence that all the Confederates in their midst were connected with these irregular bands in consequence of which we were indiscriminately outlawed. Our commander therefore was compelled to discriminate nicely between the methods of war that were legitimate and illegitimate, and to exercise continually such control over the passions of his men as would prevent their wreaking cruel vengeance upon such of the enemy as fell into their hands. The rendezvous of the company was in the mountain region along the border of Madison and Jackson counties. In the vastness of these mountains we found a safe asylum after every contact with the enemy, and from here as occasion was presented we furnished information of the enemy's movements to the Confederate forces south of the river.

There were frequent skirmishes between small detachments of our company, and scouting parties of the enemy, and from time to time many of the enemy were captured, and either sent south of the river, or released on parole. I shall not attempt, after so many years, to record each of these small engagements. A few affairs of greater magnitude I will relate.

The first of these was not creditable either to our discipline or to our courage. Soon after the company was organized, we started upon some errand the nature of which I do not now recall. Our route lay to the south, as if we would strike the river in the neighborhood of Guntersville. It was necessary to cross the railroad along which lay the largest bodies of the enemy. To avoid observation, we made a night march. Many of the men had never been under fire, and as we approached the point of greatest danger there was an evident feeling of trepidation, which increased as we advanced. Just before day we discovered that we were in close proximity to a cavalry camp. The company was halted for a moment, but before the position or strength of the enemy could be ascertained, the bugles sounded reveille. In an instant there was a panic. Vainly the officers commanded a halt and attempted to form the company in order. Both men and horses were so completely possessed by fear as to be uncontrollable. Many a man who at a later day showed the most admirable coolness and courage in the midst of real dangers, was not terror-smitten and turned and fled. As is usual in such cases as soon as the stampede began the contagion spread like fire in stubble. Soon we were all in headlong flight. Every bush and tree was magnified into an enemy; every fleeing horseman thought the comrade just in his rear was a federal cavalryman about to deal a saber stroke. We ran until daylight revealed to us our folly. In the meantime, we had become badly scattered and many days passed before the command was reunited. It is but just to state that at this time many of us had no arms.

On another occasion we received information of a wagon train approaching Huntsville on the Fayetteville turnpike, and accompanied by a small escort. By a night ride we succeeded in surprising and dispersing this party, and capturing a quantity of supplies, such as were needful.

Soon after this, we were ourselves surprised, in daylight, at a point near New Market, in Madison County, and suffered a loss of one man badly wounded and several captured. Despite our surprise and discomfiture, we retreated in good order, and escaped among the mountains.

While these events were taking place, Captain Hambrick of Forrest's Regiment succeeded in crossing the Tennessee River with his company, and united with us. Our entire force at this time consisted of two companies, mustering about one hundred and fifty men. Thus reinforced, we were enabled to act with greater boldness, and to undertake some enterprises of greater magnitude than any we had previously attempted. The enemy were using the Memphis and Charleston R. R. for the purpose of moving troops and supplies. Even when our numbers were small we had several times interfered with their use of this railroad, by removing rails at different points, so that they were forced to station garrisons near each other all along the railroad from Huntsville to Stevenson. One of the stations occupied by a garrison was the Flint River Bridge, twelve miles east of Huntsville. This covered, wooden bridge was converted into a block house and furnished with bullet proof gates at each end.

When Capt. Hambrick united with us, Bragg's army had already turned the enemy's flank, and were upon the march to Kentucky. Part of our duty now was to obstruct the retreat of the force in North Alabama, and a plan was matured for capturing and burning this bridge. Our scouts learned that the doors were kept open during the daytime and that many of the garrison amused themselves bathing in the river. We hoped to be able to get near enough to capture this bridge by a sudden dash. We dismounted in the woods and approached as near as we could under cover. Many of the Federal soldiers were bathing in the river, others were amusing themselves in various ways. We felt that the prize was almost in our grasp. Just then the sentinel on duty discovered us and fired; those of the garrison nearest the bridge rushed to their arms; the bathers in the river grabbed their clothing and ran into the bridge and the heavy doors closed with a bang. Those of our party whose guns were of long enough range amused themselves by firing a few shots. Our plan had failed, and we drew off. The progress of Bragg's army through East Tennessee now began to necessitate the removal of large bodies of Federal troops from West Tennessee and Mississippi to East Tennessee. Their line of march lay just along the line of Tennessee and Alabama. Learning of their passage through the country we moved in that direction for the purpose of interfering as much as possible with their progress and observing their movements. While watching what is locally known as the Ginn Spring road, we learned that a Federal General, ignorant of our proximity had passed with an escort of only four or five hundred cavalry. He was several hours in advance of us, but the prize was too alluring to be easily relinquished, and we followed upon roads parallel to his line of march. At night he encamped at Rock Springs. It was night when we reached the neighborhood of his camp. Nearly the whole night was spent in securing guides and getting the necessary information as to the location of the camp. When these were secured the night was far advanced and a plan was hastily communicated to the men for surprising the camp and capturing the General.

We approved as near as was prudent on horseback, dismounted and divided into two parties to attack on opposite sides. One of these parties reached its position at a fence about one hundred yards from the camp and found the Federals already astir. They waited patiently for the pre-concerted signal. Before the other party was ready for the attack the Federals had mounted and begun their march.

This officer who came so near to falling into our hands was General George H. Thomas.

We had followed him further than we could prudently go and turned again in the direction of our rendezvous. We marched rapidly by the most obscure roads and without halting to eat or rest, about nine o'clock in the morning crossed again the Ginn Springs road at a point about six miles north of New Market. As we crossed this road we observed that troops had been passing. We were halted and formed in line parallel to the road in the open woods. Captain Gurley, mounted on a large grey mare turned down the road in the direction from which the Federals had come and rode two or three hundred yards to see if others were near at hand. We saw him wheel and start back at a gallop, and in another moment we saw four cavalrymen in close pursuit. As soon as he reached our position he turned and ordered a charge. The Federals discovered us at the same moment and fled. Our column entered the road, left in front, which threw Gurley's own company in advance. We had pursued about a quarter of a mile when we ran into a body of cavalry, among whom we discharged our double barrel shotguns with fatal effects. Those of us in front passed many of them and left them to be captured by the men behind us. As we became intermingled with them in their flight we emptied several saddles. Next, we passed a wagon camp by the roadside, and then entered a long lane.

Everything in front of us was panic-stricken. In the lane we overtook a buggy containing two Federal officers. Firing on these as we came up with them, one was wounded and the other surrendered and hastily stating that the wounded officer was Gen. McCook, appealed to us for help. Capt. Gurley who was with the head of the column stopped and caused the General to be carried into a house nearby, where he expired in a short time. The fatal shot had passed through his body from the rear, coming out near the buckle of his sward belt. By whose hand the fatal shot was fired is not known, as three or four were firing at the same instant. During the pause which occurred at the killing of Gen. McCook, this writer with one other companion pressed forward and for a considerable distance kept close to the rear of the fleeing Federals. As we reached the end of the land a Federal officer just in front of me, threw himself from his horse and fled into the woods.

Being determined to kill or capture him, if possible, I turned my horse into the woods, being at a full run. About twenty feet from the road my horse ran under a swinging grapevine which caught me about the middle of the body. I was suspended for a moment in midair with my feet entangled in the stirrups until the saddle girth broke and I fell heavily to the ground. Just after I left the road my companion overtook and captured several musicians on foot, these being the first infantryman encountered.

While I was hastily repairing the effects of my disaster several of our comrades passed, and about one hundred yards further on these were saluted with a volley fired by an infantry column which had hastily formed across the road. At this volley they turned and fled, except one whose horse, being beyond control carried him into and through the column of infantry, and he escaped with no greater harm than a slight wound in his horse.

Though we had now discovered the presence of a large force of infantry we took advantage of their demoralization and deliberately returned over the ground that had been covered in the melee and gathered up the spoils of our victory. These consisted of a considerable supply of arms and other material of war, and a large number of prisoners, though many of the latter not being placed under guard as soon as captured, escaped to the woods and soon rejoined their friends.

Some parties who passed over the entire distance of our pursuit and claimed to have counted the dead gave the number as twenty-one, including General McCook. Among our prisoners was Capt. Brock of Gen. McCook's staff. Most of the prisoners were Germans and could not speak English.

As soon as we had gathered up the spoils we retreated to our stronghold in the mountains. As soon as the demoralized troops of Gen. McCook were reorganized they began to execute their vengeance upon the defenseless inhabitants of the country. Every house within several miles of the scene of strife was burned to the ground. Even the family who had sheltered and ministered their unfortunate commander in his dying moments suffered the common fate. These citizens were wholly innocent of complicity with us. The community was one in which we had not been before, nor had we been in communication with the people. It is to be hoped that this terrible vengeance was but the venting of the blind fury of the common soldiers, and that it was not authorized by the officers in command.

Among the trophies of this fight, was the sword which was presented to Gen. McCook by the Congress of the United States, which bore upon its blade an inscription commendatory of his gallantry.

The immediate results of this skirmish were highly beneficial to the inhabitants of that section, excepting those who were in the immediate vicinity and who suffered as above described. It put an end to the depredations of straggling parties and forced the enemy to keep in compact bodies in marching.

To those who were the immediate actors, it brought another benefit. Through the Federal officer who was captured, communications were opened with the Federal authorities, and our officers were enabled to show their commissions and obtain for us recognition as regular Confederate troops with all the rights of belligerents. In a few days our prisoners were paroled and these parolees were recognized by the Federal authorities.

The reputation of a brave, skillful and honorable officer of the Confederate Army demands that I, a participant in this affair, and a witness of the fatal wounding of Gen. McCook, should so far depart from the thread of my narrative as to relate the remote effects of this affair upon Capt. F. B. Gurley. The reports of this skirmish that reached the north caused great indignation. It was stated that Gen. McCook fell by the hand of Gurley himself, after he had surrendered. One report was that he was murdered while lying sick in an ambulance. Capt. Gurley was represented as a Guerrilla and a desperado.

In 1863 this officer was captured. Instead of being treated as a prisoner of war, he was incarcerated in the Tennessee State

Penitentiary and held there until the close of the war, when in the general prison delivery, he was released. He returned to his home in Madison County, Alabama. In the first election after the war he was honored by his fellow citizens with the office of Sheriff of his county. While holding that office the malice of political opponents trumped up the old charges against him and he was arrested, heavily ironed, incarcerated in jail, tried by a military court for murder, and sentenced to death. In all these proceedings there was great haste, and the conviction was entirely upon ex parte evidence. A reprieve was granted by the President until he could himself investigate the evidence, and after a careful hearing of the same he overruled the sentence and set Capt. Gurley at liberty.

The question "Who Killed Gen. McCook?" can never be answered, but this writer does not believe, nor does Capt. Gurley that he (Gurley) fired the fatal shot.

It is certain that the McCook fight was as great a surprise to us as it was to the enemy. We accidently ran into the enemy. We fought without premeditation, deliberation, plan or purpose. Our success was wholly due to the fact that (to use one of Gen. Forrest's expressions) "We got the bulge on them." Had we known what lay before us it is probable that we would have retreated without firing a gun. Or had we with deliberate purpose made a cavalry charge upon a Division of Federal Infantry would have shown us as courageous and well-disciplined as the noted "Light Brigade" whose charge into the valley of death at Balaklava will live in history, in story, and in song as long as humanity retains its admiration of valor and heroism. As I am the first participant in this affair who has ever published an account of it from the Confederate standpoint, I have thought it but just to enter into these details, that a gallant and honorable officer may be vindicated from alleged crime, and that the affair itself may be put upon record by one of the few participants who still survives.

Of the four Confederates who were nearest Gen. McCook when he fell, one was killed in the cavalry attack on Fort Donelson February 3, 1863, another was killed in battle near Kennesaw Mountain, Ga., June 9th, 1864. The other two were Capt. Gurley and the writer.

During the imprisonment of Capt. Gurley, though I was in a distant place, I communicated with him through friends and offered to share with him the hardships of persecution. This offer he magnanimously declined. I then put all the information in my possession at the command of Hon. D. C. Humphries and Mr. Benjamin Jolly of Huntsville, Ala., placed it before President Johnson, and secured amnesty both for Capt. Gurley and myself.

In consequence of the exaggerated rumors as to our strength, which were circulated among the enemy after this skirmish, they seldom moved from their garrisons except in large numbers, and we had the whole country open to us, and moved about with great freedom. Our scouts frequently fired on the enemy's pickets, and thus kept up the impression as to our strength. In this way a general engagement was prevented, our safety secured, and the country relieved from the depredations of stragglers.

THE AFFAIR AT INDIAN CREEK FORD: THE ARCHAEOLOGY OF A SMALL CIVIL WAR BATTLE

By Ben Hoksbergen and Brian Hogan

...Learned this morning that there had been quite a fight near Ellick Jones' and that the enemy had brought in 49 prisoners and several wounded men of Col. Wynn's [sic] *regiment with the exception of Capt. Jordan and two of his men ...The wounded men were badly cut up with saber cuts, as it was a hand-to-hand fight, and the enemy says the young rebels fought bravely....*

-Diary of Mary Jane Chadick December 23, 1864

Background

It was the winter of 1864. Huntsville was being reoccupied by Union forces for the fourth time. They had left town in a panic a month earlier, fleeing northeastward up the Memphis & Charleston Railroad to avoid being outflanked by the advancing forces of Confederate General John Bell Hood. In mid-November, Hood had crossed the Tennessee River at Florence on his way to Nashville to lure Sherman away from his Atlanta Campaign, but now Hood was defeated, and the Union forces were sweeping back down the railroad to cut off his retreat.

Confederate cavalry units under Brigadier General Philip D. Roddey had been covering and supplying Hood, but now were dispersed across northern Alabama engaging the advancing Union forces and delaying their advance. Roddey ordered part of a cavalry regiment under Colonel John R. B. Burtwell to advance from their camp in Mooresville toward Huntsville where they were to occupy and hold the town and await reinforcements from Colonel Josiah Patterson's Brigade. Burtwell and his Inspector General, James Irvine, rode to Huntsville on the evening of December 20 to assess the situation. As they rode into town from the west, they were met by two companies of Roddey's men who had been on picket at Paint Rock Bridge, but had been routed by advancing Union cavalry who chased them westward toward Huntsville. One of Burtwell's companies that had been on provost duty in Huntsville had retreated toward Athens. Burtwell ordered the retreating men to join his unit at Mooresville and fell back with them to regroup.

The Union force that arrived in Huntsville consisted of detachments of the 10th, 12th, and 13th Indiana Cavalry and the 2nd Tennessee Union Cavalry under Lieutenant-Colonel William F. Prosser. They pushed into Huntsville from the east on December 21, and set about resupplying and ransacking stores and houses. Soon after, Union infantry under Major General James B. Steedman began arriving from Nashville to reinforce them. Upon recapturing Huntsville, the Union troops settled down for an occupation that would last through the end of the war.

On the morning of the 22nd, Col. Burtwell advanced with at least two companies of cavalry from Lieutenant Colonel F. M. Windes 4th Alabama Regiment and detachments of the 10th Alabama Cavalry and Moreland's Cavalry Battalion to a position on Indian Creek, six miles west of Huntsville about three quarters of a mile upstream from the Memphis & Charleston Railroad Bridge. Burtwell and his officers set up camp in a house in the bluffs west of Indian Creek, while the enlisted men camped about 200 yards away on the floodplain. Leery of the substantial Union force in Huntsville, the Confederate troops hunkered down to await reinforcements from Patterson's Brigade. In the meantime, Burtwell gave the order to pile fence rails on the railroad bridges between

Huntsville and Decatur in case the Union forces attempted to advance further westward by rail.

Meanwhile, Union gunboats advanced down the Tennessee River toward Decatur, bombarding any possible Confederate positions there. The heavy cannonading to their rear and the large Union force to their front unnerved the Confederate soldiers at Indian Creek who were already receiving rumors of Hood's defeat. There was no word from Patterson's brigade, and the scouts and couriers they sent out never returned. On the afternoon of the 23rd, Burtwell ordered the railroad bridges burned, and the men settled in for an uneasy night leaving their clothes on and their horses saddled. Burtwell sent out extra pickets and ordered a scouting party to head toward Huntsville to warn of any Union movement. They held their position and waited in vain for reinforcements.

The Battle

During the night of December 23rd, a slave belonging to the residents of the house occupied by Burtwell and his officers, reacted to the harsh treatment he had received from the Confederate troops and escaped to Huntsville where he warned the Union garrison of the Rebel force at Indian Creek. Irvine, Burtwell's Inspector General, noticed the slave's absence soon after nightfall and reported it to his command, but by then it was too late. Col. Prosser had already received word of the Confederate position and was ordering around 200 of his men to advance on Indian Creek. The Union force made up of parts of the 10th Indiana and 2nd Tennessee left Huntsville at 3:00 a.m., setting off down the Decatur Road.

The night was cold, and the ground frozen, but the Union cavalry rode hard and arrived at Indian Creek at dawn, driving the Confederate pickets and scouts ahead of them.

Col. Prosser and Captain George R. Mitchell led the charge with the 10th Indiana while the 2nd Tennessee held up the rear. Col. Burtwell and his staff had arisen just before dawn and rode to the railroad bridge across Indian Creek to make sure it was destroyed, but no sooner had they returned to camp when gunfire was heard toward Huntsville. Burtwell set up a line of defense at the narrow ford across Indian Creek with Sloss Company (4th Alabama, Co F) commanded by Lieutenant Thomas J. Williams in front, "25 to 30 steps" from the bank of the creek. The other company, Company I, began forming a line on the bluff overlooking the floodplain. The formation was done leisurely since they thought that the scouts and pickets would delay the Union charge, but no sooner had the company on the bluff began to dismount to advance into position with Sloss Company when they spotted a Union saber charge driving down the tight road cut east of the creek. The Union advance began to cross the narrow ford with Prosser and Mitchell leading the charge and the 2nd Tennessee driving hard to join the fight. The Confederate company on the bluff wavered and turned, fleeing westward down the road toward Madison and Mooresville beyond. Sloss Company was only able to fire off one volley of shots from horseback before the Union charge crashed into their line, forcing them to join their fleeing comrades. The 2nd Tennessee cavalrymen used their sabers with devastating effect while the 10th Indiana clubbed at the retreating Rebels with their carbines. Burtwell and his officers tried in vain to turn the retreating column. The Confederate troops were pursued along the road all the way to Mooresville, many being cut down and captured along the way.

The small battle was little more than a rout of the Confederate force. It was primarily a saber charge, and one Union eyewitness stated "There was not exceeding one hundred shots fired on our side." Confederate casualties included 50 to 60 captured and several wounded and killed. A review of the Confederate rolls identified 51 Confederate cavalrymen captured near Madison Station on the day of the battle (see list at end of article). The account of John W. Andes of the 2nd Tennessee mentions the citizens of Mooresville reporting that about 100 wounded Confederate soldiers had passed that way. In her diary, Huntsville resident Mary Jane Chadick reported hearing that the Union occupiers brought in 49 prisoners and several wounded men from the fight. The wounded were "badly cut up with saber cuts, as it was a hand-to-hand fight." Union casualties are listed in the Official Records as one killed, three wounded, but first-hand accounts list one killed and only one wounded.

The prisoners were taken back to Huntsville where they were marched to the public square and placed under guard. Some of the captured Confederate troops were released through the intercessions of their loved ones, but the remainder was divided up and sent by rail to Union prisons. The officers were sent to Fort Delaware on the Delaware River, while the enlisted men were sent to Camp Chase in Ohio. Captain Mitchell was later commended for leading the Union charge.

Locating the Battleground

The initial battlefield survey was conducted as part of an archaeological and historical survey of around 7,635 acres of western Huntsville and eastern Madison conducted by the Redstone Arsenal Environmental Management Division to assess impacts to historic properties from the Redstone Gateway development on the north end of Redstone Arsenal. It was known at that time that the battle had occurred somewhere in the survey area, but its exact location was up for debate. Available historic maps were digitally scanned and uploaded using the ArcGIS program to electronically georectify them so that they could be overlaid on modem aerial imagery to help narrow down the location of the battle.

Original pier of the Memphis & Charleston Railroad Bridge across Indian Creek; a pier still stands on either side of the creek, even though neither is used for support anymore.

Based on a detailed account in James Bennington Irvine's wartime diary, the battle took place around a quarter of a mile away from the Memphis & Charleston Railroad Bridge across "six mile branch six miles west of Huntsville. All Union accounts list the creek as "Indian Creek." The drainage now known as Indian Creek is located about six miles west of downtown Huntsville, although the creek went by many other names in the past. It is labeled Hurricane Fork on an 1837 map and Price's Fork on the 1875 Madison County map which reserves the name Indian Creek for that portion of the drainage below its confluence with Huntsville Spring Branch. Nonetheless, there is little doubt that this was the creek where the battle took place.

The Memphis & Charleston Railroad followed the same route as what is now the Norfolk Southern line through Huntsville and Madison. The modern Norfolk Southern bridge crosses at the same place the Memphis & Charleston line crossed during the Civil War. All that is left of the Memphis & Charleston railroad bridge over Indian Creek are the two end pilings which are left intact but no longer support the bridge deck. Rock from the remaining original pilings is spread out as riprap along the north side of the bridge abutments. It is likely, but uncertain that these stone pilings are the remains of the original bridge that was present during the skirmish on December 24, 1964.

Another contemporary account by Major William A. McTeer of the Union 3rd Tennessee Cavalry states that the Union force set off down "Decatur Road" from Huntsville to attack the Confederate position. The 1861 Huntsville city map shows the main westward thoroughfare out of Huntsville as "Pulaski Road." This is where Holmes Avenue runs now. The 1875 Madison County map shows the same road as "Athens Pike" which follows the current route of Holmes Avenue westward to what is now Sparkman Drive where it comes to a fork. The southward branch of the fork is called the "Huntsville to Madison" road on the 1875 map. It followed what is now Sparkman Drive southward until it got to where I-565 is now and then turned westward toward Madison. The road angled across Indian Creek upstream from where Old Madison Pike currently crosses it. The crossing is indicated by a deep road cut on the east side of the creek, and there is still a narrow natural ford across the creek at that location. The 1875 road then passed southwest across the Indian Creek floodplain and up into the bluffs where it turned westward again, following the current route of Old Madison Pike until it branched again a mile west of what is now Wall Triana Road. The south branch of this fork is labeled "To Decatur" on the 1875 map suggesting that this was the route that was considered the "Decatur Road" during the Civil War.

These locations were compared to the first-hand descriptions of the battle allowing the battleground to be laid out on modern aerial imagery. This was viewed in ArcGIS using a hillshade model produced using high-resolution digital elevation data generated through a Light Detection and Ranging (LIDAR) scan of the landscape. This imagery was used to locate areas with minimal ground disturbance for a metal detector survey to determine if any material residue of the skirmish remained.

The metal detector survey was conducted using a White MXT Tracker E-series metal detector with an Eclipse 950 coil. The initial survey was conducted by sweeping all undisturbed ground along transects laid out every five meters. Wherever Civil War era artifacts were found, the surrounding area was swept at closer intervals in an increasing radius around each find to delineate any concentrations. Each metal detector hit was excavated. All 19th century artifacts were collected, and their find locations were electronically marked using a Trimble GeoXH hand-held Global Positioning System (GPS) unit with sub-meter accuracy. This data was then uploaded as an ArcGIS shapefile so that it could be overlaid on maps and analyzed for any spatial patterning.

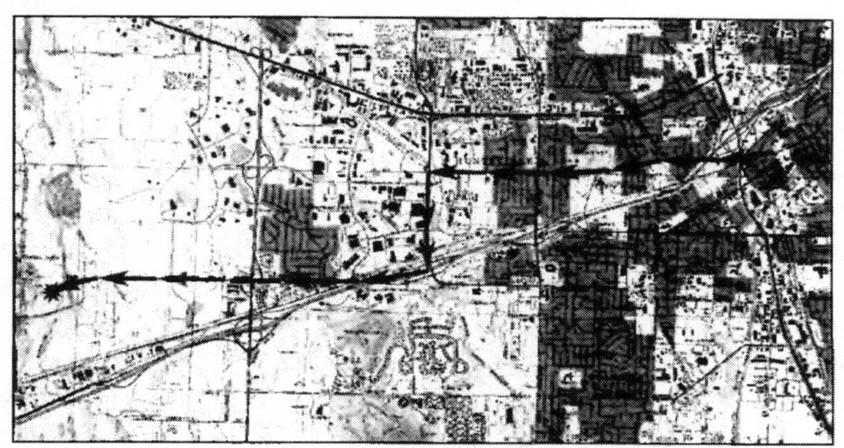

Probable route followed by Union cavalry from Huntsville to Indian Creek.

Survey Results

The metal detector survey focused on three areas (hatchered areas on map below). The first area investigated was designated Survey Area I. The survey of this area was based on Irvine's account which put the Confederate soldiers' camp on the west side of Indian Creek, "about 1/4 mile" from the railroad bridge. All undisturbed ground within this radius was surveyed. About six hours were spent on the actual survey. The vast majority of this area had been disturbed by modern construction. Four parcels (circled by a yellow line in the figure) were determined to be intact enough to be selected for the metal detector survey. All four of these parcels were on the low ridge above the Indian Creek floodplain. Each of these parcels was surveyed with the metal detector in transects spaced a maximum of 10m apart. While lots of 20th century debris (aluminum cans, oil filters, shotgun shells, modem bullets, etc.) was recovered, only two artifacts possibly dating to the Civil War period were collected. One half of a mule shoe was recovered north of a modern electric substation, and a horseshoe was collected in the center of a turnaround in the Madison Academy driveway. Both of these artifacts could have been associated with 19th or early 20th century agriculture, but the 1937 aerial photographs indicate that both find locations were not in cultivation at that time. Nonetheless, there was no evidence that there were any Civil War camps or skirmishes at that location.

The next area surveyed was the vicinity of the ford across Indian Creek which was identified through the analysis of historic maps. The west side of the creek was a parcel of mature hardwoods that was designated Survey Area 2. It was surveyed in transects spaced at 5m intervals. A total of about 30 hours were spent metal detecting this area once all the 19th century finds were delineated. The north boundary of the survey area was a deep historic road-cut which shows up as a secondary road on the 1936 quad map and may mark the original location of the historic Huntsville to Madison Road. The survey area was bound to the south by The Vintage Apartment Complex and to the east by a dense stand of Chinese privet on the Indian Creek floodplain which inhibited metal detecting. Several Civil War and possibly related 19th century artifacts were recovered in this survey area including

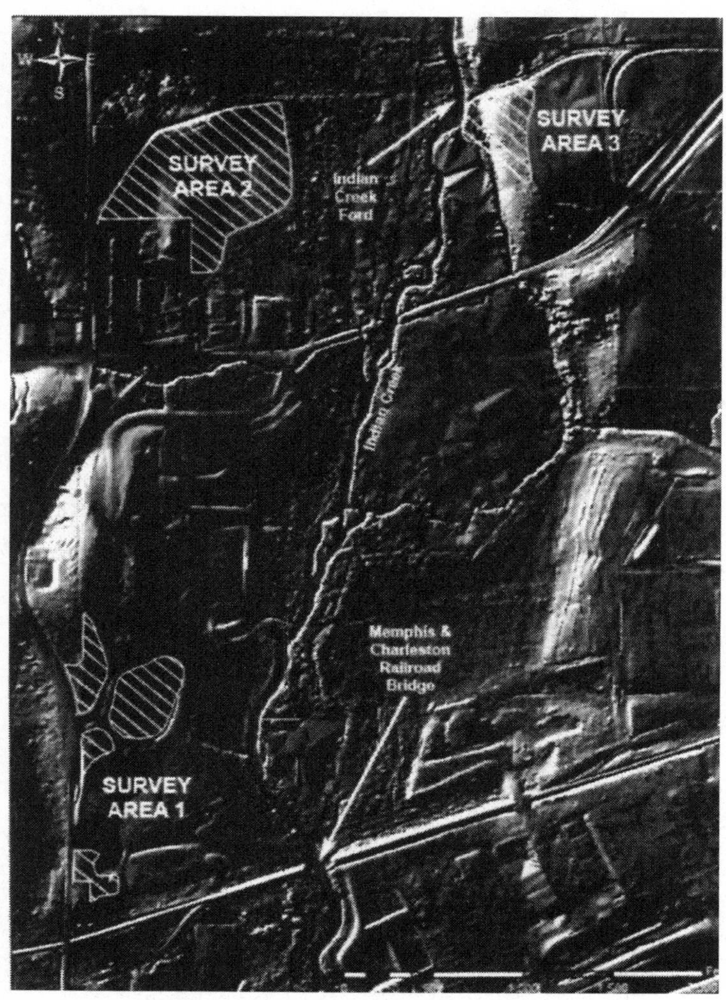

Survey areas on LIDAR hillshade imagery.

a fired Henry repeating rifle casing, a dropped Burnside .54 caliber bullet, two dropped .54 caliber Merrill carbine bullets, a melted Minie ball, a dropped .44 Colt pistol 32 bullet, two fired small caliber pistol balls, a fired pistol bullet, a Union issue knapsack hook, a Union uniform button, a civilian spur, two concentrations of cut nails, a trace chain, and several horse and mule shoes. All 19th century artifacts were plotted using the GPS, and all GPS points were uploaded into ArcGIS for distributional analysis.

Survey Area 3 was the east side of Indian Creek where the historic Huntsville to Madison Road cuts through the Indian Creek bluffs and leads to the natural ford across the creek. Only about three hours were spent at this location. The north side of the road was heavily disturbed by earth boffowing around a modern house, so the metal detector survey focused on the south side of the historic road trace. Transects were spaced 5m apart. Only three Civil War era artifacts were recovered there including a carved .44 caliber Sage bullet, a cut nail, and half of a horseshoe.

Confederate Casualties

The Confederate rolls for units that were known to be operating in this area during the Affair at Indian Creek Ford were examined to identify those captured or wounded on December 23, 1864.

4th Alabama Cavalry (Roddey's)

Armistead, George W., Pvt., Co F. - Residence in Lauderdale Co., took Oath of Allegiance June 13, 1865.

Carroll, John E., Pvt., Co. F - Wounded, gunshot wound left shoulder, surrendered, took Oath of Allegiance December 25, admitted to post hospital (Thomas Barracks) December 26, released January 24, 1865.

Flint, Samuel, Pvt., Co F - Residence in Lauderdale Co., age 19

Hendrick, Alonzo D., Pvt., Co F - Residence in Lauderdale Co., age 18, took Oath of Allegiance June 13, 1865.
Ingram, Benjamin, Pvt., Co F. - Died of pneumonia March 14, 1865 in Camp Chase, buried in Grave #1650.
Irvine, James B., Inspector General and Adjutant to Colonel Burtwell, Residence, Florence, Lauderdale County, Captured at Madison Station, December 23, sent to Fort Delaware POW Camp via Nashville and Louisville. Took Oath of Allegiance, released June 13, 1865.
Irvine, Seymour, Pvt., Co F - Residence, Florence, Lauderdale Co., Sent to Camp Chase POW Camp. Took Oath of Allegiance June 13, 1865. James B. Irvine's brother. Actually captured a few days prior to the battle - may have been serving as a vidette or scout.
Kirkman, J.J., Sgt., Co F - Residence in Lauderdale Co.
Oliver, Albert W., Pvt., Co F - Residence in Lauderdale Co.
Reeder, Reuben A., Pvt., Co F - Residence in Lauderdale Co. Actually captured a few days prior to the battle - may have been serving as a vidette or scout.
Stewart, Edward M., Pvt., Co F - Residence in Lauderdale Co., age 18, took Oath of Allegiance June 12, 1865.
Weems, James M., 2nd Lieut., Co F - Residence in Lauderdale Co.
Young, Samuel C., Pvt., Co F - Residence in Lauderdale Co., age 23, took Oath of Allegiance June 13,1865.
Jordan, Thomas B., Captain, Co I - Captured at Madison Station, December 23, sent to Point Lookout (MD) POW Camp via Nashville and Louisville. Transferred to Aiken's Landing (VA) for exchange on March 17, 1865. Other information indicates that he had been arrested April 16, 1864 by Major General Logan and held by order of Major General Sherman. Released from confinement August 2, 1864 by bail bond of $10,000. Charged with violating parole, awaiting trial.Recruited and commanded a company during the rebel army advance on Nashville.

Leedy, W.B., Sgt, Co I - Appears on muster roll, dated March 20, 1865, of a detachment of paroled and exchanged prisoners at Camp Lee, near Richmond. He was shown as enlisting in Huntsville December 1, 1864, by Captain Jordan. Leedy had been sent to Point Lookout POW Camp from Nashville for special exchange. Exchanged March 17, 1865. He had been charged with being an employee of the QM Department, US Army, and deserted to the enemy. Tried February 14, 1865 at Nashville, but was released on special exchange near City Point, VA.
Moore, Alfred, Pvt., Co I - Residence in Madison Co., age 17, took Oath of Allegiance June 13, 1865.

4th Alabama Cavalry (Russell's)

Hancock, Henry E., Pvt., Co K - Captured at Ft. Donelson Feb. 3, 1863, paroled and delivered to City Point, VA Feb 11, 1863, in General Hospital, Branch A, Petersburg, VA Feb 20, returned to duty Feb 27, 1863, then captured near Huntsville Dec 23, 1864, sent to Camp Chase via Nashville and Louisville, Oath of Allegiance June 13,1865. Enlisted at New Market, AL, age 30

Note: Do not know if he was captured at Indian Creek. May have been captured near his home. Russell's 4th not known to have been at Indian Creek but perhaps he got separated from his command and joined up with Roddey's 4th.

10th Alabama Cavalry

Littleburgh, H. Binford, Surgeon - Sent to Ft. Delaware POW Camp via Nashville and Louisville, transferred to Fort Monroe (VA) for exchange. Exchanged January 22, 1865.

Castleberry, William, Sgt., Co. B - Residence in Tishomingo Co., MS, age 35, took Oath of Allegiance June 13, 1865.

Ganong, Cornelius, Pvt., Co B - Residence in Tishomingo Co., MS, age 20.

Nunley, William, Pvt., Co B - age 31, took Oath of Allegiance June 12, 1865.

Smith, Thomas R., Pvt., Co B - Residence in Tishomingo Co, MS, age 31, took Oath of Allegiance June 13, 1865.

Landers, Josiah B., Pvt., Co E - Took Oath of Allegiance June 13, 1865, admitted to Branch A, Post Hospital, Louisville, KY June 21, 1865, scurvy, discharged June 25, 1865.

Covington, Thomas, Pvt., Co G - Residence in Lauderdale Co., age 17.

Wilson, William, Pvt., Co G - Residence in Lauderdale Co, age 20, took Oath of Allegiance June 13, 1865.

Branson, David, Pvt., Co. I - Residence in Tishomingo Co., MS, age 32.

Nance, Washington P., Pvt., Co I - Died March 9, 1865 in Camp Chase, pneumonia, buried in Grave #1699, 1/3 mile south of Camp C.

Martin, William R., Pvt., Co K - Admitted to USA General Hospital #2 at Vicksburg, MS, May 27, 1865 from Marine Barracks, acute dysentery, returned to duty June 3, 1865.

Hamilton, George W., Pvt., Co. L - Residence in Limestone Co., age 19, took Oath of Allegiance June 13, 1865.

Nelms, James L., Pvt., Co L - Residence in Lawrence Co., age 38, took Oath of Allegiance June 12, 1865.

Sholar, William A., Pvt., Co. L - Died February 28, 1865 in Camp Chase, buried in Grave #1477, 1/3 mile south of Camp C.

May, Samuel W., Pvt., Residence in Franklin Co., deserted December 23, took Oath of Allegiance March 13, 1865.

Owens, Marquis L., Pvt., Residence in Giles Co., TN, deserted December 23, took Oath of Allegiance March 9, 1865, was a conscript.

Note: Civil War Soldiers and Sailors (CWSS) lists Branson, Castleberry, Covington, Ganong, Landers, Martin, Nance, Nelms, Nunley, Smith, and Wilson as being in the 11th Alabama Cavalry. The 11th was organized by the consolidation of Warren's and William's battalions on 14 Jan 1865.

Moreland's Alabama Cavalry

Pierce, Thomas W., Asst. Surgeon - Sent to Ft. Delaware, then Ft. Monroe for exchange on February 22, 1865.
Clark, Julius F., Pvt., Co A - Died January 28, 1865 in Camp Chase, pneumonia, buried in Grave #9340, 1/3 mile south of Camp C.
Gains, H.M., Pvt., Co A - Residence in Franklin Co., Oath of Allegiance June 13, 1865.
Sartin, Langford, Sgt., Co A - Paroled at Camp Chase and transferred to City Point, VA February 25, 1865, for exchange. (alternate name: Sartain).
Cathey, Andrew D.A., Pvt., Co C - Residence in Tishomingo Co, MS, age 15.
Kay, John, Pvt., Co C - Died June 5, 1865 in Camp Chase, pneumonia, buried in Grave #2017, 1/3 mile south of Camp C. Enlisted at Dickson, AL.
Davis, James H., 2 Lt., Co D - Residence in Tishomingo Co, MS, sent to Ft. Delaware, Exchanged and released Jan. 17, 1865.
Holder, Benjamin A., Pvt., Co D - Paroled at Camp Chase and transferred to City Point, VA February 25, 1865, for exchange, in Jackson Hospital, Richmond, VA March 10, 1865. Enlisted at Warren Mills, MS.
Looney, Lowry B., Pvt., Co D - Residence in Tishomingo Co., MS.

McCoy, William F., Pvt., Co D - Died March 2, 1865 in Camp Chase, buried in Grave #1530, 1/3 mile south of Camp C.
Moore, John, Sgt., Co D - Paroled at Camp Chase and transferred to City Pont, VA February 25, 1865, for exchange, in General Hospital, Camp Winder, March 10, 1865.
Spencer, William A., Pvt., Co D - Died February 20, 1865 in Camp Chase, buried in Grave #1394, 1/3 mile south of Camp C.
Tackett, Enoch B., Pvt., Co D - Paroled at Camp Chase and transferred to City Point, VA February 25, 1865, for exchange Roddey's Escort Company.
Gurley, John S., Pvt., Co G - Residence in Tishomingo Co, MS.
Burgess, Richard F., Pvt., Co H - Gunshot wound, right side, admitted to Granger General Hospital, December 24, then sent to prison, where he died on February 20, 1865. Buried in Grave #1353, 1/3 mile south of Camp C.
Crowell, George W., Pvt., Co H - Residence in Franklin Co., age 24.
Leadbetter, Henry, Pvt., Co H - Paroled at Camp Chase and transferred to City Point, VA for exchange, in Jackson Hospital, Richmond, VA March 8, 1865. Furloughed March 9.
Norris, William W., Pvt., Co H - Paroled at Camp Chase and transferred to City Point, VA February 25, 1865 for exchange.
Patterson, A.W., Capt., Co H - Sent to Ft. Delaware January 9, 1865. Oath of Allegiance June 10, 1865.
Rogers, John H., Pvt., Co H - Paroled at Camp Chase and transferred to City Point, VA February 25, 1865 for exchange, in Jackson Hospital, Richmond, VA March 8, debilitas, Furloughed March 10. (alternate name: Rodgers).
Gable, James H., Cpl., Co I - Died May 16, 1865 in Camp Chase, buried in Grave #1972, 1/3 mile south of Camp C.

All the following were captured near Huntsville but were not involved in the battle at Indian Creek. They would have been sent as prisoners to Huntsville, then transferred to Camp Chase, via Nashville and Louisville.

Chittwood, Richard O., Pvt. - Captured December 20, 1864, Died February 20, 1865 and buried in Grave # [illegible].
Coons, Everitt, Pvt. - Captured December 20, 1864, at Maysville. Residence in Franklin Co, Oath of Allegiance June 13, 1865.
Dodson, Willis, Pvt. - Captured December 27, 1864, at Madison Station. Residence in Lawrence Co. (Note: one card says captured January 15, 1865).
Doss, James M., Pvt. - Captured December 27, 1864 in Madison Co, sent to Camp Chase, then Vicksburg MS for exchange. Admitted to General Hospital #2 from Marine Barracks May 21, 1865, remittent fever, returned to duty May 22.
Heflin, Alexander, Pvt. - Captured December 27, 1864 in Madison Co. Residence in Lauderdale Co, age 18, (Note: one card says captured December 25.).
Roberts, Henry C., Pvt. - Captured December 20, 1864 at Brownsboro, died in Camp Chase, buried in Grave #1748, 1/3 mile south of Camp C.
Yerby, Tolbert, Pvt. - Captured December 20, 1864. Residence in Fayette Co, age 18.

Stuart's Battalion

None found. Assumed not engaged at Indian Creek.

5th Alabama Cavalry

None found. Assumed not engaged at Indian Creek. Believed to have been in Decatur. (Note: Only Roll # 19 (A-L) was reviewed on the basis that if there were no captures on or about December 23 of the men on this roll that it would be unlikely to find any on Roll # 20 (M-Y). There were a number of captures December 29, 1864 at Pond Springs (Courtland), which supports the preceding statement.

RECONSTRUCTION IN HUNTSVILLE AND MADISON COUNTY, ALABAMA, 1865 - 1869

By Sarah Etheline Bounds

The Civil War was a revolution in the life of the American people. A detailed examination of the conditions in a small section of the United States following the war may lead to a greater understanding of these drastic changes. Madison County, lying in the fertile and prosperous Tennessee Valley of north central Alabama, serves as the microcosm for the study. Madison County is not an entirely typical county, but its history shows the forces and organizations that were active during the years immediately after the Civil War.

Though the events of 1865 settled the secession and slavery issues, new and more difficult problems faced the people of the Southern States in the post-war years. Immediate and pragmatic answers were needed for dealing with the freedmen; for obtaining money to buy seeds and supplies; for paying debts and taxes; and for stimulating business. Only time and the cooperative effort of all would bring solutions to these perplexing issues.

Although the population of Madison County increased from the years 1860 to 1870, the estimated population in 1866 was below that of 1860. There were 25,531 people in 1866, a reduction of 923 but an increase of 988 whites. This was due, in part, to the influx of northerners and to the departure of former slaves leaving to test their freedom or to join the Union army. The casualties of the war for Madison County were 147 killed, 214 dead from sickness, and twenty-eight disabled.

While population declined in other parts of Alabama, Madison County showed an increase in both white and former slave population between 1860 and 1870. In 1860, the white population was 11,686 and the black population was

14,768, a total of 26,454. The total population in 1870 was 31,267, white: 15,527 and black: 15,740.

The Huntsville city government, during and immediately following the Civil War, found it almost impossible to carry out its administrative functions. The needs of the people were numerous, and funds were lacking to supply even the basics of greater police protection, more water, and better fire control.

From May 5, 1863 to January 15, 1867 the minutes of the Huntsville City Council meetings were written in a ledger other than the official book, and there is evidently no existing record of these proceedings. Mayor Robert W. Coltart and eight new aldermen were elected in December, 1866, to take office on January 15, 1867. With a balance of $34.12, these officials began the task of bringing Huntsville out of a crucial time of suffering and hardship. The incomplete and inaccurate records and files made the first business meeting most difficult. The expenditures and receipts of the available records were not consistent. Since previous boards did not require the recording and the auditing of accounts, some entries, credits, and forfeitures do not appear or do not correspond.

Since early 1863, property damages against the city were extensive. Claims of above three thousand dollars were filed against the city within a week. The major and aldermen studied the books and found $808.88 due for taxes in 1865, $6,930.03 due for 1866, and $399.50 due for city licenses. Even though money was scarce and many people were destitute, they expected 75 percent of these back taxes to be paid. Some people paid the back taxes and license fees, making the new balance $396.01 by March 5, 1867. But on April 12, 1867, the mayor ordered the establishment of a new set of books, saying it was impossible to balance the books for 1866.

Before the war the city purchased shares of stock in the Memphis and Charleston Railroad, and now it became necessary to sell some stock to pay the indebtedness from some bonds due in June, 1867. Mayor Coltart went to

Philadelphia and sold sixteen hundred shares with a face value of twenty-five dollars. He was able, however, to secure only eighty-five cents on the dollar for the stock.

The financial statement of July 31, 1867, indicated a deficit of $2,881.35 because the council had received $24,728.74 and spent $27,610.09. The city had assets of $96,631 which included railroad stock, personal property, real estate, and waterworks; its liabilities were $41,461, covering city bonds, bills payable, coupons and unpaid checks. Huntsville, thus, had a liquidating value of $55,170.

The extremely low city finances required the strictest economy in management. The new mayor and aldermen displayed much courage, patience, and energy in working with the problem. The people apparently were paying back the fees for licenses, fines, forfeitures and taxes when they were able. Yet, the financial balances at council business meetings were remaining small. Although many of the tax assessments were uncollected, the financial condition improved during 1868 until the city budget had a surplus of $9,000.00.

As in most other matters, there was much optimism regarding business prospects soon after the war. The hotels reopened, but were plagued by financial difficulties. Cotton merchants hung out their signs along the west side of the courthouse square. Horse and mule trading became an important business because the animals were needed to stock the farms.

By the summer of 1866, actual improvements were not as great as expected. Construction consisted of two small stores in town and of a large warehouse and store near the depot. The courthouse and many private homes were repaired and painted. The newspapers made constant appeals for the building of small cottage-like houses for mechanics and laborers. Businessmen felt people would come to Huntsville if better residences at a fair rent were available.

Business was generally stagnant. The only town people who were busy were the lawyers and the loafers. The country people were busy on their farms. Business could not really be active until the people had something to sell. The only brisk period of trade was in the fall after the gathering of the wheat and cotton crops and the people were preparing for the winter. At this time of year the country people came to town on Saturdays in wagons and buggies, making the courthouse square a popular place to trade, to meet friends, and to get news.

The merchants and citizens protested the presence of transient traders and petitioned the city to have them taxed. They secured the passage of an ordinance which required the traveling merchant or trader to pay one percent of their sales to the city. To ensure payment, the city took as collateral two satisfactory securities, personally owned items or property deeds. The transient doctor or physician had to pay fifteen dollars for a license or ten dollars each day without a license. The merchants also obtained a prohibition against the open sale of bacon on the courthouse square, since the price was far below that charged by regular merchants.

Since very little money was in circulation, the transaction of banking and all other business was difficult. The Northern Bank of Alabama was in liquidation. The National Bank of Huntsville, chartered by the state legislature in July, 1865, had more than three-fourths of its capital stock of $100,000 furnished by money from New York. Rison Banking, a private concern with a capital stock of $40,000, made its appearance in March, 1866. Its organizers were W. R. Rison, who was previously in the mercantile business in Aberdeen, Mississippi, and Captain Samuel W. Fordyce, a Federal officer stationed in Huntsville during the war.

The first Alabama branch of the Freedmen's Savings Bank opened in Huntsville in December, 1865. These banks, serving only freed slaves, were not a part of, but were usually allied with, the Freedmen's Bureau. Bureau agents were often in charge of the bank branches. In 1868, the Huntsville branch had $5,097 in deposits and $38.02 in interest on long-term deposits. In only five months, deposits increased to

$17,603.29. By March 31, 1870, five hundred depositors had a total of $89,445.10. As indicated by these figures, deposits increased rapidly and the bank continued to prosper for several years. The Huntsville and Mobile branches of the Freedmen's Savings Bank were the largest and most prominent in the state. Nevertheless, only those in and around these cities became depositors. Those in more remote sections of the country lived in ignorance of the bank.

Another aid to the freed slaves were the rations provided by the Freedmen's Bureau under the supervision of Colonel John B. Callis, Superintendent of the Bureau in North Alabama. These rations usually consisted of white corn and bacon. The newspapers most often read by the freed slaves carried items on the issuing of the rations.

Colonel John B. Callis
Superintendent
Freedmen's Bureau in North Alabama

Rations from the government were to end in the fall of 1867, except for hospitals, orphan homes, and very extreme cases. Nevertheless, Huntsville continued to obtain rations and a soup house opened in February 1868. The time and the place of the establishment of this soup house and others over the state, seem to indicate they had a political objective of influencing the black vote. Anyone could receive soup and bread by merely appearing at the barracks near the depot. After a short operation of several months, the soup house was discontinued.

To assist the ever-increasing number and demands of destitutes, the city and county established an Alms House and Hospital in December, 1866. It was located on the farm of Robert C. Brickell, south of Huntsville, and was under the supervision of Dr. Henry W. Bassett.

The small, insufficient crops of 1865 were among the factors creating a more destitute condition. A lack of farm laborers resulted in scarcely any cotton being planted. This failure made it impossible for thousands of residents to grow crops the following year without assistance. In addition to all the man-made troubles of the farmer, such as a lack of implements and labor, nature also worked against him in unfavorable weather, rotten seeds, and insects. The newspapers described 1866 as "the wettest winter and spring and the hottest and driest summer and the worst year for farming we have had in North Alabama for a great while."

Despite these difficulties the estimated cotton crop for the year was 5,000 bales, but this was not half an average crop. At this time, the winter of 1866-67, cotton was selling at twenty-four cents per pound the highest price during Reconstruction.

By the end of 1867, the advice to the farmers was not to depend heavily on cotton. Cotton prices were low and

South side of Courthouse Square in 1867.
James Record Picture Collection,
Huntsville Public Library

continued to drop to about ten cents. Wheat was the advisable crop to plant because it brought a good price and could be used to support the needs of the people. The suggested proportion of food crops to cotton crops was three-fourths to one-fourth. The objective was to strive for self-sufficiency and then to sell the remaining crops for money and necessary goods not obtainable by individual efforts.

Mortgage sales on the courthouse square occurred by the hundreds. There was a general exodus of people toward the western states for several years after 1869. Before hard times struck, however, land deeds were secured quickly by the actual settlers under the Homestead Law of 1862. People from Madison and other counties crowded daily into the United States Land Office in Huntsville. They wanted to save their land registered under the secession state government. The Office entered 545 farms or over 4,000 acres in April and May of 1867, only one entry had been by a former slave, a woman from Morgan County.

General Włodzimierz Bonawentura Krzyżanowski Sixth Division in Alabama

The lack of transportation facilities was a serious hindrance to the rebuilding of Alabama. Fortunately, Madison County had the advantage of the Memphis and Charleston Railroad that extended across the entire northern part of the state. At the railroad stockholders' meeting in Huntsville on August 29, 1866, the statement of the total loss due to the war was $1,195,000. A second mortgage of one million dollars was made for the improvement of the railroad and for a line from North Alabama to Atlanta. Since the value of the road and equipment was $9,549,115 and the total liabilities were only $4,348,304, the railroad hoped to pay a dividend in the fall of 1867 and every six months thereafter. Considering the general economic circumstances of North Alabama, the financial condition of the company seemed excellent. Instead of paying the promised dividend, however, the stock continually dropped in value until it reached only forty-four per cent of its face value in January 1869. The projected connection to Atlanta did not materialize either. Another means of transportation was the Tennessee River. Wagons hauled goods to and from the river by the Whitesburg Pike. Stage coach lines ran between Huntsville and the river and the smaller communities, but on an irregular schedule.

General Thomas H. Ruger Command of Alabama with Headquarters in Huntsville.

A profound influence in Huntsville during and after the war was the almost constant presence of Federal forces in the city after April 11, 1862, when General O. M. Mitchel captured the city. Shortly after the war ended, the twelve counties of North Alabama were withdrawn from the jurisdiction of the assistant commissioner for Tennessee, General Clinton B. Fiske, to become the sixth division in Alabama under the command of General Waldimir "Kriz" Kryzyanwski.

The United States government-built barracks, a quartermaster office, and a commissary store at the railroad depot in 1866. Until the completion of the barracks, the homes of Huntsville citizens served as quarters for the troops, with the Calhoun house and the building on the corner of the square and Eustice Street as the office of the quartermaster.

The officers and soldiers stationed in Huntsville after the war were of the 33rd Regiment of the United States Infantry. Citizen and soldier baseball teams often played near the depot. The soldiers showed an interest in community affairs, by contributing to the Catholic building fund, by helping to put out fires on numerous occasions, and by having the military band play for fancy balls.

In 1868, General Thomas H. Ruger, the former Military Governor of Georgia, took command of Alabama, with headquarters in Huntsville. The Huntsville *Advocate* described Ruger as an officer of character, ability, and fairness, with an accurate knowledge of the political status of the state and of its individuals. When two companies of troops arrived in September 1868, there was a total of eight companies or about five hundred men in Huntsville. Most of the troops camped on the Whitesburg Pike, while General Ruger maintained his headquarters in the Calhoun house.

Unfortunately, lawlessness was a common occurrence during and immediately after the war. The Federals held Madison County for almost three years of the war, except for two short intervals when the Federal forces were flanked and forced to retire. Since the Federal occupation entirely destroyed the civil government of the town, anarchy generally reigned in the absence of military control.

The relaxation of military discipline after the war resulted in a deterioration of law and order. Many Huntsville citizens suffered robbery, murder, and arson from the soldiers and other civilians. The local traffic in whiskey was enormous. Drunken soldiers, who frequently became violent, crowded the streets. Ladies of easy virtue were also present.

Efforts to correct these evils included arresting lewd women, fining them as much as twenty dollars and moving them outside the city limits. Captain Robert Harrison, commander of the Huntsville post, requested an ordinance prohibiting the selling or giving of liquors to enlisted men. Such an ordinance passed, being amended to include minors and providing a penalty of twenty-five dollars for each offense.

In view of the prevailing disrespect for the law, Provisional Governor Lewis E. Parson received authorization to call out the militia in each county if necessary. In addition, the mayors of Huntsville, Athens, and Florence had special police power to suppress violence. Because the lawless element was especially strong in Madison County, the Huntsville mayor apparently was in the greatest need of this power.

Huntsville was one of only three cities in Alabama to have Freedmen's courts for freedmen to secure a fair and unprejudiced trial. The state courts actually became the Freedmen's courts early in 1866. A military commission at Huntsville rendered decisions in questions of property title.

While the county experienced limited economic growth, the courts had more business than ever. Both civil and criminal cases crowded the court dockets. The circuit court in September, 1866 had over seven hundred new suits. But despite the number of the legal transactions, the newspapers gave detailed accounts on them.

During the post-Civil War period, Huntsville had three newspapers, a Radical paper supported by the Federal government and two Democratic papers. The Radical, or Republican, paper was the Huntsville *Advocate,* known as the *Southern Advocate* before the war. This paper was a semi-weekly, published every Tuesday and Friday, with yearly subscriptions at four dollars. The *Advocate* was entitled "The Official Journal of the United States Government for the Northern District of Alabama," serving the counties of Madison, Marshall, Jackson, DeKalb, Blount, Marion, Walker, Fayette and entirely supported by Republican campaign funds and by appropriations from the government for printing the laws passed by the United States Congress. All bankruptcy, judicial, and legal notices for the above counties appeared in the *Advocate*.

William Bibb Figures was the editor of the *Advocate* before the war and until his death in 1872. Figures was quite active in local politics, serving as mayor of Huntsville before the war and for two terms after the war, chairman of the Fifth District Executive Committee of the Union Republican Party, justice of the peace, and registrar in chancery. Of the old whig school, he approved of the provisional government during the first term of President Grant. Figures had the reputation of being a competent editor, who reported every happening carefully and accurately.

One of the Democratic papers was the Huntsville *Weekly Democrat*, previously entitled the *Daily Huntsville Confederate*. Its editor was John Withers Clay, son of former Governor Clement Comer Clay and the brother of former United States Senator Clement Claiborne Clay. Forced to publish in secret during the war, the *Democrat* came out of hiding after the war and changed from a daily to a weekly paper.

Edited by J. J. Dew and John W. Young, the Huntsville Independent was a weekly paper established in 1855. The Radicals, its powerful opponents, said its editors were poor and unskilled and complained about the *Independent* being an inadequate and inferior paper.

Because of the intense political hatred between Radical and Democratic papers, harsh and insulting remarks appeared in the newspapers about the other papers and their editors. Some of the leading enemies of the *Advocate* were the Huntsville *Independent*, the Montgomery *Mail*, and the *Moulton Advertiser*. The Montgomery *Mail* referred to the *Advocate* as "the Black Republican organ of Huntsville - a bogus Union paper." On one occasion Figures sought revenge by advocating the erection of a statue of John Withers Clay fleeing from Huntsville as the 4th Ohio Calvary came into the city in 1862. Clay should be mounted on Jack Esslinger's mule, said Figures, and carry a black flag in one hand and a white flag in the other.

The newspapers usually consisted of four pages. The second page contained the editorial and the third page was mostly notes or comments on local business, farming or society. The publication of the laws of the United States, bankrupt notices, assignee sales, and other legal notices were on the last page or the third page. The remainder of the paper consisted of reprints from other newspapers, letters, poems, advertisements, and notices of educational institutions.

Private schools for white boys and girls and the Huntsville Female College reopened in the fall of 1865. The buildings of Green Academy, destroyed during the war, were not restored and the school was closed permanently.

Among the private schools which reopened for day and boarding students was the Huntsville Female Seminary, with the Presbyterian minister, Reverend H. R. Smith, as principal. Half of the tuition for the five month term was paid in advance. Board with tuition was $130 with ten to thirty dollars more for additional courses in ancient or modern languages, drawing, painting, or music.

First National Bank in 1870. Theophilus Clay, Cashier, is standing on the bank steps, his family carriage and driver in the foreground.
James Record Picture Collection, Huntsville Public Library

The Huntsville High School, or Male High School, also had two terms of five months each. The tuition, due in advance, varied from twenty to forty-five dollars a term, depending on the class. Board with private families in Huntsville was a hundred dollars per term. W. A. Slaymaker, the principal, said the school was inferior to none in the South and was entirely free from any sectarian bias.

The Huntsville Female College had similar terms and tuition as the Huntsville Female Seminary and the Huntsville High School. Although board and tuition were due in advance, supplies were taken for payments. Revered J. G. Wilson, the president, stated that the school offered courses in music, oil painting, German, French, English, and other useful and ornamental branches of female education.

Other schools included the Mathematical and Classical School directed by Dr. C. G. Smith; a second school which met in the rear of the Baptist Church and applied the fourteen dollars tuition toward the completion of the church building; and another school at the Catholic Church which taught English, piano, and guitar to boys and girls. Major General O. O. Howard, chief of the Bureau for Freedmen and Refugees, announced arrangements for an elementary and an advanced education at a school on Lookout Mountain, Tennessee. The program, unfortunately, was available only to white boys and girls who were the children of Union soldiers.

Many parents, mostly farmers and tenant, were unable to send their children to school because of the high tuition. Although some parents tried to teach their children at home when they had time from their work, many children of educated parents grew up in ignorance.

Before the war ended only three or four Negro schools were established in Alabama. One of these was in Huntsville on Townsend Street and another was at the Negro colony on the Plantation of former Governor Reuben Chapman, a few miles north of Huntsville. Northern societies sent teachers and missionaries to the South as the Federal Occupation continued. The Pittsburgh Freedmen's Aid Society supported eleven schools in Huntsville, Athens, and Stevenson by the end of 1865. While the society provided the teachers and the supplies, the Freedmen's Bureau aided these schools by furnishing the buildings, the rent, and the repairs. Under the terms of the original Freedmen Bureau Act, money to equip these schools came from northern donations and from the seizure and sale of cotton in the area of the school. After the passage of the Bureau Act of July, 1866, the sale of Confederate property became another source of support. It was reported that five hundred black children attended various Huntsville schools in December, 1866. The total average attendance per day for the preceding month, however, was only three hundred.

At first only Northern white teachers were employed in Huntsville's schools. Soon qualified black teachers were secured. In late 1866, there were five white teachers from the North and three black assistants from Huntsville, Thomas Townsend, Charles Henley, and S. L. Carter.

For religious instruction, the former slaves attended churches with the whites immediately after the war, and white pastors and teachers chosen by the freed slaves attended to their religious welfare and education.

One of the Northern missionaries who created ill feeling between the races was Reverend A. S. Lakin from Indiana. He was sent to Huntsville in 1866 to organize the Northern Methodist Church. Lakin tried to crush the former slaves' attempts to form their own churches, and he took over Southern Methodist church buildings for his group. Even his own congregation finally complained, charging they paid for their own lot and church but the deed was in Lakin's name. He was so universally hated that an attempted assassination was made on him and his family in 1868.

Federal forces occupied many of the churches of Huntsville during the war. Frequently, fires made in church basements for the soldiers to cook their food were carelessly tended. Only two days after a protest to the military authorities about fire hazards, the Methodist Church was completely destroyed by fire. The rebuilding of the church was typical of several congregations during the post-war days.

Although the Methodists had no definite place to worship, the Reverend A. L. P. Green came from Nashville in July, 1866, to assist in a series of meetings. With the use of Presbyterian buildings, the Methodists were hosts to 175 ministers attending the Tennessee Conference in the fall of 1866.

Immediately following these revival services, the members began active planning to erect their church within a year. Raising the necessary money required many and varied approaches. The building fund received the proceeds of the Grove Spring Tournament, the annual summer social event in Huntsville. The pastor, Reverend Thomas L. Moody, solicited funds in the surrounding states and obtained $4,500. Within two weeks after his return, rubbish was cleaned from the church lot on Randolph Street and construction began on July 15, 1867. Church services, as well as Sunday School and social events, were held in the basement of the church for several years while the sanctuary was being built. During these years the women of the church increased the building fund by giving suppers, fairs, and tableaux.

All the churches, of course, provided many social activities for the people such as picnics, ice cream parties, suppers, and fairs. Most of these events raised money to pay church debts or to build and repair the buildings. During the summer months barbecues, picnics, and fish fries were held on the banks of the Tennessee River and at many springs near Huntsville. These events were often attended by both races. Good feeling and order prevailed.

Huntsville had two annual festivals. The Flower Queen Festival, enacted by the children under the direction of their parents, was held in the spring. The summer event the Huntsville Tournament Association or the Grove Spring Tournament, was a colorful two-day celebration at the amphitheatre on Monte Sano Mountain. The pageant involved knights from the county who competed for the honor of selecting the Queen of Love and Beauty and her court. The proceeds went to some charitable project, such as the building fund of the Methodist Church. The annual circus was another event that the children anxiously awaited.

The Huntsville Hotel was the scene of Fancy Dress Soirees or balls. Only the socially elite attended, but the receipts had a charitable purpose, such as raising money for the Mason's Widow and Orphan Fund of Madison. Either the Band of the 33rd Infantry or the Spring City Brass Band provided the music for such affairs.

The two bands also gave concerts, and the pupils of various teachers performed in recitals. The students were from music teacher Professor Habick, dancing instructor Professor McDonald, or the Huntsville Female Seminary. The Opera House offered entertainment by traveling theatrical troupes and the Huntsville Thespians. Local plays were apparently well liked, with the group giving several repeat performances.

Despite the gloom and despondency associated with much of Reconstruction, there was considerable activity which brought enjoyment to the local citizenry during the period of 1865-69. The new status of freed slaves, along with other social and economic changes, of course, affected the customs, manners, reactions industries agriculture, and population of the area. But along with change came new opportunities for citizens to participate in and contribute to the progress of their community. In time, recovery was affected and Huntsville returned again to its former position as a leader in the development of Alabama and, indeed, the South.

CRIMINAL JUSTICE IN MADISON COUNTY, ALABAMA APRIL 1865 TO DECEMBER 1874

Mary G. Tumlin

The criminal justice system in Madison County, Alabama, was largely ineffective throughout Reconstruction. When the Civil War ended in April 1865, citizens attempted to re-implement pre-war leadership within their local police, sheriff, and judicial systems. It soon became apparent, however, that restoration of civil authority under the supervision of respected officials would constitute a long struggle. Chaos during Reconstruction was primarily due to radicals who were determined to reconstruct local government under the leadership of men loyal to the Republican Party, rather than conservative Democrats who had controlled the criminal justice system prior to the war. Further complicating the situation, the citizenry was confronted with intervention from outside agencies such as the Freedmen's Bureau, the Union League, and the United States Army.

Thus, the period from April 1865 to December 1874 was one of the most chaotic in the history of Madison County. As federal authorities became more aggressive, inept civil officials were appointed or elected to positions within the justice system. Carpetbaggers, northerners who supported the Republican Party, and Scalawags, local Republicans who were loyal to the Union, dominated law enforcement and the court systems. Ku Klux Klan activity abounded due to public apathy and a lack of law enforcement. Many locals, nevertheless, continued their efforts to regain control of local government, and by December 1874 the criminal justice system in Madison County had gained stability under the leadership of men who represented a choice of thepeople.

Whites began their attempt to restore civilian leadership after the war, but the Freedman's Bureau and federal troops dominated local affairs from April 1865 to January 1866. There appeared to be very little animosity towards the Bureau during this period, for the organization distributed badly needed rations to destitute citizens. In the meantime, the commander of federal troops in Huntsville received numerous complaints from people throughout the county concerning cases of assault, theft, and drunkenness.

In their first effort to re-implement civil authority, locals went to the polls in November 1865, and elected Frank Gurley, a Democrat and ex-captain in the Confederate Army, as sheriff of Madison County. Shortly afterwards, according to local newspapers, Gurley was arrested by federal troops and taken to Nashville to stand trial for murder in military court. His accusers had asserted that while serving the Confederacy, Gurley had murdered a Union officer. Even though the sheriff was sentenced to hang, orders for his execution were suspended. Many locals were concerned about Gurley's dilemma and resented the fact that the county had finally gained an officer who represented a choice of the people, only to have him abruptly removed.

Some progress was made within the judicial system during this period. The county and mayor's (city) courts were reestablished for the first time since the war. These courts were responsible for hearing minor cases which occurred within the county and within the city. The circuit court, which handled serious crimes, was also re-implemented under the leadership of William J. Haralson. Although Haralson was a Republican, he was well respected and remained Circuit Court Judge throughout Reconstruction. The courts as well as local law enforcement exerted very little authority, and people were forced to rely on federal troops for protection.

Criminal justice remained in upheaval as citizens struggled through another period of uncertainty from January 1866 to March 1867. Problems mounted as the local Freedmen's Bureau began to dominate the judicial system. Consequently, whites viewed the Bureau, which was under the direction of John Callis, a northerner, as a nuisance. While civil courts remained ineffective, a Bureau Court was established and heard numerous cases that concerned complaints filed by freedmen. An example noted in the Freedmen's Bureau Papers involved Russell Sanford, a white, who was fined forty dollars after he refused to pay one of his ex-slaves back wages.

The Huntsville Advocate reported numbers of complaints filed against unruly soldiers. The problem was so bad in 1866 that the commander of federal troops forbade citizens to sell intoxicating beverages to soldiers. Troops often experienced difficulties in their relations with freedmen. One example reported by a local paper involved three drunk soldiers who interrupted a baptism at the Big Spring. After soldiers pushed a freedman into the water, a fight ensued and the men were chased back to their barracks. Madison County, although stymied by federal authority, had an appointed sheriff, city police were reinstituted for the first time since the war, and civil courts convened haphazardly during the latter part of 1866. These accomplishments would be nullified in March 1867 when Congress placed the South under military rule.

Passage of the Reconstruction Acts by a radical Congress not only declared local governments in southern states illegal, but they also authorized military authorities to remove civil officials. Furthermore, numbers of ex-Confederates were disfranchised as well as excluded from holding public office. The progress that had been made in Madison County's criminal justice system was nullified when elected officials were removed from office and replaced by military appointees. The Union League, an organization whose goal was to solicit black votes for the Republican Party, became active on the local level. Thus, disfranchised whites looked on with dismay as freedmen paraded around the courthouse square demonstrating their new political rights.

In the meantime, crime increased, and local jails overflowed as civilians within the criminal justice system were subjected to military authority. Newspapers reported that troops were so unruly, citizens took the law into their own hands. After a soldier, James Hardy, was convicted of theft, his head was shaved, and he was tied to a cart and forced to march through Huntsville.

Problems continued as ex-Confederates were forced from the justice system. Sheriff John Coltart was removed from office by the military and replaced by a "loyal union" man. Shortly afterwards, Robert Coltart was ousted as Mayor's court judge. Coltart, a respected Democrat, was replaced by a staunch Republican, Elisha B. Clapp. The U.S. Armv Commands stated that the newly appointed judge soon proved to be a very inept individual who received bribes from defendants for ruling in their favor. The Circuit Court was also in limbo. Federal officers suspended trials because the court failed to comply with military regulations.

With the implementation of a new state constitution in 1868, as well as Alabama's readmission to the Union, people could now go to the polls. As a result of the election held in February 1868, civil authority was restored. Since many whites were still disfranchised, the Republican Party, supported by freedmen's votes, elected Radicals to local offices. Military reconstruction ended in July 1868 when these newly elected civil officials assumed office.

The period from July 1868 to November 1870 was perhaps the most violent in the history of Madison County. Unqualified Carpetbaggers and Scalawags dominated positions within the criminal justice system. Lawlessness abounded as Ku Klux Klan activity reached its peak. The Huntsville Police Department was active but plagued by complaints. According to the Minutes of the Board of Aldermen, one instance involved policeman R. B. James, who shot a freedman for no apparent reason. Although James had been suspended five times for misconduct, no action was taken in this case.

The Sheriff's Department also experienced problems during this period. As a result of the February election,

Joseph P. Doyle, a Republican, was elected sheriff of Madison County and assumed his duties in July 1868. The highest ranking law enforcement officer in the county was a weak, unstable individual who failed to act against troublemakers. Doyle's apathy towards his responsibilities disillusioned citizens who refused to accept his leadership.

An unqualified Carpetbagger was elected County Court Judge and took office in July 1868. Lewis M. Douglass, a carpenter from Oregon, had no prior experience in any judicial system. Since the Circuit Court remained under the jurisdiction of William J. Haralson, all of the judges in Madison County were now affiliated with the Republican party. Thus, civil authority was reinstituted on the local level; but the majority of office holders were inexperienced Radicals who did little to control the violence that erupted after July 1868.

The first official deaths connected to local Klansmen occurred in October 1868, when Judge Silas Thurlow, a Radical Republican, and former slave died from wounds which they received during a political rally. The *Advocate* and local court records noted that on the thirty-first of October a large number of people had gathered on the square for a Republican rally. Shortly afterwards, approximately 150 Ku Klux Klansmen rode into town. Several shots were fired by unknown persons which resulted in the two deaths. It was never proved that a robed Klansman fired the shots, and the case was finally dismissed in the Circuit Court.

Klan action increased during 1869 with the majority of reported cases filed by freedmen. It was during this period that respectable whites officially denounced KKK activity by claiming that the organization had become filled with ruffians who donned hoods and called themselves Klan members. In any event, lawlessness increased as Sheriff Doyle refused to investigate numerous complaints filed by members of both races. Since no arrests were made, Judge Haralson attempted to bring Klansmen to justice. Haralson vested a grand jury with power to summon witnesses in cases that involved Ku Klux Klan attacks. The decision was ineffective, for Sheriff Doyle failed to deliver the subpoenas.

Klan outrages increased, and citizens appealed to Governor William Smith for protection. According to the William H. Smith papers, neither federal troops nor the sheriff were reducing acts of violence. Since there was an insufficient number of troops to combat the problem, the local commander requested that Governor Smith utilize the state militia. The Governor then ordered Sheriff Doyle to assist troops in bringing outlaws to justice. There was no official indication that the Governor's orders were carried out.

Throughout 1869 and 1870, numbers of freedmen as well as some whites reported abuses by the KKK. Local papers noted one example of Klan harassment that involved a local troublemaker. Reverend A. S. Lakin, a northerner who shared a house with Judge Lewis Douglass, claimed that two men fired sixteen buckshot into his residence. Lakin was an ardent Republican who had supported the Union League.

Because of Klan outrages, Congress established a committee to take testimony from people throughout the South. The KKK Reports note the following examples of Ku Klux Klan harassment reported by citizens in Madison County. In July 1869, William Campbell, a freedman, was killed when he was shot six times by men dressed in black robes. Campbell had allegedly stolen chickens from a white farmer. Shortly afterwards, John Leslie reported that Klansmen broke into his house and shot at him eight times while they searched for guns.

The above cases are only a few of the many reported KKK abuses which occurred throughout 1869 and 1870. During such a period of crises, it was vital that respected and diligent men control the reins of government. Instead, incompetence and apathy within the hierarchy of the criminal justice stymied efforts of the few who attempted to execute their duties. Citizens, nevertheless, were determined to restore order in Madison County, and the criminal justice system gradually regained stability during the next four years.

Violence subsided in Madison County between November 1870 and December 1874 as Alabama gradually returned to "home rule." As a result of the election in November 1870, Robert B. Lindsay, a Democrat, was elected governor, defeating the incumbent William Smith. White citizens in Madison County then turned their attention to incompetent officials within law enforcement and the court systems.

The first Radical removed from office was Sheriff Joseph Doyle. A local grand jury announced that Doyle had failed to enforce laws and to investigate crimes throughout his tenure as sheriff. Shortly thereafter, Doyle resigned, and Governor Lindsay appointed John Cooper, a Democrat, as sheriff of Madison County. People were obviously tired of inept officials, and the removal of Doyle reflected a trend towards pre-war leadership.

Richard Busteed, Judge of the United States District (Federal) Court, was the next person forced from office. The District Court was responsible for those cases not covered by local or state law and was supposed to convene in Huntsville twice per year. The court had remained ineffective during Reconstruction due to Busteed's behavior. The judge was a haphazard individual who had rarely convened his court prior to 1870. Consequently, he was very unpopular with the citizens of Madison County. Busteed was finally forced to resign when faced with charges that would lead to impeachment.

According to the *Advocate*, unsettled conditions began to improve in Madison County although there was some evidence of scattered Klan activity. In July 1871 six disguised men fired into a passenger train for unknown reasons. Afterwards, several freedmen who lived on a farm stated that they were whipped by five KKK members. Another case involved Klansmen who invaded the houses of several people for the purpose of harassment. Klan attacks virtually ceased by 1872, the sheriff announced that Madison County was more peaceful than at any time since the Civil War.

The Huntsville Police Department, which had been plagued with discipline problems throughout Reconstruction inherited a new City Marshal. It appears that Britton Franks was appointed to strictly supervise. Shortly after he assumed office, Franks suspended three policemen for drinking to excess, disorderly conduct, and associating with a woman of ill repute. Perhaps the marshal's actions had a positive effect upon his men, for records indicate that officers made numbers of arrests under Franks' supervision.

Although problems still existed, criminal justice had gained stability by November 1874. Since Madison County experienced relative calm, citizens could turn their attention to the upcoming election. The majority of white Democrats could now vote, and they were determined to rid themselves of all remaining Carpetbaggers and Scalawags. As a result of the election held in November 1874, the remaining Republicans, who had been elected in 1868, were removed from office. Louis Wyeth, a Democrat, succeeded William Haralson as Circuit Court judge. Lewis M. Douglass, who had been unpopular as county court Judge was also relieved of his duties.

As Radical Reconstruction drew to a close on the local level, the criminal justice system was composed of men who represented a choice of the people. Thus, Madison County returned to "home rule" after nine years of upheaval, uncertainty, and outside intervention. Amidst this confusion, Radicals had accomplished one goal: freedmen gained legal political and civil rights for the first time. Otherwise, the Reconstruction process was largely a failure, for ill-equipped Radicals failed to cope with the problems which they had created.

THE PARDONS OF MADISON COUNTY

By Norman M. Shapiro

On May 29, 1865, President Andrew Johnson began his attempt at restoration of full citizenship by proclaiming amnesty to all, except certain specified classes of persons. This followed only weeks after the final collapse of the Confederacy in the spring of 1865 and Lt. General Richard Taylor's surrender of the last Confederate armies east of the Mississippi at Citronelle, Alabama, on May 4, 1865. Early in the war, however, the problem of the seceded states was discussed in the Congress and in the country at large and, absent any guides in the Constitution, many theories were proposed on how to accomplish this task. The background of the pardon/amnesty process, and those pardons relating to Madison County, Alabama, which are the subject of this paper, is best explained with the introduction to the microfilm publication, "Case Files of Applications From Former Confederates for Presidential Pardons, 'Amnesty Papers', 1865- 1867," which essentially follows.

Federal officials early on recognized a need for new laws to deal with rebellious acts of large parts of the Southern population. Because "treason" seemed too strong a word and death too severe a penalty for many of the acts in support of the Confederate cause, the Congress passed acts of July 31, 1861 (12 Stat. 284), and July 17, 1862 (12 Stat. 589), that fixed penalties for the lesser crimes of "conspiracy" and "rebellion." The latter act also provided for future pardon and amnesty by Presidential proclamation to be extended "to any persons who may have participated in the existing rebellion ... with such exceptions and at such time and on such conditions as he may deem expedient for the public welfare."

The first such amnesty proclamation was issued by President Abraham Lincoln on December 8, 1863. It extended pardon to persons taking an oath to support the Constitution and the Union and to abide by all Federal laws and proclamations in reference to slavery made during the period of the rebellion. Six classes of persons were excluded from the benefits of the amnesty: (1) civil or diplomatic agents or officials of the Confederacy, (2) persons who left judicial posts under the United States to aid the rebellion, (3) Confederate military officers above the rank of Army colonel or Navy lieutenant, (4) Members of the U.S. Congress who left to aid in the rebellion, (5) persons who resigned commissions in the U.S. Army or Navy and afterwards aided in the rebellion, and (6) persons who treated unlawfully black prisoners of war and their white officers. A supplementary proclamation, issued March 26, 1864, added a seventh exception (persons in military or civilian confinement or custody) and provided that members of the excluded classes could make application for special pardon from the President.

President Johnson's first amnesty proclamation of May 29, 1865 was issued after Attorney General James Speed had advised the President that while Lincoln's pardons were valid, his proffer of amnesty ceased to function with the end of the war and therefore a new proclamation was necessary. In the new proclamation, Johnson cited the failure of many to take advantage of Lincoln's earlier proclamation and noted that many others had been unable to do so because of their participation in the rebellion after the promulgation of the December 1863 amnesty. Under the new proclamation, 14 classes of persons were excepted from the general amnesty. Johnson incorporated Lincoln's seven exceptions with a few alterations and added the following: (8) individuals who had absented themselves from the United States in order to aid in the rebellion, (9) graduates of West Point or Annapolis who served as Confederate officers, (10) ex-Confederate governors, (11) persons who had left homes in territory under U.S. jurisdiction for purposes of aiding the rebellion, (12) persons who engaged in destruction of commerce on the high seas or in raids from Canada, (13) voluntary participants in the rebellion who had property valued at more than $20,000, and (14) persons who had broken the oath taken under provisions of the proclamation of December 8, 1863.

Johnson indicated he did not wish to deny pardon to many in the excepted classes, but he "intended they should sue for pardon, and so realize the enormity of their crime." There were, however, motives other than repentance in the minds of many applicants. A Presidential pardon would restore a citizen to his former civil rights and would also provide immunity from prosecution for treason and from confiscation of property. Thus, the President was soon besieged with thousands of applications, and by the fall of 1867 he had granted about 13,500 pardons.

The principal body of records reproduced in the microfilm publication consists of approximately 14,000 files containing pardon applications and related papers submitted to President Johnson, 1865-67, by persons excepted from his amnesty proclamation of May 29, 1865, together with a few applications submitted to President Lincoln by persons excepted under his earlier proclamations. The majority of applications are unsworn statements by petitioners, but there is a large number of statements sworn before a magistrate. Included with each application is an oath of allegiance signed by the petitioner and, in many cases, recommendations from prominent citizens for clemency or letters from relatives or friends containing pleas for compassion. Applications to the President through governors of Southern States bear their endorsements. In some instances, there are notations by the President or his assistants indicating action on a particular case. The individual files often contain considerable information on a pardon applicant's background, his activities during the war years, and his attitude in defeat under the proclamation of May 29, 1865, because of their ownership of property valued at more than $20,000.

In Alabama, the excluded classes included practically all Confederate and State officials, for the latter acted as Confederate agents, all the old political leaders of the state, many of the ablest citizens who had not been in politics but had attained high position under the Confederate government or in the army or navy, several thousand prisoners of war, a number of political prisoners, and every person in the state whose property in 1861 was assessed at $20,000 or more. According to the proclamation, the assessment was to be in 1865 but it was made on the basis of 1861, at which time slaves were included and a slaveholder of very moderate estate would be assessed at $20,000. In 1865 there were very few people worth $20,000. Most of the ninety-five applications originating from Madison County were based on the 13th exception. A few applied on the basis of multiple exceptions.

The reconstruction process for Alabama began when President Johnson appointed Lewis E. Parsons of Talladega as provisional governor on June 21, 1865, and one of the principal occupations of the provisional government was securing pardons for those who were excluded from the general amnesty of May 29, 1865. One month after his appointment, Governor Parsons issued (July 20, 1865) a proclamation which declared in full force the civil and criminal laws of the state as they stood on January 11, 1861, except as to slavery. An election of delegates to a constitutional convention was ordered for August 31, and the convention was to meet on September 10 (actually met on September 12) No one could vote in the election or be a candidate for election to the convention who was not a legal voter according to the law on January 11, 1861, and all voters and candidates must first take the amnesty oath or must have been pardoned by the President. Governor Parsons also ordered those men in office at the war's end to continue in their positions, and this resulted in considerable dissatisfaction especially in the northern part of the state which always had a strong "unionist" element. Instructions were given as to how a person who was excluded from the benefits of the amnesty proclamation might proceed in order to secure a pardon and another proclamation was issued by Parsons on July 25, 1865 with a list of questions by which "an improper person" might test his case and see how bad it was:

"For the purpose of those who desire to apply for a pardon, to do so with as little delay as possible, they will do well to notice the following points in their application:

1st. Are you under arrest? If so, by what authority, and with what offense are you charged?

2d. Did you order the taking of Fort Morgan or Mount Vernon Arsenal, or aid in taking, or advise the taking of either of them?

3d. Have you served on any "vigilance committee" during the war before which persons charged with disloyalty to the Confederate States have been examined or tried? If so, when and where, and how often? What person or persons were tried or· examined by you? What sentence was passed or decision made in each case? When, where, and by whom was it carried into execution?

4th. Has any person been shot or hung by your order for real or supposed disloyalty to the Confederate States? If so, by what authority did you give the order? Who have been executed by virtue of such order? When and where was it done? State all the facts you rely on to justify such action on your part.

5th. Have you shot or hung, or aided in shooting or hanging any person for real or supposed disloyalty to the Confederate States? If so, when, where, or how many? State all the facts and circumstances you rely on to justify the action on your part.

6th. Have you ordered, or been engaged in hunting anyone with dogs, who was disloyal to the Confederate

States, or supposed to be? If so, when, where, or how many? State all the facts you rely on to justify such action.
7th. Were you in favor of the so-called ordinance of secession at the time it was passed on the 11th day of January, 1861?
8th. No one is bound to incriminate himself. Therefore, the applicant can exercise his own pleasure in this behalf as to any one of the foregoing interrogatories, except the first.
9th. The following must be answered in addition to such other facts as the applicant may be advised or thinks proper to state.
10th. Will you be a peaceable and loyal citizen in the future?
11th. Have any proceedings been instituted against your property under the Confiscation Act?
12th. Is any property belonging to you in the possession of the United States authorities as abandoned property or otherwise?"

An editorial in the *Huntsville Advocate* of July 19, 1865, proclaimed:

> "Special Pardons are being sought for by those in the excepted classes in this State, as well as elsewhere, including Congressmen, Generals, late Confederate civilians, over $20,000 taxable men, &c. This is right. We are glad to see them restored to civil and property rights. We trust such cases will be made out as will induce the President sooner or later to grant them amnesty and pardon, restoration of rights of property, &c. He, we are satisfied, will not be found unrelenting, but forgiving to repentant ones, who 'henceforth' will be good and true loyal citizens to the United States. The excepted classes see the situation they are in; they

> know the confiscation act is a reality, and the courts will soon execute it, and like wise men want protection and safety from penalties. They do right to go to work to get into a safe position. Those who are not of the excepted classes, should be ready to take the amnesty as soon as the books are open, and then they are safe. Let us all get right again, and keep so - for revolutions like this are no trifle."

The confiscation laws relating to private property, mentioned above, under which the army and Treasury agents were acting in Alabama in 1865 are described in Fleming: "(1) the act of July 17, 1862, which authorized the confiscation and sale of property as a punishment for 'rebels'; (2) the act of March 12, 1863, which authorized Treasury agents to collect and sell 'captured and abandoned' property,- but a 'loyal' owner might within two years after the close of the war prove his claim, and 'that he has never given any aid or comfort' to the Confederacy, and then receive the proceeds of the sale, less expenses; (3) the act of July 2, 1864, authorizing treasury agents to lease or work abandoned property by employing refugee negroes. 'Abandoned' property was defined by the Treasury Department as property the owner of which was engaged in the war or otherwise against the United States, or was voluntarily absent. According to the ruling all the property of Confederate soldiers was 'abandoned' and might be seized by Treasury agents. North Alabama suffered from the operation of these laws from their passage until late in 1865, the rest of Alabama only in 1865." One can surmise that this also encouraged many desertions from the army during the last part of the war.

The threatened and actual enforcement of the confiscation act encouraged many individuals of the excepted classes to apply early for pardons. Another inducement was the constitutional convention which Governor Parsons had called for September 10, 1865. The old "unionist" faction of north Alabama hoped to assume leadership in the reconstruction of the state and there was some urgency to secure amnesty for influential excepted persons so they could be qualified as voters, and even delegates. A prominent participant in this effort was Joseph C. Bradley of Huntsville, Madison County, who prepared personal recommendations to Governor Parsons and/or President Johnson for most of the pardon applications from that County. Indeed, Bradley prepared recommendations for many of the petitioners from north Alabama and quite a few for individuals throughout the state. It is not known whether he was specifically asked to make these recommendations by Governor Parsons or the President or if he did it for his own political purposes. Bradley was apparently more successful as a facilitator than a politician but he knew just about every politician in the state, which is understandable considering his background.

Joseph Colville Bradley, born in Abingdon, Virginia, about 1810, was for a long time a successful Huntsville business man and planter. He was opposed to secession early and made his views known vocally and through letters to public officials in Montgomery and Washington. He was, however, a member of the rebel State legislature in 1863 and probably financed the raising of a Confederate company, the "Joe Bradley Rebels," early in the war. In his letter of recommendation to the President for clemency for Addison White, Bradley writes, "He was like myself and a good many of your other friends in this region had to talk a little for the rebels or leave the state." Fleming states that, "Bradley was a north Alabama man who had gone over to the enemy to save his property." Later in the war, Bradley was active in a group of prominent "unionists" that hoped to form a peace party and elect one of their number as governor in 1865, and Bradley was one of those mentioned for that position. After the war, his daughter, Susan, married Union General G. M. L. Johnson, one of the two Union generals buried in Huntsville's Maple Hill Cemetery. Bradley makes references in his recommendations to conversations with the President and was, apparently, a long-time friend. He was one of only nine men in Alabama whose pardon was certified "By order of the President." His petition for clemency to the President, which appears later with other examples, was dated, Washington City, June 8, 1865, and may have been delivered personally to the President. It was approved June 17, 1865, the first one approved for Madison County. The *Huntsville Gazette* of October 9, 1880, reports his death on October 6 and states, "Occupying for many years the position of a leader in the Republican party, his great ability and credit has been of unvalued service to that party and to the country, and in death both sustain a great loss."

Two other prominent men from Madison County who were called on for some clemency recommendations were David C. Humphreys, several term Alabama State Legislator and later Associate Justice, Supreme Court of the District of Columbia, and Peter M. Dox, a New York State Legislator and Judge before he moved to Alabama in 1856. Dox was a member of the State constitutional convention in 1865 and a member of the U.S. House of Representatives from 1869-1873. Bradley's recommendations, however, make the most interesting reading. He seems to know how everybody voted in 1860 i.e., whether they were Bell, Douglas or Breckinridge Democrats; how they felt about slavery; and just how strong their "secessionist" or "union" feelings were. And some of these facts were expressed in rather down to earth language.

The applications from Alabama and Madison County contain, primarily, the individual's oath of allegiance (sometimes taken more than once), the petitions or letters to the President including answers to the twelve questions posed by Governor Parsons, and the letters of recommendation. The petitions are, in general, rather similar. The individuals indicate whether they favored the union or favored secession and the various gradations thereof, how their feelings may have changed during the war, and they promise to be loyal citizens in the future. Typically a person might state that he was opposed to secession, but after a while sympathized with his neighbors and may have provided food or aid to Confederate soldiers or their families. Most, in common with the prevailing feeling in north Alabama, were unionists. A few were staunch secessionists but now, according to Bradley, were "completely whipped and recognize the new order of things." In any case, it really didn't matter for the pardons were usually granted.

Inasmuch as the persons on the pardon rolls represent, for the most part, the economic and political elite of Huntsville and Madison County during this period, it is interesting to see who they were and what they had achieved. Many of their antebellum homes still stand in Huntsville. The listing which follows includes information from the 1860 US Census Population and Slave Schedules, where available, in the following order: Name; Place and Date of Birth; Occupation; Value of real estate in thousands of dollars; value of personal property in thousands of dollars; number of slaves. The date of pardon is also given. As reproducing the complete pardon applications or even abstracts of same would require too much space, a few typical and interesting petitions will follow the listing.

Acklen. William: TN 1802; lawyer; 25; 45; 13.- Nov. 6, 1865.

Acklen was a grandson of John Hunt and a member of the Alabama House of Representatives 1826-1827 and 1830-1831, and a State Senator 1853- 1857.

Allison. John: Ireland 1803; farmer; 15; 57; 40.- Nov. 6, 1865.
Allison came to America about 1822 and was a resident of the Berkley community.

Barnard. Harriet M.: AL 1836; farmer; 130; 180; 9.- Sep. 2, 1865.
Mrs. Barnard was the widow of Dr. John D. Barnard and the daughter of Dr. David Moore, early Huntsville physician, banker, planter and legislator.

Beadle. Joshua H.: TN 1814; merchant; 25; 80; 0,- Sep. 29, 1865.

Beaslev. James A.: VA 1820; farmer; 64; 134; 0;- Oct. 21, 1865.

Beirne, George P.: VA 1809; farmer; 55; 235; 103;- Sep. 8, 1865.
Bierne was a Director of the Memphis & Charleston Railroad and Bradley suggested that pardon was urgent so that Beirne could participate on Board. Beirne applied under the 1st as well as the 13th exception as he was appointed Commissioner to exchange treasury notes for interest bearing bonds.

Binford, Henry A.: NC 1811; physician; 40; 70; 12;- Sep. 29, 1865.

Bradford, Hamilton G.: NC 1815; farmer; 21; 15; 33;- Oct. 21, 1865.

Bradford, William L.: AL 1839; farmer; 10; 16; 0;- no date.

Bradford graduated from the U. S. Naval Academy in 1856; resigned lieutenancy in 1861; joined C.S. Army and served until end of war with shattered arm; went to South America in 1866.

Bradley, Joseph C.: VA 1813; comm. merchant; 20; 230; 0-;- June 17, 1865.
As a member of the rebel State Legislature and Tax Collector, Bradley applied under the 1st exception.

Brickell. Robert C.: AL 1824; lawyer; 20; 60;0-;- Apr. 30, 1866.
Brickell later served as Justice of the Alabama Supreme Court from 1873-1875 and Chief Justice from 1875-1889 and 1894-1898.

Cabaniss. Septimus D.: AL 1815; lawyer; 20; 30; 8;- Sep. 15, 1865.
Cabaniss served in the State Legislature from 1861-1863 He applied under the 1st as well as the 13th exception as he was appointed Commissioner to receive subscriptions to rebel loan.

Chapman. Reuben: VA 1799: lawyer; 85; 200; 27;- Sep. 12, 1865.
Chapman was elected to the Alabama Senate in 1832, the U.S. House of Representatives from 1835-1847, as Governor of Alabama 1847-1849, and the State Legislature 1855-1857.

Clav. Clement C. Sr.: VA 1789; lawyer; 60; 85; 14;- Feb. 12, 1866.
Clay was a member of the Territorial Legislature in 1817, Speaker of the State House of Representatives in 1828, member of the U.S. House of Representatives, 1829-1835, Governor of Alabama 1835-1837, U.S. Senator 1837-1842, and Chief Justice of the Alabama Supreme Court, 1843. Confiscation proceedings had been instituted against his lands.

Collier. Charles E.: SC 1805; farmer; 25; 46; 0;- Dec. 15, 1865. Charles Collier was a brother of Henry Watkins Collier, Governor of Alabama, 1849-1853.

Coltart. Robert W.: AL 1822; merchant; 0; 0; 5;- Sep. 29, 1865. Coltart was Confederate States Marshall and applied under the 1st and 13th exceptions. He was Mayor of Huntsville for several terms.

Davis. Nicholas. Jr.: AL 1825: lawyer; 25; 25; 14;- Sep. 22, 1865. Born in Limestone County, Davis was commissioned a lieutenant in the Mexican War. He was elected to the State House of Representatives in 1851 from Limestone County. He moved to Huntsville in 1853 and served as solicitor from 1850-1860. He was a member of the secession convention.

Davis. Zebulon P.: KY 1816; farmer; 5; 30; 22;- Oct. 21, 1865.
Zebulon was a brother of Nick Davis and Mayor of Huntsville 1859 and 1860. He applied under the 1st exception as he was appointed Receiver of Public Monies.

Donegan. James J.: Ireland 1800; farmer; 138; 175; 47;- Sep. 22, 1865.
Donegan applied under the 1st as well as the 13th exception as he was Receiver of subscriptions to a loan to the Confederate government which were payable at the Northern Bank of Alabama of which he was President.

Echols. William H.: AL 1834; pardoned Nov. 22, 1865.
Echols graduated West Point in 1858, resigned his commission in March, 1861 and served as Major of Engineers in the Confederate forces until Aug 25 1865. He was later President of the First National Bank of Huntsville. As a graduate of West Point, Echols applied under the 9th exception

Fackler. John J.: VA 1802; comm. merchant; 14; 150; 17;- Jan. 4, 1866. Fackler was Joe Bradley's business partner.

Fariss. John L.: VA 1810; farmer; 20; 43; O;- Oct. 21, 1865

Fearn. Robert: TN 1830; farmer; 100; 145; 13;- Nov. 4 1865. Robert Fearn was also a lawyer and a nephew of Dr. Thomas Fearn.

Fennell. Isham J.: NC 1812; farmer; 30; 100; 74;- Sep. 29, 1865.

Ford. Marianne Mrs.: VA 1806; farmer; 35; 45; 69;- Dec. 23, 1865.

Hammond. Ferdinand L.: TN 1814; farmer; 50; 150; 5;- Oct. 21, 1865. Hammond, a Confederate States Agent in 1863 and a member of the rebel State Legislature in 1861 and 1863, applied under the 1st and 13th exceptions.

Harris. George M.: AL 1821; physician; 35; 75; O;- Sep. 29, 1865. Harris was also a planter and cotton manufacturer.

Harris. Louisa M. Mrs.: GA 1820; farmer; 52; 118; 113;- Oct. 4, 1865. Louisa Harris was the wife of Stephen W. Harris.

Harris. Stephen W.: GA 1818; farmer; 52; 118; 113;- Sep. 29, 1865. Harris applied under the 13th exception and his property was registered as abandoned.

Hewlett, Thomas H.: TN 1810; 18; 25; 0-;- Jan. 24,1866. Hewlett applied under the 1st and 10th exceptions. He was a Confederate Conscript Agent and left his home and went across the Tennessee River to farm.

Hobbs. Isham H.: VA 1815; 15; 50; 44;- Oct. 21, 1865.

Holding. William H.: O; O; 89;- Sep. 29, 1865.

Hollowell. William D.: NC 1800; farmer; 14; 18; 0;- Oct. 17, 1866.

Hundley. Mary E. Mrs.: AL 1836; farmer; 18; 46; 34;- Oct. 21 1865.
Mary Hundley was the wife of Capt. Orville M. Hundley of Wheeler's Cavalry.

Jolley. Benjamin: VA 1810: farmer; 8; 61; 20;- Sep. 12, 1865. Jolley was a personal and political acquaintance of President Johnson.

Jordan. Fleming: GA 1804; physician; 50; 230; 134;- Jan. 4 1866. Jordan was also a wealthy planter.

Kelly. Russell. J.: GA 1806; farmer; 53; 77; 76;- Sep. 29, 1865.

Lacy, Theophilus: NC 1805; farmer; 20; 80; 66;- Sep. 29, 1865.
Theophilus Lacy was Cashier of the Northern Bank of Alabama.

Lanford. William: 1797;- Sep. 29, 1865.

Lanier. Burwell C.: TN 1821; farmer; 14; 33; 9;- Sep. 29, 1865.

Lesslie, William: AL 1825; physician, 0; 0; 0;- Sep. 29, 1865.

LeVert, Francis J.: VA 1791; merchant; 10; 80; O;- Sep. 29, 1865.

Lewis. David P.: VA 1823; lawyer; 42; 185; 33;- Sep. 29, 1865.
Lewis was formerly a resident of Lawrence County and was Governor of Alabama, 1872-1874.

Lowe. Mattie Mrs.: AL 1841; housewife; 0; 30; 0;- Oct. 21,1865.
Mrs. Lowe was the widow of Robert J. Lowe, lawyer and state legislator, 1859-1861. He was a private in the 4th Alabama and died of "camp fever."

Lowry. John T.: AL 1822; merchant; 10; 14;- Oct. 7,1865.
John T. Lowry was a member of the firm of Lowry & Hamilton.

McCallev. Thomas S.: VA 1808; farmer; 94; 160; 48;- Sep. 29 1865. Thomas McCalley was also a dry goods merchant.

McCallev. William J.: VA 1821; farmer; 40; 65; 11;- Jan. 4 1866.

McDonnell Archibald: AL 1815; farmer; 49; 99; O;- Se p. 29, 1865.

McDowell. Priscilla W.: VA 1805;- Jan. 4, 1866.
Priscilla McDowell was the widow of William McDowell who died June 9, 1865. In the 1860 Census: William McDowell, VA 1801; comm. merchant; 12; 142;14.

Malone. Nashville: NC 1800; farmer; 29; 42; 0;- Jan. 4, 1866.

Mastin. Francis T.: AL 1813; farmer; 40; 35; 77;- Sep. 22, 1865.

Mastin. Gustavus L.: VA 1815; farmer; 21; 40;- Sep. 22 1865.
Francis T. (Frank), Gustavus L. and James H.(below) were sons of Captain Francis Mastin. According to the 1860 Slave Schedule, Gustavus and James jointly owned 43 slaves.

Mastin. James H.: VA 1815; farmer; 20; 35;- Sep. 22, 1865.

Mills. Thomas B.: LA 1836; 0; 0; 0;- Sep. 27, 1866.
Mills was formerly Sailing Master of the U.S Sloop of War, *Brooklyn*. He resigned after Sumter and entered Confederate service. Lt. Mills was captain of C.S.S. *Sampson* in the Savannah River. He applied under the 1st and 13th exceptions.

Moore. Beniamin T.: NC 1813; lawyer; 39; 80; 0;- May 17, 1886.
Moore was Clerk of the District Court of the Confederate States in the Northern District and applied under the 1st as well as the 13th exception.

Moore. David L.: AL 1838; farmer; 14; 180; 85;- Oct. 12, 1865.
Moore was a son of Dr. David Moore. He served six months in the Confederate Army and then provided a substitute.

Moore. Samuel H.: AL 1843; student; 60; 27; 0;- Sep. 7, 1865.
Samuel H. Moore was another son of Dr. David Moore. He was a private in the 4th Alabama Infantry for thirteen months and then lieutenant in the 20th Alabama Infantry.

Moore. William H.: NC 1822; lawyer; 120; 150; l;- Nov. 3, 1865.
William Moore's property had been confiscated.

Neal. George W.: AL 1816; banker; 10; 125; 8;- Dec. 29, 1865.

Norment. John H.: GA 1800; farmer; 3; 10; 2;- Jan. 4, 1866.
Norment was commissioned U.S. Postmaster at Berkley in 1847 and continued as Confederate Postmaster. He applied under 1st exception.

Patton. Charles H.: VA 1806; farmer; 120; 400; 0;- Sep. 29,1865.
Dr. Charles Hays Patton was also a physician and manufacturer (president of the Bell Factory Cotton Mill). He and John Patton below were brothers of Robert Miller Patton, Governor of Alabama from Dec 1865 to Jul 1868. Robert Patton was a resident of Huntsville from about 1818 until 1829 when he moved to Florence.

Patton. John: VA 1814;- Sep. 29 1865.

Patton. William R.: AL 1819; farmer; 12; 25; 0;- Sep. 29, 1865.

Peete. Samuel: VA 1795; farmer; 30; 65; 0;- Sep. 29, 1865.

Powers. William: VA 1788; farmer; 30; 61; 65;-
Oct. 21, 1865.
Powers served in the War of 1812.

Rice. Marv P. Mrs.: VA 1800; farmer; 15; 60; 17;-
Nov. 9, 1865.
Mary Rice was the widow of Elisha H. Rice.

Robertson, John M.: MD 1804; minister; 32; 25; 5;- Mar. 15, 1866.
An Episcopal Minister, Robertson was arrested by the Federal authorities for "praying for the President of the Confederate States." He was imprisoned and then transported across the Tennessee River and forbidden to return. His property was cited for confiscation (presumably for abandonment).

Robinson. James: TN 1805; lawyer; 9; 33; O; Aug. 14, 1865. In his recommendation, Bradley states that Gov. Parsons wanted to appoint Robinson Chief Justice of the Alabama Supreme Court. This James Robinson was a first cousin of brothers James B. and John Robinson, below.

Robinson. James B.: VA 1810; farmer; 15; 32; 0;- Sep. 15, 1865. James Robinson also owned large properties in Marengo County, Al. His home, Forrest Field, which later burned, was supposedly similar to brother John Robinson's Oak Lawn.

Robinson. John: VA 1803: farmer; 40; 83; 0;- Sep .15, 1865

Sales. Dudley: VA 1782; farmer; 24; 83; 0;- Apr. 30, 1866.

Scruggs. John W.: AL 1818; comm. merchant; 40; 30;0;- Oct. 21, 1865. Scruggs was a member of the Alabama State Legislature, 1863-1865.

Severs. Stephen B.: AL 1830; blacksmith; 0; 1; 0;- Aug. 29, 1865.
Severs had a contract under the U. S. and then the Confederate government to carry mail between Huntsville and Montevallo, and applied under the 1st exception.

Sheffev. Lawrence B.: VA 1819; physician; 10; 15; 12;- Aug.17, 1866. Proceedings had commenced to confiscate his land.

Sledge. Oliver D.: NC 1801; farmer; 117; 172; 94; Oct. 21, 1865. Sledge's property had been cited as abandoned.

Spragins. Robert: AL 1824; circuit clerk; 8; 14; 0;- Sep. 29 1865.
Spragins had moved across the river to safeguard the court records and applied under the 10th exception.

Springer. Josiah: 1N 1808; farmer; 11; 32; 21;- Jan. 4, 1866.

Strong. Charles W.: VA 1825; farmer; 36; 46; O;- May 16, 1866.

Taber. William B.: CT 1811; manufacturer, 25; 35; 0;- Apr. 10, 1866.

Taylor. Morris K.: PA 1812; farmer; 2; 3; 0;- Oct. 21, 1865.
Taylor was appointed Tax Assessor and applied under the 1st exception.

Timmons. William H.: AL 1840; farmer; 0; 0; 0-;- Oct. 21,1865

Todd. David H.: KY 1832; merchant; 0; 0; 0-;- Jun. 22, 1867
Todd was Abraham Lincoln's brother-in-law. He served in the Mexican War and was Captain, Co. A, 21st LA Infantry.

Toney. Edmund: VA 1805; farmer; 39; 50; 52;- Jan. 4, 1866.

Townsend. Parks L.: AL 1835; farmer; 30; 75;- Sep. 29, 1865.

Turner. James B.: VA 1814; physician; 10; 51; 43;- Oct. 2, 1865.

Walls, Allen: SC 1802; farmer; l; 17; O;- Jan. 4, 1866.
Walls was a U.S. and then Confederate Postmaster and applied under the 1st exception.

Watkins, James L.: GA 1814; farmer; 200; 210; O;- Sep. 12, 1865.

White, Addison: VA 1824; farmer; 91; 115; 16;- Sep. 12; 1865.
Addison White served in the U. S House of Representatives from Kentucky from 1851 to 1853.

White. Thomas W.: VA 1818; farmer; 85; 75; 15;- Aug. 19, 1865.
Thomas White was Mayor of Huntsville in 1881 and 1882 and a brother of Addison White.

Wiggins. Richard A.: NC 1810; O; O; 9 4;- Jan. 4, 1866.

Withers, Augustine J.: VA 1805; farmer; 53; 47; 13;- Sep. 29, 1865.

Transcripts of typical examples of amnesty petitions from Madison County Including letters of recommendation from Joseph C. Bradley appear below. One is Dr. James Blunt Turner, who favored secession, and another is Alcuin Eason, who opposed secession. Following these are the rather detailed petitions (also with Bradley recommendations) of "unionist," David P. Lewis, and "secessionist," Septimus D. Cabaniss. A photocopy of Cabaniss' actual pardon signed by President Johnson is also shown. It is interesting to see how these two distinguished gentlemen coped with their diverging viewpoints. Lewis served as Republican Governor of Alabama from 1872-1874 and is one of the five Alabama Governors buried in Huntsville's Maple Hill Cemetery. It is interesting to note that Lewis joined Cabaniss' law firm after his term as Governor.

The last example is Bradley's petition which is dated Washington City, June 8, 1865, and may have been delivered personally to the President. It was approved June 17, 1865, the first one approved for Madison County. Bradley was one of only nine men in Alabama whose file action was certified "By order of the President." It should be noted that as prominent southern Republicans, Bradley and Lewis were also considered to be "scalawags."

To His Excellency, Andrew Johnson, President of the United States, Washington, D. C.

Your Petitioner James Blunt Turner respectfully represents unto your Excellency, that he is now and has been for the last forty years & upwards a citizen of the State of Alabama and in the county of Madison. That he is by profession a physician: That he has never served in the Confederate army, or been connected with it in any capacity: Nor has he ever held any civil office under said Government: Yet he acknowledges that his sympathies were with the South, during the Rebellion.

Now that the rebellion is closed, your Petitioner readily accepts the new order of things in regard to slavery, and promises that he will become in the future, a peaceable and loyal citizen of the Government of the United States, with all the rights and privileges of a citizen restored to him, which he may have forfeited by his former sympathy with said rebellion. Your Petitioner is not under arrest. Nor did he order the taking of Fort Morgan or Mount Vernon Arsenal, or aid in the same, or advise the taking of either of them. Nor has he served in any Vigilance Committee during the War, before which persons charged with disloyalty to the Confederate States have been examined or tried. Nor has any person been shot or hung by his order. Nor has he shot or hung or aided in the same - any person for real or supposed disloyalty to the Confederate States. Nor has he hunted or aided in hunting any one with dogs, for real or supposed disloyalty to the Confederate States. Nor have any proceedings been instituted against his property under the Confiscation Act. Nor has any of his property been taken possession of by the United States Authorities as abandoned property.

Your Petitioner further states, that he may be included in the 13th exception of your Proclamation, dated May the 29th, 1865; as the estimated Value of his taxable property may be $20,000. And now he having taken the oath of amnesty, as prescribed by the Proclamation, before alluded to; he prays your Excellency to grant him a special pardon, according to the provisions thereof.

s/ James B. Turner

Sworn to & subscribed before me
This 29th day of August 1865
s/ John H. King
U.S. Commissioner for the
Nor Dist of Alabama

****

Huntsville,Alabama
Sept 4 1865

Gov'r L. E. Parsons
Montgomery, Ala

The petitioner, Dr. James B. Turner, of this County is a man of character amongst us. He was in 1860 a Secessionist & supported that policy. He now acknowledges himself whipt, and is willing to conform to the present condition of affairs. If the President will grant him a pardon he says he will make a true and loyal Citizen of the United States Government. It is my opinion that…if he lives 100 years he will never again be caught in another Rebellion.

Yours respectfully,
s/ Joseph C. Bradley

****

EASON: To His Excellency, Andrew Johnson, President of the United States:

The undersigned, a Citizen of the United States, residing in Madison County, in the State of Alabama, where he has lived for upwards of fifty years, respectfully petitions for the benefits of the amnesty and pardon offered by your Proclamation bearing date the 29th day of May 1865. The necessity for this Special application arises from the fact, that my taxable property if assessed, would probably exceed $20,000 in value, thereby including me in the 13th Exception to your Proclamation. I am not included in any other of its exceptions. A planter by occupation, I remained at my home during the entire rebellion. I never held office under the so-called Confederate Government, civil or military. Nor was I a soldier in any of the armies of the Confederacy. I was opposed to the ordinance of Secession whereby the State of Alabama was attempted to be taken out of the Union. But when my State, and a majority of my neighbors drifted into the rebellion, my personal sympathies followed them, and under the influence of those sympathies, I may have contributed to aid those engaged in the effort to establish the Confederate Government, but never by conviction or in sentiment have I been a secessionist. I am not under arrest, nor have I been accused of treason, or for inciting insurrection or rebellion against the United States, nor have any legal proceedings under the laws of the United

States providing for the confiscation of the property of persons engaged in the late rebellion, been instituted against me. I also acknowledge the overthrow of the late rebellion, and accept the consequences following that overthrow to the peculiar institutions of the South. And besides taking the amnesty oath prescribed by your proclamation - a certified copy of which oath accompanies this petition - I hereby pledge myself to support, and in future defend, the Government and Constitution of the United States, and the Union of the same under the Constitution.

Madison Co: Ala, near Huntsville, 11th August 1865.

s/ Alcuin Eason

Sworn & subscribed before me
this 11th day of August 1865
s/ John H. King
U.S. Commissioner for the
Nor Dist of Alabama

****

Huntsville, Alabama
August 11 1865

Gov'r L. E. Parsons
Montgomery, Ala

The petitioner, Alcuin Eason, was among one of the strongest Union Men in the County & done all he could to oppose the secession of our State from the Union. After the rebellion commenced Mr. Eason sympathized with the people of his own State & may have contributed something to the Confederate cause. Mr. Eason will make a loyal citizen of the United States Government.

Yours Respectfully,
s/Joseph C. Bradley

****

LEWIS: To His Excellency Andrew Johnson, President of the United States of America

Your petitioner David P. Lewis, a citizen of Huntsville, Alabama, formerly of Lawrence County, Alabama, begs leave to represent to your Excellency, that he owns taxable property over the amount of twenty thousand dollars.

Your petitioner was elected to the Convention of the State of Alabama, in 1860, from the County of Lawrence, as an avowed union man, in opposition to secession & disunion. His speeches and circulars in connection with James S. Clark, his co-delegate, were unequivocal & undisguised over the subject. As a member of the Convention, he was one of the Committee who opposed the report of the Committee presenting said ordinance, & presented a minority report against said ordinance. He voted against the ordinance of secession & and in favor of referring it to a direct vote of the people. Under special instructions from his constituents, he and his co-delegate affixed their signatures to the ordinance.

Petitioner was elected by said Convention a member of the Congress of the so-called Confederate States. He did not solicit the same, and as is well known to the members of the Convention from North Alabama, did not know that he would be nominated. He did not know that he would be thought of in that connection, & was never consulted in reference to it. He accepted the office at the request of union members of the Convention, who desired that some members of the Provisional Congress to be of their political faith. The records of said Congress will show that petitioner did not vote for the Constitution of the so-called Confederate States. Nor has petitioner ever taken an oath to support the same, nor any other oath in conflict with his loyalty to the United States of America. On the adjournment of the State Convention, petitioner resigned his seat in the Provisional Congress & was succeeded by Hon. Henry C. Jones of Florence, Ala.

In the excitement which followed in the Spring of 1861, petitioner connected himself with a volunteer company, raised for twelve months service in the Confederate Army, of which he was elected Captain. Said company was never mustered into service, nor accepted by the Confederate authorities. But on being required to enter the service for three years or during the war, as Captain of the same, he disbanded it, & it dispersed, & the members then went home, as citizens. No oath was administered to any member of the Company.

Petitioner then became convinced that the points aimed at by Secession leaders were something entirely beyond the rights of the States or of Citizens under the Constitution of the United States, & he kept aloof from any voluntary participation in a plan which his heart nor judgement never for one moment, sanctioned, nor approved.

In December 1862, petitioner was offered, unsolicited, a Lt Col'cy in Roddey's Regiment of Confederate Cavalry, which he promptly declined. He submits the papers connected therewith as part of this petition.

In the Summer of 1863 petitioner, being a few months under forty five years of age, became liable to conscription, & without solicitation, through the kindness of Hon. Joseph C. Bradley of Huntsville, Ala, received the appointment of Judge of the 4th Judicial Circuit, in which he then resided. He accepted it, & held the office until he became forty five years of age for the express and sole purpose of exemption from liability to Service in the

Confederate Army, resigning the same to take effect on Jan'y 1, 1864. Petitioner never took any oath of office (the Commission was sent by hand) and Dr. Carlos Smith, now a citizen of Huntsville, then of Lawrence Co, in which petitioner resided, & Wm. Skinner of Franklin Co, both men whose loyalty is & always has been above suspicion, both of these know, that he resigned said office for the reason that he would embarrass his conscience & duty by taking the oath of office, & that he deemed it wrong to hold the office after the necessity of avoiding present conscription had passed. Petitioner further states, what is notorious in his circuit, that the honest, conscientious, & correct discharge of his imperative judicial duty, in disposing of many cases of application for relief under Hab. Corpus, provoked from certain secession officers not only censure, but threats of arrest & violence, as he was frequently informed, though petitioner avers that he could in no single case have handed the petitioner over to the Conscript Bureau without committing plain & manifest perjury. The records of said trials may be found in the Circuit Courts of Lawrence and Franklin Counties.

Immediately after the petitioner resigned, the conscript act was raised to the age of fifty years. While on the bench, petitioner had become the owner of a mill. And to avoid going into the rebel service, he obtained a detail as miller, & personally attended to the mill in that capacity for the sole purpose of being exempt from liability to rebel service. But in consequence of being engaged as attorney in prosecuting a writ of Habeas Corpus (as he supposes) to liberate Capt. Rand of Franklin County from the rebel service, he received a peremptory notice from the Conscript Agent that in November, "he (petitioner) would be obliged to go into the (rebel) Army." Thereupon petitioner made his escape to Decatur, & has ever since been in the Federal lines, going to Tennessee with Gen.

Granger's Command when North Alabama was evacuated. The original letter of S. C. Timothy, Conscript Agent, is made a part of this petition.

Petitioner is the only descendant of an aged mother (73 years of age) his only surviving parent, for whose sake alone he remained at home as long as he did. But when a necessity demanded a separation, he chose to come into the Federal lines from principle & convictions of duty.

Petitioner further shows that there are no indictments, nor proceedings of any nature against him, nor have there been, in the Federal tribunals, nor has any of his property been confiscated, nor seized, nor any steps being taken to that end, by the Federal authorities, to his knowledge or belief; That he now & always has preferred the Union of the States to any other projected or possible form of government; That he not only heartily accepts, but prefers the emancipation of the slaves & if he had the power would not remand them to servitude; That he rejoices at the overthrow of Secession and treason & will give the Federal Government his unqualified & active support in reestablishing the authority & dignity of the Union against all enemies & in reorganizing the industrial resources & prosperity of the South.

Petitioner prays the Special pardon of Excellency restoring him to his rights of citizenship of the United States, & his rights of property.

(s) David P. Lewis
Sworn & subscribed to before me this 9' day of August 1865.
(s) John King
US Comm N.District of Alabama

****

Huntsville, Alabama
August 9, 1865

Gov'r L. E. Parsons
Montgomery, Ala

Hon D. P. Lewis is one of the most loyal men to the United States Government in North Ala. Recommend the President to grant him a pardon without delay as the Union party here needs his influence and services at this time. Judge Lewis can be relied on in any statement he may make in his petition.

Yours Respectfully,
s/Joseph C. Bradley
s/D.C. Humphreys
s/E.E. Douglass, Marshal
North. Dist. Ala
s/J.J. Giers

****

CABANISS: To his Excellency, Andrew Johnson
President of the United States

The undersigned, Septimus D. Cabaniss, a citizen of Huntsville, Alabama, aged about fifty years, and by profession a lawyer, believing that he is within the first, and possibly the thirteenth, exception of your Excellency's Amnesty Proclamation of the 29th Day of May, 1865 makes this his Special application for a Pardon thereunder, and respectfully submits the following statement of facts for your consideration.

He was a private in the Military Service of the Confederate States, having belonged to the class of troops known as Alabama State Reserves; was paroled at Marion, Alabama, on the 16th Day of May,1865 by order of Gen'l

Grierson, to whom he voluntarily surrendered after the capitulation of the Confederate troops in Alabama.

That in the spring of the year 1861, at the request of Memminger, then acting as Secretary of the Treasury of the Confederate States, in connection with three other citizens of Huntsville, he acted, for two or three weeks, as a Commissioner for the receiving of Subscriptions of Stock in a loan to the Confederate States known as the "Fifteen Million Loan," and supposes that he was, whilst so acting, a domestic agent within the meaning of said first exception; but he states, that he never held, or sought, any other office or agency, civil, diplomatic, or military, under said Confederate Government; and that agency was unsolicited on his part, and without compensation.

That he will not be worth Twenty Thousand Dollars, after discharging his pecuniary liabilities and does not think it certain that his taxable property is worth Twenty Thousand Dollars; but at this time it is difficult to arrive at a satisfactory opinion as to the value of several Species of his property; and it may be assessed at more or less than Twenty Thousand Dollars.

That so far as he knows or believes, no proceedings have commenced against any of his property under the Confiscation Act, nor is any of it in the possession of the United States Authorities as abandoned property. Some of his property, consisting of household furniture, cattle, plank & post fencing, materials of frame buildings, and some other articles of perishable property, were taken and carried from his residence for the use of the Federal Army, as he is informed & believes; but he does not know what has become of it, nor does he expect to seek its restoration. His losses, however, as a consequence of the war, will, as he believes, be more than twice as much as he is now worth. He presumes that it is not improper to state, in this connection, that his wife and six minor children are all of frail constitution, and that his own health is becoming infirm.

He further states, that whilst he does not construe the Tenth (10th) Exception of said Amnesty Proclamation as being intended to apply to any persons whose homes were within the Confederate States, and especially not to those in said States who left their homes before they fell within the Federal Military lines; yet, having learned that a different construction is placed upon it by Attorneys at Law residing in Huntsville, the undersigned, in deference to their opinions, and for greater certainty, thinks it proper to state in this application that during, & for many years prior to the war, his home was in Huntsville Ala; that upon the reported approach of the Federal Military Forces toward Huntsville in 1862, and again in 1863, he left his home & went South of the Tennessee River, leaving his family at home where they continued to reside during the whole period of the war.

That he left Huntsville mainly because he was at the time a member of the Alabama Legislature, elected after the Secession of the State, and he did not think it proper that he should, whilst holding that relation to the people of his County & State, voluntarily fall under the control of the Federal Authorities.

That after the term of office as a representative had expired, and he had become liable to Military Service under an Act of the Confederate Congress passed in February, 1864, he was enrolled in the Military Service of the Confederate States in the class of troops known as Alabama Reserves, & continued in that service until he was surrendered & paroled as aforesaid; but he did not pass beyond the Federal Military lines when leaving his home, nor was he at any time after at his home whilst it was within the said Federal Military lines, until he had been paroled as aforesaid. He admits, however, that when leaving his said home as aforesaid, he was friendly to the said Confederate Government, and disposed to aid it.

In conformity with the suggestions of Governor Parsons, he further states that he is not under arrest; that he did not order the taking of Fort Morgan or Mount Vernon Arsenal, or aid in the taking, or advise the taking of either of them, no person has been shot or hung by his order, for real or supposed disloyalty to the Confederate States, he has not shot or hung, or aided in the shooting or hanging any person for real or supposed disloyalty to the Confederate States, he has never ordered the hunting, nor engaged in hunting anyone with dogs who was disloyal to the Confederate States, or supposed to be so.

He never served on any "Vigilance Committee" but in as much as that term and "Committee of Safety" are generally regarded as synonymous, it is perhaps proper that he should state the fact that in the latter part of the spring, or early part of the summer of the year 1861, he did serve for a short period of time on a Committee which, according to his recollection, had the latter name, and in as much as he is aware now, as he was then, that such committees have been most commonly, in times of excitement, the instruments of the bad passions & prejudices of others, rather than a safeguard against them, and being always averse to doing anything not in conformity with law, he deems it due to himself to state the circumstances under which it was organized, & to say that he would not have consented to serve upon it but for his knowledge of the high character of the gentlemen associated with him for intelligence, integrity & discretion, and the belief that the existence of that Committee could serve to allay excitement, and to prevent less discreet persons from taking the law in their own hands.

In the winter & spring after the election of Mr. Lincoln, there was an apprehension in the minds of many of our citizens, & especially the Ladies, that there would be an insurrection among the slaves. This increased, after the companies of Volunteers had gone to the Confederate Army, leaving no military organizations in the county. To allay this excitement, nearly every male citizen of Huntsville & vicinity between the ages of fourteen & eighty years, voluntarily united in a Military Association, forming a small battalion.

As a consequence of this uneasiness & the state of the country, there was, as is usual in times of high excitement, a disposition on the part of some of the community to take the law in their own hands; and when the Military Association was formed, it was agreed that it should be under the control & direction of a Committee of nine citizens, selected at the time of its organization, who should be charged with the duty of investigating any matters which the safety of the Community might seem to require. Several startling reports were brought before the Committee of insurrectionary plots which, when calmly investigated, proved to be without foundation; and a considerable excitement was also aroused against several persons charged with, or suspected of, disloyalty to the Confederate States; but it was allayed by the Committee, and no one was punished, except one person whose name is not now remembered. The sentence in his case was, that he should, within a certain time, leave the County or State, & not return.

According to the recollection of the undersigned, it was proved that this person had been in Huntsville but a few months, was a gambler by profession, & came from Memphis or New Orleans. Robert K. Dickson, a citizen of Huntsville, was also before the Committee, charged with uttering disloyal sentiments. The facts charged against him were investigated. The Committee advised him to be more discreet in his language, & he agreed to do so in future. Excitements arose against others who were charged with disloyalty, & were allayed through the instrumentality of the Committee; but the undersigned does not recollect any other persons whose cases were tried; and he is satisfied that the object of the Committee in those cases was prompted by a desire to preserve good order in the Community, & not to punish persons for their political sentiments. A large majority of the Military Association, &, according to his recollection, a majority of the Committee, had been opposed to the secession of the State. He does not remember how often he served on said Committee, was probably at eight or ten meetings - possibly more; they were held in Huntsville.

He states that he was in favor of the Secession of the State at the time the ordinance of Jan'y 11, 1861 was passed, but not in favor of it in the form in which it was passed. He was not in favor of it unless it should be manifest that a majority of the people of the State were in favor of it; & he desired that the ordinance should be passed subject to its ratification by a vote of the people; but not believing that the ordinance was rendered invalid because it was not submitted to a vote of the people, he gave it his support.

He thinks it is not out of place to add that he was opposed to the disruption of the Union so long as he had a hope that the antagonism between the two sections could be removed. Having despaired of that after the election of 1860, he sincerely believed that it was best for both sections that they should separate. He preferred separate State Action to the Co-operation policy, because he believed that there could be no effectual co-operation among the slave States, whilst in the Union, without the formation of a compact which would be obnoxious to the Constitution. He was not influenced by a hatred of the people of the Northern States, & would have preferred a Convention of all the States of the Union prior to separate State action, if he had believed it practicable to get it. He never engaged in political life until the year 1861, when with some reluctance he consented to be a candidate to represent his County in the Alabama Legislature, he was elected, & served out his term, but refused to be a candidate again. He will be a peaceable and loyal citizen in the future. He has taken the oath of Amnesty prescribed by your said Proclamation, which is herewith enclosed.

The premises considered, he respectfully asks your Excellency to grant him Amnesty and Pardon, with restoration of all rights of Property except as to slaves, and such other relief in the premises as you may be authorized to grant.

s/ S. D. Cabaniss

Sworn to & subscribed before me at Huntsville Alabama this 18th day of August 1865.
s/ John H. King
N States Commissioner
N District of Alabama
****

Huntsville, Ala
August 18, 1865

Gov'r L. E. Parsons
Montgomery, Ala

The petitioner, S. D. Cabaniss, I have known from boyhood, has always been considered an honest and industrious citizen respected for candour [sic] & truthfulness.

I believe he was honest in his politics for I have great confidence in him as a man, but surely he was a deluded one, which I often told him was a fact patent to my own mind....He believed that the perpetuity of slavery depended altogether on the seperation [sic] of the Slave from the Free States,- hence his delusion in regard to his extreme States Rights view. Cabaniss is a clever man and

neither would he personally or politically do any person injustice, and knowing the man as I do, I believe that he was honest in politics, and done what he did from an honest conviction of heart & conclusion of his mind. Whenever Cabaniss will take the oath of allegiance or amnesty he will observe them strictly, & I believe hereafter he will make a true and loyal Citizen of the United States Government. The suppression of the Rebellion has so completely cured him of his delusions and corrected his errors - that henceforward our Country will find him a good Citizen. He gives up the Negro & secession questions. I therefore recommend him for Executive clemency.
With Respfy
Yr Obt Svt
/Joseph C. Bradley

****

BRADLEY: Washington City, June 8, 1865.
To Andrew Johnson, President US
The undersigned, a citizen of Madison Co. Ala will respectfully state to your Excellency that he has never been in the Military service of the so-called Confederate States. That he was opposed to the attempted secession of Ala from the Union and done all he could to defeat the ordinance of Secession. That after the Presidential election of 1860, he was in favor of the inauguration of Abraham Lincoln as President of the US & zealously advocated a Submission to his Administration. That after the Convention of Ala had passed the ordinance of Secession, he Telegraphed the delegates from his County to retire from that body, & that North Ala would resist the action of the Convention. The Telegram was suppressed by the late Jere Clemens, until after the Convention took a recess for a few weeks, when the Delegates from Madison

returned to their homes in the recess a public meeting of the people of the Co. was called, & in said meeting your petitioner introduced union resolution which were indignantly voted down & resolution passed instructing Nick Davis, one of the Delegates to sign the ordinance of secession. When Tennessee voted sepperation [sic], the union men in North Ala, as they considered had no alternative left - but to submit to the action of the State Convention, or leave the State. Your petitioner among a large number of other union men, in our action. submited [sic] - but not in our feelings & opinions, which are openly and publicly declared, regardless of consequence to ourselves -until overarmed & overpowered by Confederate Troops & authority. Your petitioner was offered many Military & Civil offices under the Confederate Government all of which he declined except one, The Collectorship of the War Tax for Ala. This office he at first declined, but being persistantly importuned by the best union men throughout the State to accept the office so as to give men of their belief some protection, your petitioner yielded to their entreaty, accepted the office, and afforded all the protection in his power to union men against secessionist & Confederate Troops. Your petitioner, immediately after appointing sub-Collectors and assessors, resigned the Chief Collectorship & refused to accept one cent of the salary of the office. Your petitioner is now a member of the Rebel Legislature of Ala, and on all questions, the record will show that his votes in that body were cast with the Union Conservative party. Your petitioner, on all occasions, aided with money & advice, the Families of union men who had to flee from Confederate to Federal lines in Ala, and in every instance when called on, regardless of threats from secessionist and the Confederate Authorities has been the bail & friend of every union man that has been arrested or indicted in the Confederate Court of Ala for Treason or violation oflaws.

Your petitioner in his heart has never entertained any malice or rebellious feelings against the US Government, and he trusts that it will not be considered out of place in your petitioner to call the attention of Your Excellency to the fact that at heart he has never been considered by the union men of Ala in any other light than a loyal man to the Federal Government. The undersigned is sincerely desirous of returning to his allegiance to the United States Government and to be reinvested with rights of Citizenship and having accepted the office of Chief Collectorship from the State of Ala as above stated from the Rebel authorities or powers, and by reason thereof, is excepted from those entitled to avail themselves of the benefits of your proclamation of May 29th 1865, now for his relief your petitioner respectfully submits the foregoing statements of facts for your consideration and decision of his case, preying [sic] Your Excellency to extend to him the Clemency of the United States Government, by the exercise of the pardoning powers in his behalf, vested in you as President, for all offenses committed & from all penalties incurred by reason of his participateing [sic] as before stated in said Rebellion - indulgeing [sic] the hope of a favorable decision your petitioner as in duty bound will ever prey [sic].
(s) Joseph C. Bradley
(Statement not sworn)

****

On September 7, 1867, Johnson issued a second amnesty proclamation narrowing the number of excepted classes to 3 and reducing the number of those unpardoned to about 300. His third proclamation which excluded only Jefferson Davis, John C. Breckinridge, Robert E. Lee, and a few others, was issued July 4, 1868. On Christmas day of that same year, Johnson's final amnesty proclamation was extended "unconditionally and without reservation" to all who had participated in the rebellion.

House of Representatives Executive Document No. 16, 40th Congress, 2d Session, dated Dec 4, 1867, is a final report of the names of persons who lived in Alabama, Virginia, West Virginia or Georgia and pardoned by the President from April 15, 1865 to that date. The report has been reproduced as a book and lists the names, the exemption under the amnesty proclamation of May 29, 1865, by whom recommended, and date of pardon. For Alabama, the report does not, in all cases, accurately reflect what is in the application files. The President in the end granted pardons to nearly all persons who applied for them, but not a great number applied. The total number pardoned in Alabama from April 15, 1865 to December 4, 1868, was less than 2000, and of these most were those who had been worth over $20,000 in 1861 and had provided aid to the Confederacy. Before the general amnesty of 1868, 1456 of these people (of whom 72 were women) were pardoned. How many of this class of excepted persons did not ask for pardon is not known.

AN EXCERPT FROM THE "CIVIL WAR ADVENTURES OF BISHOP HENRY C. LAY"

By The Reverend Emmett Gribbon

Editor's Note: Because of the tremendous influence which the Reverend Henry C. Lay had among the citizens of Huntsville during his eleven years as rector of the Church of the Nativity, his activities during the Civil War are of interest to those who are associated with the religious and cultural life of Huntsville today. The longer piece by the Reverend Gribbon covers a six-year period and Bishop Lay's travels through many states. This excerpt covers only the brief span of time of Huntsville's first occupation.

The holocausts of war have in every age uprooted and sent wandering non-combatant peoples....This is the story of Henry Champlin Lay, the Episcopal Bishop of Arkansas who for the years 1862 to 1866 was a Displaced Person, and whose odyssey carried him through 14 States, twice into Federal prisons, twice across the battle lines under a flag of truce [and] in the field as a Confederate Chaplain. In Philadelphia in the fall of 1865, he was instrumental in reuniting the Episcopal Church in the South with the Church in the North.

This narrative has been quarried from a fascinating mass of manuscripts and printed material listed in the Southern Historical of North Carolina as the "Henry C. Lay Papers."

Henry C. Lay was born in Virginia in 1823 and was educated at the University of Virginia, graduated with an M.A. degree at the age of 18, and at the Virginia Theological Seminary in Alexandria he took both the first and second year courses during his first year and entered the senior class his second year in residence. On the 10th of July in 1846 he was ordained Deacon by Bishop Meade and began his ministry at Lynnhaven parish, near Norfolk. The following May he married Elizabeth Withers Atkinson, who was also a native Virginian, and that summer accepted a call to be Rector of the Church of the Nativity in Huntsville, Alabama. Although the young couple's roots were deep in Virginia, they soon found Huntsville a real home and made many devoted friends there. Huntsville was to become a haven of refuge for Mrs. Lay and their children in time of need, and for many years, they thought of it as "home" even when they lived elsewhere. Shortly after their arrival in Huntsville, Bishop Cobbs of Alabama ordained the young Rector to the Priesthood, and for eleven years, he labored diligently in that vineyard.

In October 1859, the General Convention of the Episcopal Church met in Richmond, and Mr. Lay was one of the delegates from the Diocese of Alabama. Henry Lay was elected by the House of Bishops to be the Missionary Bishop of the Southwest, a missionary district which included the state of Arkansas and the indefinite limits of the Indian Territory to the West.

By November 16, 1859, Bishop Lay was in Memphis headed west, but his wife, who was expecting a baby, and their three children were to stay in Huntsville until he could decide where he would settle in Arkansas and rent or buy a place to live. Arkansas had only a few Episcopal congregations and fewer clergy at this time.

Travel in Arkansas proved to be slow, uncomfortable, and uncertain from the moment he crossed the Mississippi. We will not follow Bishop Lay's arduous journeys through his vast diocese except to note that he decided to establish his residence at Fort Smith on the western border of Arkansas. The Bishop returned from his first trip in Arkansas and spent four weeks in Huntsville, fortunately being there when his wife gave birth to a son.

In the summer of 1860 having packed their belongings for the arduous journey, the Lays uprooted themselves from Huntsville and by rail, steamboat, and stage pushed through the wilderness of Zion to Fort Smith. Shortly before Christmas of that year they moved to a house they bought in the village.

Enough land went with the house so that they had room to keep pigs, chickens, and a cow and have a vegetable garden. Although unable to borrow the money needed to purchase this property because lenders were unwilling to lend amid the uncertainties of the times, a providential gift of $500 from his cousins in Virginia enabled the Bishop to buy and move. A few weeks later the Southern States began to secede, and Southern authorities began to seize Federal forts and arsenals. Fort Smith was surrendered by its garrison without a fight on April 24th (1861). This happened while the bishop was in the southern part of the state, and he hurried home to be sure his family was safe. Fort Smith was taken by Arkansas forces less than two weeks after Fort Sumter had fallen and the war had begun.

Two letters to his wife expressed the Bishop's sentiments of sorrow and foreboding. On April 19th he wrote, "I am distressed as a man can be at the civil war now opening on us - have advised the clergy to disuse the prayer for the President. I am now Southern, Secession and all that. But I could weep day and night for the misery before us and the folly that has brought us to it." The next day he wrote, "But my heart is so sad for the country. Dark days remain for us and our children. There is little on earth to hope for now in our day. The issue is very clear - I go with my own people - and am ready, if it would do good to lay my life down in resisting Abraham Lincoln."

When the war developed its full fury, the people of Arkansas, as did people everywhere in the South, found the old patterns of life broken up. The Bishop travelled incessantly visiting his congregations, counselling his clergy, and raising money to keep the missionary work alive. In Virginia his two brothers and numerous other relatives of his and those of Mrs. Lay's entered the Confederate Army.

He himself travelled back to Virginia in the fall of 1861 carrying with him his eldest son, Henry Champlin Lay, Jr., then eleven years old. Henry was left at a small boarding school at Mt. Laurel so that he might receive a proper education. Back in Arkansas the Bishop spent the winter of 1861 - 1862 in more travelling through his Diocese, but the work was discouraging. Many congregations were having difficulty paying the clergymen's salaries. One clergyman was facing bitter antagonism because he happened to have been born a Yankee. Other clergy had left to be chaplains, or just left in discouragement. One of the Bishop's special projects had ended in failure.

As the war drew closer to Fort Smith, the Lays were bereaved by the death of their son, Thomas Atkinson, named for Mrs. Lay's uncle, the Bishop of North Carolina. In his journal Bishop Lay records in mid-February 1862, "At 4-1/2 p.m. fell on sleep our saintly child, Thomas Atkinson." But to bereavement was suddenly added new worries and fears. On February 18th the journal records, "Today we hear that the Federal Army is advancing. Gen. McCulloch declares that he will make his stand at Boston Mountain some 30 miles hence. Expecting to remove my family I committed little Thomas to the earth in my garden—Present Mrs. Sandels, the grave-digger, my wife and two servants. I read the service."

They had difficulty getting away. The Bishop tried to rent a stage but failed. He preached twice in Fort Smith first on "The Disciples in a Storm," and then on February 28th, the Fast Day appointed by President Davis, on the text "Thou dids't hide thy face from me." On March 2nd, he baptized the month-old child of his two slaves, John and Clarissa, and finally on the 5th the whole family including the slaves left on the river steamer *Tahlequah*. After a week on the Arkansas River, they reached Little Rock.

The Bishop believed himself quite fortunate in selling his house back in Fort Smith for $4,500 in Confederate bonds. Having sold the house, and since he had decided to move permanently to Little Rock eventually anyway, he sent for his furniture.

On March 29th they left Little Rock on the steamer *Notrebe* and reached Memphis three days later. After a week of visiting and church services there, they left by train. As the journal records, "We left Memphis at 6-1/2 p.m. passing Corinth on the night of the second day's battle, and with some detention reached Huntsville at midday."

It was Bishop Lay's plan to leave his family in Huntsville while he himself went to New Orleans to administer Confirmation and otherwise assist the Church in Louisiana. The uncertainties of the war situation in Mississippi and Louisiana changed Bishop Lay's plans, and he decided to wait in Huntsville for better prospects. He and his family stayed with their dearest friend, a lady of some wealth, Mrs. Mary Rice. The children called her "Grandma," and she became the cause two years later of one of the Bishops' most unusual travelling adventures. Mrs. Rice was more than happy to fill her big empty house with the Lays. When her son John had died the previous fall, Mrs. Lay had written the Bishop, who was then in South Carolina, "I think with a sort of awe, of one poor human creatures' have [sic] such affliction. A husband and thirteen children & now to be alone in her house with not one left."

On the morning of April 11th Federal forces under the command of General Mitchel swooped into Huntsville and seized the railroad. During the rest of the month no services were held in the churches as all citizens were restrained within the picket lines. On May 2nd twelve prominent men in Huntsville were arrested and "put into confinement under guard." One of these hostages was Bishop Lay who was locked up in the Probate Judge's office. Then followed two weeks of conferences, exchanged notes, consultations with each other, and interviews with the General. General Mitchel was determined to get his distinguished hostages to sign a statement which he drew up and which read in part, "We disapprove and abhor all unauthorized and illegal war; and we believe that citizens who fire upon railway trains, attack the guards of bridges, destroy the telegraph lines and fire from concealment upon pickets deserve and should receive the punishment of death."

The hostages were just as determined that since they themselves were innocent of such hostile acts, and since the General laid no charges at all against them, they would not sign but wrote in reply, "We respectfully disclaim the responsibility of condemning to the punishment of death any of our countrymen for acts, the method, motives and circumstances of which are utterly unknown to us." This statement was signed by the eleven other hostages and below their signature was added, "I subscribe to the above with the explanation that I am a citizen of Arkansas, accidentally in Huntsville. Henry C. Lay."

Having reached this impasse, General Mitchel let his prisoners have visitors, and food was sent to them by their families, but the harassment of enforced restraint continued. In one of eleven notes to his wife, which Mrs. Lay kept, the Bishop wrote, "We have no chance of getting away tonight, except Dr. Fearn who is released. It is all an attempt to mortify and humiliate us. Let us possess our souls with patience." In another, "We agree to keep our counsel for the present. Your chief anxiety must be that we may behave ourselves like men and Christians. There will be a trial of moral power. We must trust in God & keep good cheer." After an interview, which the twelve had with General Mitchel, Bishop Lay wrote, "He had no charges against us, he said, but arrested us to show that he would arrest anybody. He sent for us to make us use our influence to promote amicable relations between his army and our people. He proposed conditions of release to us in writing. These were considered by the whole 12, and we declined subscription. We must take the consequences. I know not what they will be. I am very quiet & easy in mind. The way of duty is very plain—and to do nothing is easy."

For a while visitors were allowed the hostages, but in two notes the Bishop wrote, "I do not think it would be well for you to come here, much as I would like to see you." And, "I don't like to see ladies come. Lucy [his seven-year-old daughter] might be alarmed at the bayonets around us." The General decided to be more stringent with his uncooperative captives, and so Mrs. Lay received one day a scrap of torn yellow paper on which in familiar handwriting she read, "I am in solitary confinement. Alone yet not alone. Open notes from you may pass. In the morning send clean clothes, looking glass, shaving things, brush, etc. Some writing paper. God bless & keep & comfort you all. The room is clean & airy."

The prisoners were allowed renewed opportunities for conference with each other, and they finally decided they were willing to condemn illegal acts of war in general terms. They had made their protest, but continued imprisonment would do no one any good. The General accepted their watered-down statement, and after thirteen days of confinement released them.

Three weeks later Mrs. Lay had a "confinement" of her own, but a different and a happier kind. On June 3rd, she gave birth to her seventh child, a boy weighing eleven pounds who was given the name of Beirne, the family name of Huntsville friends. The happiness of Beirne's safe arrival was soon overcast with sorrow when on July 5th the journal records, "our little daughter Lucy died," and next day "was buried at 6 p.m. Mr. Banister officiating."

Editor's Notes: In October, Henry Lay travelled to Virginia on personal and church business. The other eleven citizens confined to the Courthouse were: William McDowell, William Acklen, A. J. Withers, George P. Beirne, William H. Moore, Samuel Cruse, J. G. Wilson, Thomas S. McCalley, Gus L. Mastin, Stephen W. Harris, and Dr. Thomas Fearn. From time to time, other prominent citizens were held in jail, the most prominent of whom was former Governor Clement Comer Clay.

EDWARD DORR TRACY: EVOLUTION OF A SOLDIER

By Kenneth R. Wesson

More than one-half million men died in the American Civil War, and the large majority of them are little remembered today. Much relevant history about them remains to be written, however, inasmuch as many of the less-renowned Civil War manuscript collections belonging to these obscure Civil War veterans have yet to be transcribed and chronicled. One such collection centers in the letters of Edward Dorr Tracy, a Confederate whose career was punctuated with frequent promotion until he was killed in battle. His knowledgeable correspondence to his wife and associates unfold the development of the man as a soldier, his aspirations and ideals, as well as his prejudices and faults. Collections such as Tracys merit not only investigation, but also exploitation as an important part of Civil War history.

Information regarding Edward D. Tracys early life is remarkably scarce, and the sources are often contradictory, but some background is known. Edward Tracys father, Edward Dorr, Sr., was trained in the law, and early in the nineteenth century he migrated from Norwich, Connecticut, and settled in middle Georgia. The elder E.D. Tracy was soon chosen Judge Advocate for the district surrounding Macon, Bibb County, Georgia. In the late 1820s Tracy, Sr., married Susan Campbell, the sister of the prominent Mobile jurist, John A. Campbell; Susan was to be the mother of Edward Dorr Tracy, Jr.

Tracy, Jr., was born November 5, 1833, in Macon Georgia, and his early life was a virtual model of good fortune and achievement. Being a blend of New England and the South, and of the upper-middle class economically, it was not unfair to assume that Tracy was a respected young man within the

Macon society. He received his early education at private institutions and later attended the University of Georgia, in Athens, where he was graduated in 1851 with an A. B. degree, at the age of only seventeen. Two years later, he received a Master's Degree. Tracy studied law in his spare time, was admitted to the bar, and began practice in Macon at the age of twenty. Presumably owning to his father's political affiliations, Tracy was able to greatly expedite his career by obtaining a partnership with the established and respected law firm of Judge D. C. Humphreys of Huntsville in 1855.

When Edward Tracy migrated to northern Alabama early in 1855, he was an attractive young man, twenty-one years of age, tall and slender with brown hair. A promising lawyer, reared in the chivalric tradition of the Old South, Tracy undoubtedly attracted the attention of many ladies in antebellum Huntsville.

Predictably, he was married (February 19, 1855) to one of Huntsville's prized young socialites, Ellen Elizabeth Steele. Ellen was the daughter of the renowned architect and planter, George Steele, and his wife Eliza. The marriage joining Tracy and Ellen took place in Steele's famous Huntsville home, Oak Place. The Tracys subsequently made their residence in the bride's family home.

During the succeeding five years, the Tracy family grew both numerically and socially. Ellen gave birth to four children; two of the four died in infancy, however. The Tracys adhered to the Presbyterian faith and were devout in their religion. Edward Tracy had been a member of the Presbyterian Church in Macon and he transferred his membership to Huntsville in 1857. He was included on the original Board of Directors of the Madison County Bible Society, organized on July 24, 1859, and he also became a member of the Masonic Order. Socially, the Tracys became closely associated with the Clay family including Clement Claiborne Clay, Jr., and his wife Virginia; and Hugh Lawson Clay and his wife Celestia Comer Clay. Celestia was a native of Macon, and probably was acquainted with Tracy there.

Further, Tracy was associated with Leroy Pope Walker, a prominent lawyer of the city, both cordially and professionally. These friendships influenced Tracy politically and otherwise. The family evidently developed materially as well for by 1860 the Tracys owned five slaves.

The close association Tracy had with the Clays in social life carried over into politics as well. After the Charleston and Baltimore Democratic conventions, and the split of the Democratic Party in 1860, C.C. Clay, Jr., strongly supported the Breckinridge-Lane "Southern Bolters" ticket as "the only candidates who could preserve the rights of the South. Tracy, though not a candidate for public office during the late 1850s, campaigned diligently for the Democratic Party's candidates. After the party divided he also backed the Southern Democrats and was an alternate elector for the State-at-large on the Breckinridge-Lane ticket. During the campaign Tracy acquired a brilliant reputation for oratory while on speaking tours in the northern counties.

Not all North Alabamians agreed with the Clays and Tracys, however, and Union sentiment was strong in the area. Most Unionists, also called Loyalists or Tories, lived in the hill counties of the Tennessee River Valley – "a cancer in the side of the Confederacy." These regions contained few slaves, produced little cotton, and would have little to gain from a Confederate victory should a war develop. These people later formed Union units in the state. They were also torn between Breckinridge and the national Democrat, Stephen A. Douglas. Many feared that should the extremists gain control of the state, the area's commercial relationship with Tennessee would be endangered; to them it was "unthinkable to server their relations with the Union when their sister states to the north… had no intention of seceding." There was considerable apprehension that the northern counties might secede from Alabama and join Tennessee. As an indication of their economic fear and their loyalty to the national Democratic Party, Madison County gave 1,300 votes to Douglas and only 591 to Breckinridge in the presidential election.

After Lincoln's election and South Carolina's departure from the Union, the secession question reached a point of decision in Alabama. Though the Alabama Convention voted for secession by a large majority, Cooperationists and Unionists in North Alabama met in Huntsville and passed resolutions instructing Madison County delegates to retire from the convention if the Ordinance of Secession were not submitted to popular vote. Some leaders proposed civil war rather than submission to the Ordinance. Tracy wrote to C.C. Clay, Jr., who was an ardent immediate secessionist that "Lincoln's inaugural... breathes war" and Hugh Lawson Clay predicted: "There will be a successful attempt to excite the people of North Alabama to rebellion against the State and we will have a civil war in our midst." Although this intra-state warfare never fully materialized, Unionist opposition continued and was stronger in 1865 than in 1861.

In early March, however, at a Huntsville mass meeting, the secessionists triumphed and passed resolutions whereby the Unionists pledged to support the new government. Tracy was present at this meeting and quite immodestly communicated his role therein to Clay, Jr. Tracy had asked for a reading of the resolutions and pronounced them "exceedingly obnoxious."

"I told the chairman...that I was rather uncertain as to my status in the meeting, the call was addressed to the Freemen and I myself one of 'em but wished to know of him whether it was a 'free flight.' He said he supposed it was; whereupon I went in. I made fight on the preamble and resolutions, separately and collectively, spoke for more than an hour and...made a first-rate speech....After a vain attempt to harmonize the whole question was put, 'shall [the Unionist] resolutions be adopted.' The ayes were feeble the nays tremendous.

A decision was called for, and our majority was so overwhelming that the president decided by a glance that the decision was in our favor...My resolutions scratched off in the heat of the fight were then put and went like a tornado. The action of the meeting is important not so much from what was done, as from what was not done, to wit the meeting refused to censure our state convention format submitting the ordinance of secession back to the people..."

By April, 1861, events were moving so rapidly that most Cooperationists and Unionists, though hesitantly, were following the general trend of the Confederacy. Thus, conscious of the direction in which the political currents were flowing, Tracy predictably joined the "rebels" and the Southern cause would play a major role in his life from this point onward.

Even prior to the firing on Fort Sumter, military units had been formed throughout Alabama. Early in March 1861, Tracy wrote to Clay, Jr.: "I am hesitating whether to apply to [President Jefferson] Davis for a position on his personal staff or to take my chances with the volunteers." Many volunteer units elected their own officers, more on their popularity than military skill, and named their own units. Representative groups were christened the New Market Rebels, Minute Men, Joe Bradley's Rebels, Madison County Cavalry, and Ward's Battery. Tracy joined the North Alabamians and was elected captain of the unit on April 26, 1861, at Huntsville. This unit later comprised Company I of the Fourth Alabama infantry Regiment. The local populace was proud of its volunteers, newspapers published lists of those who joined and donations were given to outfit the new soldiers. In May, 1861, Madison County political leaders contributed $1,000 toward equipping the local units. These green recruits usually departed in high spirits and in a lighthearted manner, "making it appear much like an excursion."

Immediately after induction the North Alabamians were transported to Virginia for their military training. They left Huntsville by rail on April 29, were delayed in Chattanooga, Tennessee, and reached Dalton, Georgia, on May 1. At Dalton they joined with nine other companies and continued toward Lynchburg, Virginia, for camp and drill. From Lynchburg the new recruits traveled to Winchester, arriving at Harper's Ferry on May 14, where they would remain for a month.

Captain Tracy's first impression of Harper's Ferry was not a favorable one, though he seemed to enjoy the camp life there. To Tracy, the environs resembled "a Washington City on an insignificant and contemptable scale: both hitherto and dependent on Federal patronage and therefore both servile and corrupt." Tracy wrote lightheartedly, however, of the former city lawyer rising early, drilling until night, and sleeping on the ground, "with sword and pistols by his side." As more troops arrived from the Southern states, Tracy enjoyed the pleasure of being reunited with many old friends among the Georgians.

Many of Tracy's letters exhibit patriotism and dedication to the Southern cause. He viewed the Confederate motives as just, based on the principles of liberty (though he failed to mention the slavery issue), and sacred in the eyes of God. For ten years he had believed that the North's purpose was to degrade and make vassals of the Southern people. He regretted the recourse to war, but he did not shrink from it. With typical Southern flair he wrote: "We must be prepared in this day of our Country's great peril and distress to submit to individual sacrifices of pleasure, comfort, property and everything except honor." He also expressed his willingness to die in defense of the South and asserted that no one would be ashamed of his conduct in battle. Tracy was confident (perhaps overconfident) of Southern victory, however, and agreed with many others that the war would be a short one.

Though devoted and loyal to the Southern cause, Tracy was also well-informed and he realized the potential destructive power of the industrial North. Still he doubted that the South's subjugation would greatly profit the North, as any surplus of goods on hand in the Northern states would be exhausted in the effort. He predicted that the Confederacy would emerge from the conflict "exhausted and faint...but with the cordials of Liberty in Government and Trade...it would recuperate." Tracy also realized that the war would take many lives, but remained staunch in his opinion that "disunion from such a miserable, fanatic, vulgar race as our grandeur brethren will be cheaply purchased at any cost."

Captain Tracy's fiery patriotism and loyalty remained strong in these early weeks of the war, but the military policy adopted by the Southern leaders disturbed him and made him critical. Actually, the captain was ignorant of the exact circumstances, for if he was aware of the game of military chess being played by the commanding generals he did not reveal such information in his letters. In early June, Tracy expressed doubt that a fight with the Yankees would ever occur and wished for an end to the war. He wrote his wife: "the only fights are such as are improvised among our own boys."

Even as Tracy expressed his impatience, however, the new commander at Harper's Ferry was engaged in combative exercises. General Joseph E. Johnston did not trust the defenses of the Ferry and declared his wish, to General Robert E. Lee, to command "a movable column, and not one tied by the leg to a stake." Moreover, Harper's Ferry was in danger of being surrounded by Union forces and in order to avoid this situation Johnston concluded to evacuate Harper's Ferry and remove to Winchester, important for its rail junction and access to General P.G.T. Beauregard at Manassas Junction.

The departure from Harper's Ferry presented the army's first opportunity for battle. Federal General Robert Patterson crossed to the west bank of the Potomac and Johnston's troops were held in a line of battle to receive the attack. Patterson re-crossed the river, however, no battle occurred, and Johnston proceeded toward Winchester.

Early in July, another opportunity for battle was presented when General Patterson's troops gathered at Martinsburg, Virginia. The Confederates marched to within five miles of the town to meet them, but after four days Johnston chose not to attack the town and on July 6 he ordered the retreat back to Winchester.

Captain Tracy evidently did not understand the military maneuvers, nor the geographic factors involved in these episodes, and he was incensed because the Confederates had not attacked. Concerning the first opportunity he wrote: "We are doing a good deal of hard watching, which men who affect military character called 'strategy,' what it really is I will not say, other than that we expected a battle yesterday, and marched in a direction opposite to the enemy." Tracy summarized the events of early July in a letter to his wife:

> "It was soon apparent…that our General had no intention of advancing on them, and I never had the least idea that they would advance on us. And so, we stood for four or five days tantalizing each other…yesterday Gen. Johnston issued an order to the troops complimenting them for their gallantry, saying that for four days we had offered battle to a largely superior force with they had declined, that an attack by us would involve a loss entirely out of proportion to the object to be attained and therefore we would fall back…"

Tracy lamented that his army was "not even within the sphere of the War Department's ground operation, but rather being employed simply to hold the enemy in check." He wrote that his only duty was "to obey orders, know nothing and think nothing, and to trust in the wisdom of inferiors." His anxious wait for battle would not be a long one, however.

By mid-July, Federal General Erwin McDowell was ready to move on Manassas and General Johnston's troops were to be involved in the coming encounter. After Midnight on July 17 Johnston received a telegram from Richmond ordering him to evacuate camp at Winchester and to proceed to Manassas Junction, where Beauregard had appealed for assistance and reinforcements. Johnston called his subordinates together and decided to depart the following day. On July 19, McDowell attempted to force a passage at Bull Run Creek (near Manassas Junction), but was repulsed by Confederate artillery, losing forty men in the effort. McDowell stated that he would "hereafter examine the location of the enemy's battery before engaging them." Meanwhile owing to the general confusion, and his lack of rations and information, McDowell retreated and bivouacked on July 19 and 20, while Johnston proceeded to the rendezvous with Beauregard.

For Captain Tracy the journey to the battlefield and preparation for the fight were taxing ordeals. In the early morning of July 18 his company had been ordered to prepare for a "long, heavy and forced march." He hastily provided for the sick men in his unit and began the advance in the late afternoon. "We marched all that night and the next day," Tracy wrote, "and arrived at Piedmont after night… nearly dead with hunger, thirst and fatigue." The men were then allowed to break ranks and sleep, amid a steady rain. At 1:00 a.m. the Confederates were aroused and ordered to board a train, which arrived at Manassas Junction at 10:00 a.m. on the morning of July 20. After a short rest Tracy's company was marched two miles into the country and allowed to recuperate the balance of the day and night. Still skeptical of the "Cry of Wolf," they began the march again on the morning of July 21, "eight or ten miles on double quick time."

This movement must have been extremely difficult for Tracy, for he confessed that he was hardly able to walk, ill with fever and other camp diseases, and his tongue was "furred." Nevertheless, the destination was reached, battle lines were formed, and the soldiers were told to wait. "I was so utterly exhausted," wrote Tracy, "that I was willing to rest immediately in the range of rifle and cannon." He also remembered his great thirst for water, but there was no time and the soldiers were quickly ordered to advance. Tracy recorded: "We were told to load as we went, and that the enemy were right before us. We marched up a hill, in an open field, and, just at the brow, were ordered to lie down, fire and load, fire and load…"

Captain Tracy's initial exposure to battle proved threateningly fierce. He flamboyantly began a letter to his sister: "I have seen a battle in all its terrible, magnificent horror. I have seen dead men and wounded men. I have heard the roar of cannon, the sound of bomb, the rattling of mustering…around and over my head, without being either killed or frightened…" He wrote that his company had been ordered to the "hottest" section of the battlefield and had been exposed to fire "from front and flank" for an hour and three quarters. Federal Colonel William T. Sherman's battery also emerged on their front, supported by a large number of infantrymen, and delivered a constant and murderous fire. Proudly, Tracy wrote:

"I stood up in the front rank, rallying my men when the troops were lying down. I saw man after man of my company fall dead at my side, and others wounded. Our position was a most hazardous one, but well did we maintain it. At last we were flanked on the left, and then from three sides… We fell back, our men falling as we retired."

After retreating about one quarter of a mile, Tracy encountered two wounded comrades and attempted to assist them. He first discovered the colonel of the Fourth Alabama, Egbert J. Jones, who had been wounded twice - once in each thigh. Tracy attempted to carry the colonel to safety but found that he did not have the strength to lift him. He called for volunteers to help remove Jones and persuaded three young soldiers to follow "in what was certainly a perilous, and what those who had no stomach for it denounced as a mad enterprise." When Tracy was returning to the battle he encountered Major Charlie Scott, of the Fourth Alabama, who had also been wounded in the leg. The captain likewise assisted this officer to a wooded area of safety. After the battle both men were retrieved and neither was thought to be mortally wounded.

When Tracy returned to the battle, he found the dissipated troops being reformed by General Barnard Bee. Tracy noted that his company, "or the fragment that remained unkilled, unwounded, or undispersed... were like sheep without a shepherd." General Bee, as he could find no other portion of his brigade, placed himself as acting colonel of the Fourth Alabama. Bee expressed his confidence that the Fourth would stand by him and, locating himself at the head of the reduced column, returned into the thick of battle. Bee was wounded almost immediately and died the following day. Tracy related that the Fourth was "his (Bee's) pet regiment and I suppose he died as he would have desired, leading a charge."

After a long and exhausting battle, of which the result was doubtful for most of the day, the Confederates emerged victorious. Generals Johnston and P.G.T. Beauregard had exposed their lives as freely as the common soldier and by their heroic daring had given confidence to the troops. Finally, in the late afternoon, the issue was settled and the Federals were retreating.

Tracy recorded the withdrawal of the Union soldiers in illusory terms:

"Panic stricken and demoralized, the invading hosts fled in every direction, followed by our cavalry that mowed them down like a ripe field in harvest time. Back and back they fled, throwing away their arms, knapsacks, food, everything that impeded their flight. What a contrast between those terrified and flying, and the grand army so carefully prepared, so admirably equipped for the great advance movement."

Prisoners captured by the Confederates told of congressmen and other notables who had come out from Washington with their wives to rejoice over the certain rout of the Rebels. Tracy commented that the congressmen were said to have been trampled in the dust by their flying army, "their dead Samsons...rotting in the sun....May the God of battle be praised for their single and glorious defeat."

But victory had been costly to General Johnston's Third Brigade, with over four-hundred men either killed or wounded – almost one-third of the regiment. Tracy wrote that his company had suffered more severely than any other (except the Florence, Alabama, company) with six dead and sixteen wounded. His unit had been exposed to rifle fire eight or nine times and to cannon all day. He wrote, however, that his men had "stood fire most gallantly."

Though Tracy admitted that the dead and wounded were terrible features of battle, his persistent thirst for water seemed overwhelming. He revealed only humanness when he reiterated that "the most excruciating torture was the intolerable, insatiable, and burning thirst for water. Great God how thirsty we were." They drank from mud puddles, where they could find them, and in the midst of the hottest fire men forgot everything except their desire for water. "On all sides," he wrote, "from wounded and unwounded, the cry went up, 'water, water, water'."

Tracy ended his account of First Manassas with assurances to his sister of his good health, ultimate Confederate victory, and a revealing statement concerning his progressing maturity as a military man. Despite his lengthy exposure to battle action, and fatigue, Tracy wrote that he was "entirely well" at the end of the day. Further, he optimistically announced that complete Southern military success was assured. He wrote that one more similar defeat of the Yankees would enable him to "hang up my sword and return to Blackstone." Earlier in his letter, however, he had expressed himself in such a fashion that only an intimate might realize the statement's importance. Obviously having extensively analyzed his feelings after the battle, he had written: "I felt none of the sensations I've often described of extreme nervousness at the first and indifference afterwards - I was neither nervous nor indifferent." Edward Dorr Tracy had become a soldier.

Tracy would continue to achieve militarily throughout his short career as a soldier. Beginning as captain, he was handed steady promotions until he reached brigadier general in August, 1862. Tracy served in Mobile with Leroy Pope Walker, under Braxton Bragg, and was cited for bravery and courage at the Battle of Shiloh. As operations focused around Vicksburg and the west, in early 1863, General Tracy and his five Alabama brigades were sent to Port Gibson, Mississippi, south of Vicksburg, to check General Ulysses S. Grant's movements in the area. Grant crossed to the east side of the Mississippi River and the Battle of Port Gibson ensued. In the early hours of this desperate Confederate attempt, Tracy's colonel, Isham W. Garrott, of the twentieth Alabama, wrote: "A little before 8 o'clock our brave and gallant commander, General Tracy, fell near the front line, pierced through the breast, and instantly died without uttering a word."

Tracy was apparently buried first in Port Gibson, for it was not until after the war that his remains were transferred to Macon, and there interred near his father in the distinguished Rose Hill Cemetery. In March, 1913, the Federal Government sponsored a sculptured monument of General Tracy, located in the Vicksburg National Military Park in Vicksburg, Mississippi. And, consistent with the tendency of Southerners to make martyrs of their fallen warriors, these words have been ascribed to General Tracy:

"Snatched, all too early, from that august Fame, Which on the serene heights of silvered Age, Waited with Laurelled hand."

Edward Dorr Tracy was a gentleman reared in the Old South tradition; a devoted husband and father; ambitious, yet one whose strong sense of duty applied not only to man and country, but to God; and one who harbored firm personal convictions; not the typical Southerner by any means, but not extraordinarily unique for his time.

"MY VERY DEAR WIFE": THE LETTERS OF A UNION CORPORAL

Brian Hogan

Author's Acknowledgement: I want to take this opportunity to thank Ranee Pruitt, Archivist at the Huntsville-Madison County Public Library and Pat Carpenter of the Library's Heritage Room for their help in preparing this article. Ranee transcribed a number of Henry Ackerman Smith's letters to his wife, and Pat tracked down the authors of the poetry quoted by Henry in several of his letters.

Henry Ackerman Smith was born January 30, 1837 in Westmoreland County, Pennsylvania, and baptized as an infant into the Lutheran Church. He was educated in public and subscription schools. At an early age he flirted with the idea of engaging in a seafaring life, but relatives dissuaded him. He then apprenticed as a clerk in a retail store in Greensburg, Pennsylvania, the county seat of Westmoreland County. After a year he was released from his contract, and went south into that part of Virginia that later became West Virginia. There he worked on a farm and also taught at a school on Bingaman Creek, a branch of the Monongahela River, before returning to his father's home in the autumn of 1856.

A devout man, Henry attended both morning and afternoon Sunday school at the United Brethren in Christ Church, and soon began teaching the afternoon class. In 1856 he enrolled as a student at Allegheny College, a Methodist college in Meadville, Pennsylvania, a small town in the French Creek Valley about 30 miles south of Lake Erie. He later attended Latrobe, Pennsylvania Normal School for several months. Henry subsequently passed a teacher's examination and received a Certificate of Qualification to teach in Pennsylvania schools. His first teaching post was at a county school near Youngstown, Pennsylvania.

In the spring of 1859, Henry moved to Jessamine County, Kentucky. Jessamine County, whose county seat is Nicholasville, is located in the Bluegrass Region about 20 miles south of Lexington. Early settlers in this area were mostly German Protestants who came in large part from Pennsylvania and Maryland. There he boarded with the family of William Nixon and Elizabeth Hoover Potts and their seven children, and taught in three local schools until the outbreak of the Civil War. In 1860, he was licensed as an Exhorter in the Methodist-Episcopal Church South, and was licensed as a Preacher later that year.

On April 2, 1861, Henry married Almina Clay Potts, the daughter of his landlord and a former pupil. Almina, who was born December 26, 1845 in Jessamine County, was barely past the age of 15 when they married. (In Henry's letters home, he referred to Almina as "Minie.")

Kentucky, whose population was divided in its loyalty, attempted to remain "neutral" when the Civil War began. However, after Confederate troops occupied Columbus on September 3, 1861 and Union troops countered with the occupation of Paducah shortly thereafter, all hopes of remaining "neutral" vanished and the state legislature voted to remain with the Union.

Henry cast his lot with the Union and enlisted as a private in Company D, 21st Ohio Volunteer Infantry, on October 12, 1861 at Camp Dick Robinson, near Nicholasville. Captain Matthew Ewing commanded Company D, and Colonel Jesse S. Norton commanded the regiment. The 21st Ohio was assigned to the 3rd Division, Army of the Ohio, commanded by Brigadier General Ormsby McKnight Mitchel, when Major

General Don Carlos Buell commanded the Army of the Ohio.

Twenty-First Ohio Volunteer Infantry: September 1861-September 1862

The 21st Ohio Volunteer Infantry was originally organized as a three-month regiment, and was mustered out on August 12, 1861. It was reorganized as a three-year regiment on September 19, 1861 and mustered in at Findlay, Ohio. The regiment received marching orders a few days later, was supplied with arms at Camp Dennison, Ohio on October 2, and marched the same day for Nicholasville, Kentucky. The regiment remained there for ten days and was then ordered to march to McCormick's Gap to join General Nelson's command. During that campaign, only one engagement occurred: On November 8, 1861, Confederates attempted an ambush at Ivy Mountain but were "foiled and whipped," mainly through a flank movement executed by the 21st Ohio. The Confederates were driven from that line and the whole command returned to Louisville, reaching the city in November.

The army was reorganized in December under the command of General D.C. Buell, and moved to Bacon Creek and Green River, where it remained in winter quarters until late February 1862. The 21st Ohio marched on Bowling Green as part of General O.M. Mitchel's 3rd Division, and played a role in driving the Confederates from that strong position. Then moving directly on Nashville, General Mitchel summoned the city authorities to surrender, "which demand was promptly acceded to." Colonel Kennett of the 4th Ohio Cavalry took possession of the city on March 13. Four days later, General Mitchel's column moved out on the Murfreesboro turnpike, occupied Murfreesboro on

March 19, and remained there until April 4, 1862 when it moved on to Huntsville, Alabama.

The entire command moved from Fayetteville for Huntsville on the morning of April 10. Arriving the next morning, it drove the Confederate forces from the city, captured 300 prisoners, 16 locomotives, and a large number of freight and passenger cars. General Mitchel inaugurated "[t]he most vigorous measures...Expeditions were sent in every direction, railroad bridges burned, and every precaution taken against surprise." On or about April 20, Captain Milo Caton, Company H, 21st Ohio Volunteer Infantry, was sent to Nashville in charge of a group of Confederate prisoners. Upon his return he was surrounded by Morgan's Cavalry and, after a hard fight, Captain Caton and his company were obliged to surrender. The whole party was sent to Richmond, and Captain Caton remained in Confederate prisons for over a year. On May 28, 1862, the 21st Ohio moved to Athens to relieve Colonel Turchin, and remained there until August 28, when it moved again to Nashville.

Letters written between March 7, 1862 and August 1, 1862

Henry Smith wrote about all those things that soldiers have always written home about - the weather, the food, the tedium of camp life, his health, and gripes about Army leadership, who he thought were not doing all they could to bring the war to a successful, speedy conclusion. He was proud of his accomplishments, such as his prowess in cooking, his promotion to 2nd Corporal and squad leader, his commendations for keeping his squad tent clean and orderly (for which he received praise from General Mitchel), and his success in reforming his tent mates from the "vice of swearing," and leading them in hymn singing at night. He was disappointed by not being able to find a substitute so he could return home to "his Minie," who had asked him to return, and further disappointed in not being able to get a furlough. But most of all, he wrote how much he loved his Minie!

Henry (or Harrie, as he signed his letters) wrote some 28 letters to his "very dear wife Minie" during this period. The letters of most interest are those written during the Union occupation of Huntsville and Athens, Alabama, and are published here in detail.

Transcribed Letters from Henry Ackerman Smith to Almina Clay Potts Smith

21st REGT. O.V.U.S.A.
Col J. S. Norton Comp. D
Camp Jackson, near Nashville
March 7, 1862

My dear wife,

I embrace this opportunity of writing you a few lines informing you of my continued good health hoping that this letter will find you all enjoying the like blessings. Although nothing of interest has occurred since the last of such agitation as might be addressed to fill up these blank pages with anything of interest to you all, yet in performance of a most pleasant duty I make the attempt.

Several wet, cold & snowy days have occurred recently, very cold indeed for this season and latitude and some of the boys thought that we must be on the other side of warm weather as the further we advanced into Tennessee the colder the weather has become. This morning was clear and cold but since the day has become warm and pleasant and we hope the cold north wind and storms will soon disappear and give peace to the genial warmth of the Southern Sun. There has been a gradual accumulation of forces here until now there are five divisions and I presume there cannot be short of sixty thousand men. Discipline is so strict that we are not allowed to go beyond the lines of our division, which is as I presume a necessary evil. If it was not so I could find some acquaintances in some of the Kentucky Regiments and in all probability in some of the Pennsylvania Regiments in camp. If intercourse were thus allowed I might spend a pleasant hour which would enhance the tedium of camp life.

We seem to be now in the grand center of rebel supplies, besides the provisions captured upwards of thirty thousand tents were taken and many of us are sheltered by rebel canvas. We are now receiving much better provisions than we did on the march from Green River to this place. As I look round me and examine the culinary department of my domicile I see crackers in abundance, light bread, beef, ham, bacon (side-meat), rice, coffee, tea, flour, sugar, lard, soap candles &c. These are the edibles of my Mahgeret[?] and I know you will say that as far as substantials are concerned we have plenty and variety for the present.

The most prominent furniture we have is muskets & these we know how to use to perfection, almost. Well my dear Minie we have no drawing rooms to welcome guests and no costly cakes to treat them to. No cots of downy softness to bid them recline &c. but with good health we have those things that you do not enjoy at home. We can lie down in the most indifferent places and enjoy a good night's repose and with danger staring us in the face we can sleep sweetly and dream perchance of those so dear at home. So I have often dreamed of you darling. Besides we enjoy a good appetite for the most indifferent food and so we plod along and daily look forward till these troubles will end and all opposed to our government will be ashamed of themselves. But the day is waning and I must prepare for Dress Parade. We have drawn two months' pay and in my next I will send you some as I do not think it safe yet for money to be sent per[sonal] mail and no other way presents itself yet.

I cease writing at present and I will write the remainder on tomorrow if I have time. Till then I remain your ever loving and affectionate husband, H. A. Smith

March 9, '62

My dear Minie,

I could not fulfill my promise to finish this letter on yesterday as unexpectedly to myself I was detailed to go on Guard. So this beautiful Sunday morning I will attempt to do so although I may fail as losing sleep has the effect of stultifying the intellect. You ask me whether I prefer Tennessee to Kentucky? Under existing circumstances, I do not. Had I found you my dear here, had I wooed & won you here, I might have preferred this state. But though there are beautiful landscapes and nature has lavished her gifts with a profuse hand and even nature has been further improved by the hand of art yet the fields are not so green and smiling. The hills and valleys do not bring up so many sweet remembrances of the past and because you, my sweet flower, do not reside here I again say Tennessee does not present the attractions to me that Kentucky does. Do not be discouraged dearest Minie, be of good cheer and I will soon be with you I sincerely hope. You are now in the home of your youth and under the sheltering care of your good parents, there I expect to find you on my return. So do not pine and think the time long, for every fond pulsation of your good little heart meets an answering one in him who has risked everything for your eventual good.

I cannot have my miniature taken now for the reason that it is impossible to go to Nashville. Otherwise would I comply with your request immediately.

Well, my dear, I do not think of anything else to write so I must stop, wishing you to give my kindest remembrances to Mr. & Mrs. Potts and all the family. I hope cook's ear will get well without impairing her hearing. Write very soon sweet Minie, be prudent and obedient to your parents, ask the counsel of our heavenly Father & pray for me.

I remain your true and loving Husband Harrie

P.S. I enclose $5.00 & will send more in my next.

How strange and sad the scenes of life
As year by year time moves along.
First peace and then in mortal strife
A nation mourns in tears of blood
Not so it was three years ago
Though short the time has seemed to be
Then there was no nation's foe
But each rejoiced that he was free
A stranger sought a welcome place
Among the ones he thought was kind
His early friends he did forsake
For those he did expect to find
A northern girl had fanned his brow
A northern sun had browned his cheek
But nature gave a healthful glow
And plighted vows gave happiness
Then came the dreadful cry of war
To arms! to arms! ye bravest ye bravest
Your nation calls you from your homes
To save her from the threatened doom
Then flocked around the nation's flag
A long array of hearts so true
While those who left the flag to droop

With foul intent were far from few
But each day did that same proud flag
Advance again from state to state
While rebels quailed beneath its power
To think of retribution hour.

Do not think me an enthusiast dear Minie. I am for the government as long as it affords us protection but as soon as it is destructive to us I would cast it from me & trample it in the earth & only submit to it under a force of circumstances.

No more. Address H.A. Smith in care of Capt. Ewing Co. D, 21st Reg., O.V. U.S.A. via L & Nashville R.R.

Camp Jackson near Nashville, Tenn
March 15th 1862

My dear wife,

I embrace a moment of leisure to write you a few lines expressive of my state of feelings at this time & c. I am well as usual bodily but depressed and sad mentally. With victory everywhere crowning our banners, I am now weighed down with grief. She to whom I owe my existence and cared for me through all my infantile years is no more.

I received the notice on last evening in a letter from my brother stating that she died on the 6th inst between eleven and twelve o-clock. Now that I am motherless, all the past seems to rush into my mind. Many a time when by my wild freaks I merited chastizening that kind mother shielded me from harm. Many a time when I, careless of myself, would have run into exposure a kind mother ever ready would be present to give me good advice. Often she would share with me what would be most acceptable to herself. Now this kind and indulgent mother has passed away. My brother writes that we must not take it too much to heart, as our loss is her gain and we must look forward to a meeting beyond this world of trouble in a world where there is no separating.

Oh, my mother! Would that I could have had but the sad consolation of receiving her dying blessing and of dropping tears of grief upon the clay that conceals her sacred remains.

But she is gone from me forever and day after day as I awake from my slumber it is with the sad recollection that I am no longer blessed with my mother's good counsel. The thought has occurred to me that it was well for me if I could bury in oblivion the recollection that I had lost my kind & good mother. But no if every thought cost a thousand pangs keener than so many darts, I would not tear from my mind the recollection of the many good and kind deeds of my mother. I have always had the thought that I could bear almost any loss better than the loss of my mother and Sweet Minie as I am stricken with grief at my loss I have been so selfish as to intimate that I alone am the loser in this sad calamity. I know the blow will even reach you my dove, but on account of your slight acquaintance you cannot experience my loss but you can sympathize with me.

Now my darling I must have a share of the love and advice of your good and kind mother and she must have the place my own dear mother so recently occupied in my affections.

The extent of this love can only be second to that which shall always be yours my darling.

But I must dismiss this sad subject for the present and I next introduce one, which has been conducive of profound regret and alarm. It is with reference to the message of President Lincoln. If the matter introduced goes no further it is well, but you may be sure darling that before I go south for the purpose of subjugating state to the injury or destruction of my own states I will go back to Kentucky and assist in stopping her bleeding wounds, but I am in hopes and I firmly believe that we will soon enjoy peace and harmony again and if we are blessed with wise and prudent men as representatives we can live as in years gone by. But if madness or wild insanity prevails and wakes bitter animosity & once causes strife between the sections then I am prepared to say that the north and the south cannot live together any more. What is the opinion of Mr. Potts as to the near-approach of the end of the war? I rest firmly in the belief that soon this foolish war will close and we will be united again as we were five months ago.

As far as I have observed the marks of the destroyers are not so prevalent here as in Kentucky. Every effort is being made to keep the property of citizens inviolate and as far as I have seen there is no discrimination for opinion sake. With a governmental policy like this, if the estranged affections of the people cannot be enlisted then indeed we may give up the contest, but already the salutary effect may be seen and from the election returns it will be seen that the majority of the people of the state are still for the union notwithstanding the secession papers asserted the contrary. Tennessee will soon be entirely redeemed from rebel rule.

Since I wrote last we were once more out on picket duty and the position we occupied was extremely critical. We went about two miles in advance of any other picket guard and as there were only two companies of us we were in some danger being surrounded and taken but the night passed off without any alarm and morning appeared wet and gloomy and since then up to this the weather has been rather wet but warm and agreeable. Wet weather as I have said is most disagreeable to the soldier in camp. This is a world of mishaps and as spirits take their flight from this to another world it is but the severance of bonds that bind us to this world and which will prove ties to draw our hearts affections upon our heavenly homes. Oh, Minie it seems I cannot forbear writing of this dire calamity, and you must excuse me as it is but the flow of thought and the natural expression of a heart that beats in accordance with a heart temporarily absent but seemingly present. I ask you sweet wife to sacredly keep mother's miniature for my sake so that I can still look upon the face of her who cared so well for me. She was about 60 years of age.

I am about to part with my old and faithful musket and I can hardly reconcile myself the loss. I have kept it bright as when I left home and for a long time it was pronounced the prettiest gun in the regiment by the adjutant. Now there are several companies armed with bright muskets. Tomorrow we will exchange our muskets for French rifles, a very effective gun, and as we are to have an advanced position we will use them if an opportunity occurs.

By the way, there seems very little probability that the rebels will show us much fight in this quarter. But I must close this imperfect letter. I enclose $5.00, in my next I will send you more. I wish you to tell me when you receive this as well as the five I sent in my former letter if it came to hand. Write very soon and often sweetest one, give my love to Mr. and Mrs. Potts and the family.

Kiss Ninnie & Kate for me and tell Annie that she must be a good little girl and see how good she can read when I get home. I am not forgetful of Bennie and Middie and I hope they too will have improved in scholarship. Nerve your heart my darling a few short weeks yet and I hope to be restored to you. Direct via L and Nashville R. R. Your affectionate Harrie

Camp Van Buren near
Murfreesboro, Tenn.
March 24, 1862

My Dear Wife,

I once more embrace a moment of leisure to write you a line to inform you and all the rest where I am and what we are doing &c. We marched from camp Jackson on the morning of the 18th inst. and by a circuitous route we came to this place on the morning of the 21st.

The reason of our being compelled to go by a round about course was owing to several bridges being destroyed by the renegade Morgan of Lexington, Ky. During the forenoon of the second and third mornings of our march we were exposed to a drenching rain. Since we came here the "clerk of the weather" has shown himself considerably by having a very cold spell. It has snowed a very little almost every day and altogether it has been very disagreeable indeed and I may fail in writing you an interesting letter my dear, if so you must excuse me on account of cold weather.

My first theme will be the description, or what I shall intend as a partial delineation of what I have seen of middle Tennessee.

The country between here and Nashville must certainly be the most delightful in this state, and if it becomes any better or prettier, I may eventually be compelled to say that it exceeds even central Ky. The style of building, though it is very tasteful and chaste, is not so substantial as in Jessamine and Fayette Counties. After traversing a delightful turnpike road for the distance of ten miles we made a tum to the right at an angle of about thirty degrees, while on our left might be seen a wide scope of country which, had it been drawn according to nature, would have immortalized any painter of scenery. Imagine yourself my dear Minie standing upon a slight elevation, and receding from you by a gentle declivity were fields needing only the touch of nature's green with here and there, a "lowing kine," and beasts of burden too, while intermingled were groves of cedar and other trees of many variety. As if to finish the picture so that even the adept in artistic skill could find no objection. At each end were placed elevations having shady groves and pleasant walks, resplendent in all that could satisfy him who seeks for nature's poetry. But still not content with so fine a picture another touch of the pencil must be added ere it is considered complete, or left for man to behold. Beyond the elevations before alluded to as if to shade the fancy picture in our front, lay a ridge or small mountain, seemingly about the height of Chestnut ridge which you will recollect of seeing while you were in Pennsylvania. From the General to the private all had to look and feast the vision upon this picture. One time only before had I seen a landscape so fine and varied, and nothing that man can make can possibly fill the mind with such emotions, and no eloquence can stir up the mind so sensibly to the fact that the maker of all these things is our heavenly father. Shortly after the scenes just narrated, we entered a grove of timber, and then another scene of grandeur met our view. For the distance of two miles the trees approached the side of the road, and with their overhanging branches of evergreen formed almost a canopy while as far as the vision carried us we could see a moving mass of men and teams, while the intervening distance disclosed a real pretty little town, delightfully nestling among the numerous cedars (as if to hide its handsome appearance) bearing the poetical name of Laverne. With such ornaments and unexceptionable country in fertility - who can say else than it is a delightful country to live in.

We encamped at night by the side of the first cotton field we had yet seen in our march. But on the next day field after field was passed, and now I should judge we are in the center of the cotton region of middle Tennessee and I had no idea that there was so much raised in the entire state as I have seen in the last twenty miles.

The country seems very prolific in everything that central Ky. abounds in, in addition to the cotton, and in richness it is evidently as good and in some instances I think much better. The houses in the country are mostly of wood, though brick houses do not infrequently occur. The style of building is of a peculiar kind which I denominated Southern.

Murfreesboro is a pleasant town situated on the Stone River, in the midst of a most delightful country, having railroad communications with the principal cities of the state. It was for a number of years the capital of the state but it owes its chief importance to the productive region with which it is surrounded. Our camp is surrounded with pleasant fields and groves, while the blooming trees & flowers despite the cold gives it a pleasant appearance. We are about two miles from town and are engaged in repairing the bridges over the river, which our vandalic opponents burned. This will occupy us for some time and Madame Rumor says we will not go any further, as there is every indication of a general caving-in of the rebels. But I am not one to be seduced by such ideas and I bide the time, believing however that ere long this hateful war will come to a final end.

Well my dear I have not received a word from you for some time-but as there will be a mail today I hope it will carry at least one sweet letter from you and some papers. News of an outside character is so exceedingly scarce that papers half a month old are read with an avidity, showing our destitution in that line.

Personally I am well as usual and in the enjoyment of fine spirits when I contemplate the near proximity to the end of the war, and the happy meeting we will have when we can enjoy each other's society. One thing more and then I will cease writing for the present. I earnestly beg a continued interest in your kind prayers as well as that of the church. Forget me not at night and when you rise, and when you are in the sanctuary of God. Be unceasing in your duties to your God. Be kind and very obedient to your parents, and faithful to your brothers and sisters. By doing so you will make yourself happy and happify those around you.

Now my dear I will bid you adieu for a time, promising to write again before many days. Hoping in the meantime to hear from you. Write your address:

H. A. Smith
In care of Capt Ewing
Co. D. 21st Reg. O.V.
via & Nashville R.R.
Or via Nashville Tenn

I am forever your affectionate Husband Harrie

Camp Van Buren
Near Murfreesboro, Tenn.
March 28th, 1862

My Very Dear Wife,

Although not a week has passed since I last wrote in accordance with your request I resume my pen to inform you of passing events, and by consulting my stock of items I must confess, it looks like a failure-sure. By placing credence upon camp rumors, I might furnish an abundance of subjects. These rumors record and confirm some of the most absurd notions to which your Jayhawker story does not furnish even an example. One day peace is about declared and next the (bogus) tidings come that we will have to stay for forty years if the war lasts so long & c. Yesterday the rumor was afloat that our army on the Potomac had gained a brilliant victory, today they sustained a disastrous defeat by the same source.

I rely solely for information upon newspapers and headquarters announcements and these come few & far between. Occasionally I am led to consult my own judgment upon the conclusion of all these troubles and I am safe in saying the beams of peace or adjustment are beginning to be apparent.

This state I believe is as thoroughly rebel as any with perhaps two or three exceptions. And the people here say that "they wish that the war was settled in one way or the other." Now this is a tacit acknowledgement that should it be decided in favor of the old government they will be satisfied. I will be much surprised if Governor Johnson will find much or any difficulty in restoring the state to its allegiance.

Another reason for believing that the war is approaching a focus is the avidity in which the Federal currency is taken by the citizens, while they either refuse their own or take it at a vicious discount. The frequency of desertions from the rebel army may be adduced as another reason. Small as these promises may be, it shows that the rebel pulse does not beat with that confidence it did but three or four months ago. Take courage darling Minie the promise of a brighter day is ours, and that the day of promise is not far distance is each day becoming more and more apparently. Patiently live in hope dearest for a few days more and then I will come to you.

You spoke dearest about Morgan having Gen. Mitchel in his power. The opposite is the fact. Gen M had fairly entrapped Morgan and the latter hoisted a white flag, and produced a prisoner to be exchanged. Of course Gen M could not hold him a prisoner as he bore a flag of truce. It is generally supposed that Morgan intended to capture a large number of our teams, but upon discovering that they were full of soldiers he had necessarily to alter the plan of operations.

Morgan is bold and wary but he will run against a snag some day that will make it all day with him (or all night perhaps).

You spoke of a rose bush which was already blooming. It is doubtless a treasure as they are very rare. Take care of it but take still better care of "my rose" for surpasses all others in every way. You have given your shrub a real pretty name and I hope it may be constantly in bloom, reminding you that as constant as the beauty of the rose, so constant is the Union in its protection to its subjects. But dearest I am not unaware that this letter is a dry and uninteresting one to you but as nothing transpires in camplife, except a regular routine of business-which you style nothing.

Believing that you do not know what we do each day I will relate to you our daily duties. First we have regular guard duty occurring every ten or fifteen days. This takes twenty-four hours and unfits him for duty by losing sleep for the next day. At five o'clock we are called from our beds to roll call & to prepare for breakfast. From ten to twelve we drill. Next is dinner then from two to four is afternoon drill. At five we have dress parade & after supper is roll call. This divides the day in such a measure that by the time you rightly begin to write you are called to the performance of duty so that the opportunities of writing are not so abundance as you supposed. Besides we are now engaged in building a couple of bridges to build which will take us several days more, and the details to this work are very numerous.

The weather has become warm and already the vegetable world feels the effect of a warm and genial sun. It seems strange that such a beautiful country and such a vigorating atmosphere can be, and yet our country is humiliated to the dust by the war demon in our midst. May God in his justice break up this cruel strife as his wisdom will decide to be equitable and just to both sections, so that peace may be established again.

My health is good as usual, but, with the spring songsters making even the atmosphere pregnant with joyous sounds, it makes me chafe to be once more free to return to you that I may enjoy the sweets of your presence, the encouragement of the conversation and the congeniality of domestic life. But when the wants of my country come up and demand my service, I am compelled to acknowledge the justness of its demands and sacrifice all the pleasures consequent upon a release from service. Be brave and firm my love my Minie till I come, be obedient to your parents and perform their wishes, be kind to your brothers and sisters. Let your first and last thoughts each day be fixed upon that God who sustains us even to the last moment of life, and while you offer your adorations to him do not forget me in your sweet murmurings of prayer.

Kiss Ninnie and Kate for me and remember me to all. My kindest wishes for Mr. and Mrs. Potts & family. Don't forget to send me newspapers.

Direct via Nashville, Tenn. Your affectionate Husband Harrie

Camp Van Buren near
Murfreesboro Tenn
April 2nd 1862

My very dear wife,

I write this letter not because I have anything especially of interest to communicate to you. But in commemoration of our union, which you well recollect one year ago this day occurred. One source of sadness only, mars my joy and that is that I am unable to celebrate the first anniversary of that union which gives me so much happiness in your sweet and endearing society. But as Fate has decreed it otherwise we must each make the best of it biding our time that these cruel troubles will soon cease and we be allowed peacefully to journey through life. I am sorry to say that one of my military family has fallen a victim to disease & death. He died on the morning of the 29th and was buried on the same day near nightfall.

His disease was inflammation of the brain occasioned by being detailed for duty too soon after his recovery from a former sickness. His name was William Henry Bordner of Wood County Ohio. He had many noble characteristics, and was an industrious man, but I am sorry to say like too many in the army, he was profane and sometimes vulgar in his conversation. I can only add a passage reputed to David. "May God have called him like a wanderer home."

I carved his initials on a board to be placed at his head. Thus W. H.B. 21st O.V. Co. D. He reposes far from his friends and home, but there is one parting consolation that he died at his post, and like a true soldier he fell at the van of the host, a voluntary sacrifice to the cause of his country.

The weather here is very dry and warm, and if it were not for a fine breeze we should now be enjoying a real summer atmosphere.

As it is, some persist in saying that it is as warm as harvest time in Ohio. I do not suffer as yet from heat though I do not expect to escape it after while. We will leave here in the course of a few days, so says Madame Rumor, but as the bridges we have been building are about to be finished I cannot see what will keep us longer than a few days more.

One march will be in the direction of Chattanooga but as there are several damaged or burned bridges between this place & that it will fall our lot to repair them, as we are the pioneers or advanced troops on this road.

The forests are beginning to assume the verdure consequent upon spring and right welcome will it be to all of us, who have been immured in muslin houses all winter, to now look out upon woods and fields clothed in green. But more welcome will be the intelligence that the war is ended and we are to turn our faces homeward.

Minie I long so much to see you that I suppose you must send me your pretty face in return for the one I send you in this mail. If this one goes safely through you will have your soldier, but I reckon you will be disappointed in my not having a beard when I had it taken. I became disgusted with my beard long since and go without. Tell me what you think of the picture, and whether uniform improves my appearance or not. I neglected to say in my last letter that I received your letter so that I have now had two sweet little letters from you since I came here and also four papers from the 17th to the 20th ult. These afforded me much pleasure in reading as they occupied my otherwise idle hours.

In my next I will send you five dollars and so on for several weeks. I would send it all at once but thereby I would lose all if robbed. This mode will insure the safety of a part at least. I presume the state-money due me for the last school I taught can soon be drawn, if so have it drawn and if you do not need it give it into your father's care as well as this I send you from time to time.

Minie dearest do not think hard of my protracted stay and believe it is a necessary absence for I have not changed my mind as to the necessity of my being thus cut off from the society of those I love, and for whom I have endured a winter residence in tents and laid even life at the service of my country. But dearest think not that for a moment I have experienced any joy in my new relation for even after the din of battle had ceased at Ivy and we were the victorious possessors of the field, it was a sad sight to see the sons of Kentucky slaughtered by those who were a few months before equally the sons of Kentucky.

With these feelings I will hail the day when my country shall say that I have done all required of me, and even before the war is ended if I can be honorably discharged or if I can get a substitute I will joyfully set out on my return to the object of my love, my own sweet Minie. How gladly then would I return to the state of my adoption there to abide.

So keep a good heart my darling and pray that this war may come to an early end. God alone can avert the destruction of our land and nation and to him we must lift up our hearts and pray.

Well Minie dear I will not weary you with more of this uninteresting writing and you must please excuse my palpable want of interest and probably I will be better able to write you something of interest next time. I am very slightly indisposed but I hope to be well by tomorrow.

Direct via Nashville Tenn to your ever affectionate Husband Harrie PS. Give my love to Mr. & Mrs. Potts & family. Be very kind obedient to your parents brothers & sisters & write soon your Harrie.

Camp Harrison near
Shelbyville Tenn
April 8th, 1862

My very dear wife,

I embrace a moment of leisure to address you a letter, which I would have done on yesterday, but I was detailed to go on guard, consequently I had to defer writing till now.

Since my last we have made another advance and we are now fifty-five miles south east of Nashville and twenty-five from Murfreesboro.

On the morning of the 4th inst we set out from Camp Van Buren and had it not been for a drenching rain we would have enjoyed the march as one of the most pleasant we have yet made. The land on each side of the road for the most part was under a high state of cultivation, but occasionally the forest would form a bourne on each side of the road, when the overhanging branches would form a canopy, delightfully cool in contrast with the vernal rays of sun, which even now gives us an occasional touch of summer heat. The land is more undulating than any I have yet seen in this state, while an occasional hill is observant in the distance. Consequently there is more variety of scenery than on our previous march. Once and again a bold rocky point would jut out to the roadside and again the surface would decline into a pleasant plain, apparently productive to an almost superfously [sic] extent. Again a palatial residence would peer out amidst surrounding foliage, while the numerous cabins are indicative of a large force of servants.

The people generally seem to be busily engaged in agricultural pursuits, which bespeaks a desire to live, while the farms farther north are seemingly left to take care of themselves. This latter fact may be owing to the circumstance that the people of this county generally are noted for their firm adherence to the union. Shelbyville is a fine town fully as large as Murfreesboro though the buildings throughout are not as handsome as the latter.

Our passage through town was like an ovation. The people lined the sidewalks and numerous tiny flags were displayed while the "hurrahs" for the Union were frequent, all indicative of a loyal constancy to that union for which we have sacrificed our present enjoyment in hopes of a future peace and quietude. So mote it be.

Well dear Minie we are once more in camp though I have not the least idea that we will stay here more than a day or two more, this adduction I arrive at from the fact that there is nothing doing here, and there has not been any armed rebels in this vicinity for some weeks. Our next destination will be

Decatur, Huntsville or some other point in Alabama. On last Sunday I in company with one of my messmates went into the country and when I saw the smiling fields, and delightful forests, waving their branches on which was the first verdure of spring. All these rejoicing in the vernal rays of the sun, seemingly brighter because I was out from the restraints of camp life. When I saw these things I asked the question whether it was possible for war- hateful- interencine [sic] war to be tearing at even the vitals of this beautiful country. Soon the distant booming of a gun or the long roll of the drum awakened us to a remembrance of the fact. It would be a matter of impossibility for me to describe my feelings while I was thus enjoying my freedom. Suffice it to say that as by a natural impulse I was led on till I had gone probably five miles by the circuitous route I traversed. Then I halted at a neat looking farm house and after conversing awhile we were invited to take dinner which we accepted most willingly, as a "home made dinner" is quite an improvement on our patent ones in camp. I did not ask my friends whether they were for the union or not but from their general conversation they would be satisfied to enjoy the peace we once enjoyed, at almost any price. I almost forgot to say that my hosts were from our own state Ky and seemed much pleased to hear that I was from the same state. I came very near finding a friend the other day as were about four miles back from here. A gentleman & lady, about middle aged in life, inquired if Harry Smith was in the company, and [page missing]...so darling Minie you must not forget to write regularly. I depend a great deal upon you and your sweet advices.

My kindest remembrances to Mr. & Mrs. Potts & the family.

Let me know of everything that passes of importance. I hope to be home soon and then assist in the labors in which others are striving and I seem to be doing nothing.

Do not forget your duties dear Minie to your God and to your parents. Honor and act in obedience to the desires of your kind parents, and be a gentle and affectionate sister as you are a good and kind wife. Oh my dear I so much long for the end of these troubles that I may enjoy your sweet society once more. I hope you have received my miniature and that if an opportunity presents itself that you will send me yours unless the war will end very soon.

Direct as before Via Nashville to your Affectionate and ever loving Husband Harrie

21st REGT. O.V.U.S.A,
Col. J. S. Norton
Comp. D
Camp near Huntsville, Alabama
April 12, 1862

My very dear wife,

I embrace this opportunity to write you a letter as we may leave and I may not have another chance for some days. We left Shelbyville on the morning of the 9th inst and after a march of 26 miles we arrived at the town of Fayetteville, Lincoln Co. Here we remained till the next day Meridian when we marched over the hills to the southward and bivouacked about ten miles south of town. When we were about seven miles from town I was ordered to take twelve men and go back to where the teams were and carry two days rations into camp. Of course, this looked like a forced march ahead. I overtook the regiment about 10 1/2 o'clock at night & at 3 A.M. next morning we set out for Huntsville, a distance of 21 miles over a miserable road, crossing streams of quite a number. Notwithstanding all these obstacles we arrived here at 4 o'clock P.M. Thus we made a distance of about 60 miles in two days and a half. The country through which we passed during the last three days differed considerably from any we had yet seen in Tennessee. The country gradually became hilly but the soil was rich & well adapted to cultivation and would be one of the finest grazing counties in the state with some care. These hills covered with trees covered again with verdure of different shades while the Dogwood & June ber[r]y trees appearing as white as snow. The Wahoo with its blooms of red altogether making a variety more beautiful than my pen can paint. The buildings here were of a very inferior quality though here and there a more modem building is found which alleviates the otherwise tedium of sameness. Fayetteville is about as large as Nicholasville and is the County seat of Lincoln Co. The buildings are of a good quality and generally large and substantial, indicative of a good deal of wealth. After we had gone about ten miles south of Fayetteville we found the country to our front more open and level and after we crossed the state line it gradually became level, while on the left at a distance of 5 or 6 miles could be seen the Western range of the Cumberland Mountains. Soon after we came into the state we could see a difference in the soil and the plantations seemed to extend almost as far as the eye could reach. Minie I believe as much as I have seen of Alabama I can justly say it exceeds even our own beloved Kentucky in several respects. The soil seems to be of such a superior quality and its adaptation to the raising [of] all kinds of grain & cotton makes it a lovely country. Well darling we are now between two rebel armies and we hold the railroads or route of communication between the two. We are held in instant readiness to repel any attack that may be made upon us. And if they come we will give them a good account of our division.

We captured from 15 to 20 engines besides a large number of cars here together with 250 prisoners.

I am unable to say how soon we will get any mail or how soon I will have an opportunity of sending any letters to our friends but as soon as a chance occurs I will send this. In the meantime I will write you what is transpiring should it be of interest. I have an idea that we will be here for some time or till the country round us is cleared of armed rebels.

The people around here are not rebellious enough to burn their cotton in accordance with the instructions of the rebels in power as I saw quite a number of bales on our yesterday's march. Well dearest there is some Scare among our officers as we are not allowed to take off our accoutrements and the guns are out in stacks in front of our tents, all in fighting trim. Well I must confess that everything looks as peaceful as I could desire around us but this may be the calm before the storm if this windy day could be called a calm.

I cannot tell you anything about Huntsville as we are encamped just before the town and we are not allowed to go into it, but the suburban houses are large and elegant bespeaking the same in the town. I will at- tempt to describe it as soon as I get a chance to see it.

Formerly I believe I have neglected to request you to retain these letters as I will have use for them when I get home. Capt. Ewing has re- quested me to write a sketch of the travels and services of the 21st Reg., these letters will aid me in doing so.

Our division is here alone and the discipline is not so strict now as when we were attached to the Corps de Arme or the grand army, which was the case when we were at Nashville. I cannot but wonder at the apparent infatuation of the people in these states. We have a Secesh letter here written in Marshal County, Tenn, March 15 and in it is a statement that they (the rebels) would have the city of Nashville in a week from that time. At that time they were in full retreat and it seems strange that the people did not know it. It is by this system of misrepresentation that this rebellion is kept alive. The people are told of victory after victory that never had an existence and, believing it, they cannot see why they should act otherwise. We must teach them a few more wholesome lessons and they will get their eyes open.

My dearest Minie I will soon conclude this hastily written and poorly composed letter, but I must once more exhort you to remain pure in your thoughts about eternal life, true to your vows to God, and to honor thy father and thy mother with a sweet obedience of conduct to their wishes, to be a gentle and kind sister to your brothers & sisters, so living that I may embrace you as a model of perfection and Christian virtue. This dearest is the highest object of life and when we have passed over the weary marches of this world we will rest forever in the Paradise of God. In your daily offerings to God do not forget me in your prayers. Give my love to Mr. & Mrs. Potts & the family.

Send me papers frequently, Minie dear, I have only received the four I spoke of in a former letter. Direct as before till further instructions and I am forever your faithful and loving Husband Harrie.
P.S. I enclose $5.00

3 o'clock P.M.

Dearest, we have just received the glorious news from the Corinth Victory.

21st REGT. O.V. U.S.A.
Col. J. S. Norton
Comp.D
Camp Taylor, near Huntsville, Alabama
April 15, 1862

My very dear wife,

I once more embrace a moment of leisure to write you a letter to let you know how we are getting along &c. Our mail facilities are yet so limited that only occasionally we have any chance to send letters but I presume in the course of a week we will have more regularity in this respect. Since I wrote last I have passed through the city of Huntsville while I was going out on picket duty. I am much pleased with the town, while the elegant buildings of both a public and private kind are indicative of wealth and good taste. The streets are a model of beauty, being wide and shaded on both sides with evergreens & many other trees of nameless variety. The public square is a pleasant retreat while the stately courthouse rears its massy [sic] walls in bold relief among the numerous shade trees by which it is surrounded. The town itself is not quite as large as Lexington though in width and airiness of streets, in architectural taste in buildings & in ornamental beauty, Huntsville surpasses the latter. I cannot say that the surrounding country surpasses Fayette Co., Ky. for that I believe to be impossible but the region around this town is fully equal to it. The Poet would say that this surpasses Ky. as beyond the beautiful landscape only a few miles are the Cumberland Mountains, rising like a huge wave out of the plain which extends to its very base, the tops rearing their heads among the clouds, while the sides are covered with trees now covered with the beautiful verdure of spring.

The danger to which we were exposed when we first came here has disappeared. The rout of the rebels at Corinth and the destruction of the railroad northeast of this have made it impossible for the enemy to close in upon us without a considerable delay by which time we will be abundantly re-enforced. Our position when we came here I will now state as the danger has passed by. We came here with six or seven thousand men, when the rebels could have had seventy thousand here in as many hours, when the odds against us would have been ruinously large. Again the communication between this place and the rebel army at Corinth was uninterrupted as their wounded was sent to this place and places north of this. Had our forces been repulsed there we could have been crushed.

Well sweet Minie I believe the day of deliverance is at hand and we will not have to endure the pangs of separation much longer. I perceive many of the old citizens voluntarily taking the oath of allegiance which I look upon as a good sign that the contest is about given up.

I was much disappointed this morning in not receiving a letter and papers by mail from you but as only a few letters came through I persuaded myself that this was not a regular mail. The last letter I had from you was dated March 17, or nearly a month ago so there must be tree or four letters and as many packages of papers on the way for me.

I have thought more of home within the last week than I have done during any previous week since I have been away, probably on account of its probable near consummation and oh how I longed for a final discharge from service that I might once more join you and enjoy your sweet smiles and society. How lovely you appear to me as I bring to mind your sweet ways that have so enlisted my affections. But I miss you darling and when- ever I see one of your sex I think of you, my ideal of loveliness, goodness, and virtue, now my sweet, brave, little angel you must wait a few weeks or perhaps months and then I will come to you. I have done my duty by giving my country my services in the days of her peril, then I will do my duty to you by staying by your side. Occasionally we find citizens here so determinately secesh that they will not traffic with our men but these are rare and generally have friends in the rebel army. I have been in the habit of sending out to the country almost every day since we have been here for milk &c and find the people very reasonable in their prices generally.

Well my darling I have run out of language to note and I will quit now and should anything occur before I send this poor letter I will add a post-script. Write very often & send me papers. Be sure to send me papers having accounts of the great battles. Direct as before via Nashville, Tennessee. Forget not your duty to God nor your love and obedience to your parents, brothers and sisters. Give my love to. Mr. & Mrs. Potts & the family. I am not forgetful of all their goodness to me. Hoping to hear from you all very soon I am your ever-loving Husband Harrie.

April 16

Well sweet Minie we are town folks now and although we are thus situated I am no better satisfied than I was when I wrote the first part of this letter. We stand a good chance of staying here while others move forward and do the work of putting down the rebels. The fact is we are the Provost guards of the city of Huntsville, Alabama.

Now dearest you may not understand our duties & twill try to explain. Our Colonel is a sort of a Military Magistrate and is called the Provost Marshal and we are a sort of a police to guard the town and enforce the laws and we go by the name of Provost Guards. You will readily understand me dearest although you do not take much interest in military affairs. There has been a number of wounded rebel officers come here and give themselves up to General Mitchel since the battle near Corinth and from everything I can see there will be a grand cave in before the fourth of July. I am informed that half or more of the people of this town are in favor of the Union as it was before these troubles began. So do not be surprised my dear if you hear shortly that we are on our way home. Oh won[']t I be glad & won[']t you dear.

I enclose $5.00.

Write soon and often. Forget me not in your prayers to God. I am affectionately your Husband Harrie

Camp Taylor
Huntsville, Alabama
April 18, 1862

My very dear wife Minie,

It is just two months since we left Nashville, Tenn. and here we have been cooped up for almost a month with a little spice by way of change to make it agreeable or interesting if possible. This is Sunday - not one of those pious Pennsylvania Sundays wherein one is not allowed to whistle or sing a song but to look sentimental. Nor one of those pleasant Kentucky Sundays wherein the conventionalities of society not only allow those above mentioned acts of irreverence but even to improve the future so far as to talk love &c.

But this is a warm or hot soldier's Sunday, peculiar to them alone. We have so degenerated from the first estate that many would not know the day of the week were it not for some good genius who does not romantically whisper "It is Sunday" but shrieks it as if telling it to a brigade of noisy schoolboys. For my part I wish I could convey myself from this place to your side dearest and then I could enjoy my Sunday as I trust I shall enjoy many ere long.

As I ended my last letter in praise of my excellent health and scarcely had I sent the letter to the mail, when the messenger of ill fortune came and said "boast no more." The same evening I felt unwell and deeming the matter indifferently I supposed the symptoms would pass away with the night but in the morning I found myself very unwell indeed. Still refraining from taking medicine I passed the next 24 hours, the most painful of my life. Then I was glad to summon medical advice and in a short time was relieved to some extent of pain but I was very much prostrated with weakness and now though I am on a fair way of absolute recovery I have not the strength to walk but a short distance at a time.

Do not be alarmed dearest Minie, my sickness was not dangerous though very painful and only one thing forbids my early recovery which is the indifferent fare, which is not what any one would desire after an abstinence of nearly a week. I expect next time I write to be entirely recovered. Notwithstanding my pain of body during the last week I have had moments of great hap[p]iness. In my waking hours I was thinking of you Minie dear, and when I composed my self to sleep it was to dream and converse with you. In my dreams and conversations you looked so like you used to that I was all joy, and the remembrance would give me pleasure for hours after I awoke, as I would endeavor to repeat in my mind what had transpired in sleep. The only sadness that occurred was to think that it was not a reality. If I do not get well soon I will come to you darling and then I know I will get well.

We get the Louisville Journal now tolerably regular the fourth day after publication. I must for once depart from my custom and write you only a short letter, which I know sweet one you will excuse under existing circumstances.

There is nothing of interest transpiring at this point & no news occurring at all. I expect to hear from you as soon as a mail train comes through and you know that will be a pleasure to read your sweet letter.

Remember me warmly to Mr. & Mrs. Potts & family. I would like to see them all.

But my first offerings of love to dearest and everything but honor will I risk to see you. Be a faithful and loving child of God and to your good parents, anticipate their desires with your compliance and be exemplary to your brothers & sisters that they go not astray. Write frequently. Inform me how much money you received from me and whether you have collected the State money due me. You must get your father to attend to that if he pleases. Direct as before to Mitchel's Division, via Nashville, Tenn.

Your own faithful and loving Husband Harrie

Camp Taylor
Huntsville, Alabama
April 20th, 1862

My very dear true wife,

I once more embrace an hour of leisure in the very pleasant duty of writing to you as by so doing I have my mind fixed upon you and it gives me very much pleasure to thus think of you. This pleasure arises from several sources. First and above all the unceasing and unchanging affection that prompted me to select you as my first earthly friend, the sharer of my joys. My comforter in grief my adviser in the days of my prosperity. My counselor in the time of my adversity and trial and the wife of my bosom, second, the heroic patriotism and pure philanthropy that prompted you to permit of our separation till the hordes rebellion are driven back in ruin and disgrace. That the proud banner under which we have lived and has made us a great people may once more wave "oer the land of the free and the home of the brave." Not a part enjoyed its benefit but every one within the jurisdiction of government as it was one year ago. I cannot forbear remarking here that signs of the times indicate a gradual establishment of our proud republic and though I regard the fighting as over, or will be when you get this, there will doubtless be considerable marching to be done yet as it will require the presence of a military force in the capitals of the several states to keep the rabble in check.

There is really very little danger to be apprehended now, only a careful watch over our appetites to forbid the eating of too much delicacies and drinking too much water when warm or exhausted by heat. On this score not, a hint is requisite on my part to secure vigilance and with a healthy frame I expect to weather the storm if no unforeseen accident intrudes itself.

Yes, dear Minie each march takes me farther from you and my mind feels the truth [of] your remark but I am comforted by the reflection it brings us nearer to the completion of these troubles and when we are once released it will require a long time to reach home.

I am anxious to go forward as by that means we can either expel them (the rebels) from the country or make them lay down their arms.

Your last letter that I received was written two weeks ago today though a part was written on the following morning. That is the latest news I have of reliability. I received another sweet letter from you written a few days previous to the one above mentioned and a paper dated Apr. 5, all on yesterday and you better believe that I am well satisfied with the mail for once. Then this is Sunday, not a beautiful, bright, sunshiny day with birds of beautiful plumage dancing from branch to branch of trees redolent with verdure but a wet, dirty, dripping, blue, tiresome day, one well adapted to give a man the ennui and wish the war, tents, guns & knapsacks and everything that looks like regulation, in Dixie.

Well sweet one there is one thing that we can do and will do on such days as this and that is we think and sigh for home. Not that we would desert our post or have any inclination to do so but we think those stay at home guards might come out on wet days to relieve us and let us go home awhile, that is till the rain is over. I mean the young men who have time and could have come as well as not.

Well Minie dearest this is a funny letter. I have an idea and I expect you will smile when you read it and I want you to understand that though the day is wet and I just came off guard I am in a tolerable good humor. Why, I can hardly tell but I reckon it is on account of your dear little letters. Well you could not exhaust my patience for I could read a letter from you as long as the book of Genesis and not get tired. Speaking of being on guard reminds me that I have had my breakfast and on this wise I received it. In my duty of patrol guard on last night there was a boy about 17 or 18 years of age placed in my charge who had acted indiscreetly on coming into town from a visit to the country. This morning the gentleman had to go to breakfast and as I was eating mine, consisting of fried bacon, bread, cheese and onions (green onions) I was informed that he was ready to go. I crammed my half uneaten lunch into my haversack to finish it when I returned. After a walk of several squares we arrived at his residence, a plain looking brick building but inwardly reflecting taste and good order. After I had been in the house a short time breakfast was announced and it was insisted by both mother and son that I should take breakfast with them. After attempting to excuse myself on the plea that I had my breakfast in my haversack I sat down and partook of a bountiful meal of ham and eggs, corn bread, biscuits, milk, tea &c. During the time that elapsed while we were eating I found out that the Madame was a Kentuckian and seemed to think that we ought not fight against the south.

She had one son in the army and seemed heartily tired of the war and wished that if the Federal government was going to establish its authority that it would be done quickly. I could but re-echo this sentiment for I cannot be at ease of mind till I rejoin you again my dear love. I promised to show the lad all necessary kindness, saw him well situated and promised to see him again before I finally left town. As patrol guard I promenaded the streets of town a great deal on yesterday and the more I see of town the more I am impressed with its beauty and pleasantness.

Well my dear I am well and have written regularly all the while from three to five days apart so that if you have not heard from me it has been the fault of the mails and not mine. I hope you will get all my letters. Well my dear I heretofore have forgotten to say that roses and many other kind of flowers have been in bloom ever since we have been here. I have no idea that they are so beautiful as yours nor so sweet as you are but they furnish a variety from the dull routine that surrounds camp life and adds a degree of freshness to what otherwise would be barrenness. I am here led to use a remark that I overheard and it is true most certainly, "that to read about a battle and its daring deeds and to live in canvas houses all sounds very well, but to realize them is quite a different thing." The poetry of war is to read its history but the "reality" robs war of all its interest.

Well dearest I have written you a rambling letter and probably it will fail to interest you. But I will still write every few days and of this be assured, you have my full and unbounded affection, increasing if possible every day of our painful separation. In the meantime my sweet Minie keep your coinage bright till the day of deliverance. Live as becomes a daughter of God & of your good parents. Love and esteem them by a studied obedience to their wishes and forget not your sisterly love to your brothers and little sisters.

Now my dearest I must bid you goodbye for a few days and then I will advise you again of what occurs. Write soon dearest and advise me of all that occurs.

My kindest regards to Mr. & Mrs. Potts & the family. Address as formerly.

I am with the greatest respect your sincerely affectionate Husband Harrie.

Camp Taylor
Huntsville, Alabama
April 24th, 1862

My sweet wife,

Just coming off guard I will improve an idle hour in the pleasant pastime of speaking to you through the medium of the pen, and though so few days have elapsed and so little of interest has occurred since I wrote last that I have no anticipations of finishing the letter today. Indeed my mind seems utterly barren of thought so that I will surprise myself if I am able in writing anything that will in the least interest you, my sweet little dear. But as that is the ostensible object I must comply the best I know how and use the utmost of my zeal in that behalf. Now my dear I almost fear you will say of me what I used to say of my brother John, that he used at least half his paper in writing excuses but the fact is I am afraid that even my excuses will not excuse my lack of interest.

The beauty that surrounds me as I am writing, for I am seated under the shady boughs of a cedar almost half a mile from camp, reminds me of a pleasant walk I had a few evenings since, when I sauntered from camp winding my way up the bank of the pleasant little creek on which our camp is located. I have not had fancy enough yet to inquire its name but I will do so when convenience offers.

This stream seems to thread its way through a beautiful plain and the land contiguous is seemingly as level as the surface of the placid waters of the creek. I but wish you could see a sight like that on either side of it. I am sure that you would pronounce it beautifully grand.

Small but pleasant cottages are studded thickly over the plain while the ornaments, which seem like a necessary appendage to all homes, gives the whole the appearance of a rural village. The common immediately along the creek with its herds of sheep and cattle grazing presented such an appearance as a poet might delight in or an artist might wish to paint. Here and there I stopped to look at a strange tree or to pluck a rare flower for "Many flowers unknow[n] stood in my pathway there," and thus in contemplation or in conversation with nature I passed a very agreeable hour, only wanting you sweet Minie to have made my walk perfectly congenial. All the beauty around me together with the quiet demeanor made me almost believe against my own senses that war scenes had never approached near or that the human pulse had never beaten differently from what now characterizes it.

In speaking of Alabama a citizen of an adjoining county informed me that this was the garden spot of North Alabama and that Huntsville owes its importance to the fact that its location is as healthy as it is beautiful, and that it is a place of much fashionable resort. It looked very like a garden as I walked abroad with its flowers and fields of grain, now in head, promising a good harvest if rust does not destroy it, which I am told it does more or less every year.

I brought my walk to a close after I had gone near a mile where several boys were fishing and by their cheerful demeanor I came to the conclusion that they did not care whether the war lasted or not. I could not help wishing that all were as innocent of doing the country a wrong as they. With innocence like theirs there is no discrimination. They mix as readily with us as they do of their own citizens.

Well my dear I cannot but smile at the enormous retrenchment that has taken place here in your sex. You must excuse me, I mean in crinoline. Whether the stock of hoops is exhausted or that they are considered as contraband of war or that it has been a patriotic retrenchment remains to be known. At all events the outfit of a lady in these parts has grown beautifully less. Perhaps hoops were considered a Union fashion and if so there are yet a few Unionists here for some still adhere to the famous custom.

Well my dear I have exhausted my stock nonsense and you will *now* have to wait till tomorrow or next day for the rest of this letter and I hope by that time to get one from you.

Oh yes dearest I think the specimen of your dress you sent me will make a nice gown (that is the part you did not send me.) I consider your selection one of taste and hope to be home in time to see you wear it. I yet cannot say definitely when I will be home but as soon as I can go I will not delay a moment.

April 26

Dear Minie,

Without any special subject in view I resume my pen this morning in order that I may send this letter by the earliest mail. I have no definite idea when we will get any mail and until then we cannot know what is going on in the outside world.

One thing we do know that is the rebels are threatening our position here but we have *no thought* that they will attack us, We have a front defense here along the Memphis & Charleston R.R. of upwards of one hundred miles and we will necessarily have to contract our line of defense if attacked.

In pursuance of this plan the Eighth Brigade stationed at Tuscumbia under the command of acting General Turchin had to fall back to Decatur where the R.R. crosses the Tennessee River. If the troops have to fall back any further the bridge will be burned as everything is prepared for the emergency. We have no fears for the safety of this place and have no idea that the rebels will risk an encounter with us although they outnumber us considerably.

We have had a considerable fall of rain within the last week which has swollen the streams & rendered our camp muddy and disagreeable. However a few hours of the warm sunshine generally dries up the mud and renders us cheerful and the earth dry enough to be agreeable.

The rebels at this place are very confident that they can hold Corinth and keep our army in check. They are also skeptical in reference to our recent victor[ie]s especially at Pea Ridge in Arkansas and at Island 10. This is owing to the fact that their press is not permitted to publish any news of a discouraging nature. They claim victories where they suffered the most flagrant defeats and by this system of lying they seduce the minds of the people at home to believe that they are on the high road of gaining an easy independence. But the day will soon come when the least semblance of an army will be broken up and then they must surrender at discretion or be hunted down like wild beasts of the desert.

One thing I am glad of, that is our own state that has suffered so much from the numerous camps is effectually cleaned out of Rebel forces and I hope ere long that peace will be so restored that there will be no need of any armed force within her borders, If these Gulf states but suffered as Kentucky has then they would reap, in my opinion, as they have sown. But where Kentucky has suffered spoliation there, these states have been protected, and nowhere has camp discipline been so strict as it has been ever since we left her borders.

If Tilford Bruner is in the 21st Regiment, Ky. Vol. he is still in Nashville. Or was there at last account. I wish they were at this place for I have no doubt that I could find quite a number of acquaintances in the ranks.

Stevenson, Jackson Co., Alabama
May 1st, '62

You perceive dear Minie that I am no longer at Huntsville that has abounded with my praises heretofore and that almost a week has passed since I wrote the former part of this letter. Stevenson is about 50 miles N.E. of Huntsville and is at the junction of the Memphis & Charleston and Nashville and Chattanooga Railroads. This is a small town and the country around is mostly hilly though the valleys between the hills are pretty and very fertile. We came 42 miles by R.R. and 8 miles on foot. At present we are quartered in houses, our tents being left behind. We have not retreated from Huntsville but merely moved a few regiments here while the bridges in this locality are repaired and also to guard the Railroad.

I was at church on last Sunday and was delighted to sit in a regular church and hear preaching. I worshiped at the Presbyterian Church which is a very fine church building and the sermon was an elaborate and unexceptional discourse.

The scenery about here and between here and Huntsville is fine in the extreme and there is an endless variety between the hills and mountains, to use the extravagant language of the citizens, with their dark green foliage and the pleasant valleys with their fertile fields with waving grain & excellent pasturage. We have taken about 50 prisoners here in several skirmishes and others are being brought in daily. I received a letter from brother Mike and he and his family are well.

I have written this darling in a hurry as I expect to go on guard shortly but in a few days I will look around and then I will write again. I hope to hear from you soon and to get some papers. Direct H.A. Smith In care of Capt. Ewing, Co, D, 21st Reg. O.V., Mitchel's Division, via Nashville, Tenn. Goodbye dear till I again write. I am forever your affectionate Husband, Harrie

Let no consideration keep you from your duty to God and to your good parents. Remember me in your prayers. Your Harrie

Camp Taylor
Huntsville, Alabama
May 6th, 1862

My very dear wife,

I once more seat myself to write you a letter to inform you of my doings, whereabouts &c. I have just returned from the funeral of one of the soldiers of this regiment. We buried him with military honors and I had the sad office of Pallbearer the occasion.

At the conclusion of my last letter you found me at Stevenson about 50 miles N.E. from this city. Hardly had we become comfortably situated there and just at dark we received orders to return to this place saying that the rebels had affected the passage of the Tennessee River in large force. Now as we were too late to chase the rebels at Stevenson we concluded that a fine chance would present itself there. But fate willed it otherwise, the rebels were defeated before we came here and fell back to the other side of the river.

We are gradually becoming masters of our position and though the rebels were closing in upon us the only thing that resulted from it was the loss of some mail matter &c, together with a few prisoners.

Our Capt. who was at home on a furlough (to get married) came back on last Saturday and as he made the acquaintance of Morgan at Pulaski, Tenn. he was very unpleasantly told that he was a prisoner of war. Capt. Ewing however was a good match for Morgan. The latter was presented with a huge bouquet of rare flowers and this our Cap. stole from him and would have taken his sword but it would not go into his trunk which Morgan politely refrained from examining. He was allowed to keep his side arms and is now a paroled prisoner expecting to be exchanged in a short time. I was on picket duty on yesterday and heard what I reckon is the waking up of the mind. The people here are beginning to place the cause of these troubles on the right ones and as these sentiments prevail the cause of rebel insanity must inexorably be forever ruined.

This morning a national salute was fired in honor of the triumph of our armies in Virginia and New Orleans and Madame Rumor says that Mobile and Memphis have also fallen. I know that they will and it is only a question of time but I do not believe they are ours yet. I am anxious to hear the news and feel that we are sadly behind the times here. Any paper received here a week after its publication is considered late news and read with the greatest avidity.

I am glad you have received my miniature as by it you see my homely visage as I appear in my regimentals. Now I want you to stop saying that your face is ugly won't you my dear? We are not encamped where we were before we went to Stevenson as our present encampment is upon a beautiful Schoolhouse lawn, pleasantly shaded and just at the outskirts of town. (Editor's Note: Greene Academy) We are once more policemen as the people here were not satisfied with any other than Col. Norton for Marshall and the 21st Reg. for guards. Before we went away the citizens presented a petition numerously signed to Gen. Mitchell asking him to leave the 21st Reg. here as permanent guards. This is under the force of circumstances and if we were in the power of rebeldom I have no doubt that they would see us comfortably in prison. But you see the grand game is about to be played out and the race to the ruin of many is almost run and even the most arrant rebels (women excepted) are forced to respect us.

I was present with a squad of prisoners on Sunday last when a number of ladies called upon them, bringing flowers, edibles &c at the same time enjoining upon them to be good rebels. I believe I am safe in saying that if Jeff. Davis, Beauregard, or half of organized rebeldom had been there they could not have confirmed so much treason as these incognito traitors did!

I am credibly informed that the soldiers of this section are heartily tired of this war and would come home if they could.

There is another that would do the same thing, dearest, and will seek every convenience to do so. This I would do not because the cause has become distasteful, or the labor too irksome, but to gratify you and to attend to those duties that now seem necessary to be done at home.

I have spoken of this vale as being beautiful - a garden. It must be in such times as this that it might be termed a "vale of tears" for surely in the absence of war this delightful spot must be nought but an Edenlike place where joy introduces the morning & refined pleasure dismisses the day, but for all this I would prefer Kentucky, the home of my love.

The people here are experiencing the folly of their ways. When the rebels threatened our wings at Decatur & Stevenson and we sent reinforcements to each place from here the rebel women would call out from their doors "Good bye Yankees" and other such epithets thinking that we were retreating but to their astonishment no doubt we are here yet and will remain so unless driven away and it will take 25000 men to do that. The men here became so violent in their expressions that Gen. Mitchel ordered them to go instantly to their houses or he would cannonade the town. This was the state of affairs when we came from Stevenson and under the circumstances we assume the police duties of the town, and we will succeed.

Last night at midnight we were called from our beds to repel an imaginary attack but it was a false alarm. There is something so particularly unpleasant in being called out at night from a warm bed into the chilly air and stand probably an hour to see whether there is any reality in the alarm or not, that once satisfied anyone for a lifetime, yet these things are getting uncomfortably frequent with us now in this hot bed of secession.

Well dearest, I have forgotten to say that I am real well and indeed I never enjoyed better health. I want to hear from you soon again. I reckon Morgan got one of your sweet letters that should have been mine. The last one was dated the 23rd ult, the one before the 8th ult. Send me some [Louisville] Commercials.

Now my sweet darling, do not neglect your faithful obedience to your Creator & to your good kind parents. Let your daily prayers arise to God for our entire safety from sinfulness and for our wellbeing in this life. Be a kind affectionate sister to your brothers and sisters. I have nothing more at present.

Write soon. Your faithful and affectionate Husband, Harrie

Camp Taylor
Huntsville, Alabama
May 12th, 1862

My very dear wife,

I received a letter from you today written on the 19th of April and which I had accused Morgan of stealing but it has come around all safe only a little after time.

I likewise received three Commercials a few days ago for which you have my kindest thanks.

I perceive by the letter received today that my letters have not been reaching you regularly. This has been the fault of the mail and not mine, for I have written every five or six days ever since I left Nashville and never have I written less than 3 sheets during that time. But I will dismiss this topic hoping that by this time you receive my letters tolerably regular.

Since I wrote last we have had another of those sudden expeditionary journeys that characterize our stay here. On the night of the 9th ult we received orders to march at 10 o'clock P.M. and with utmost haste we packed up, called in guards, and were off. This was done so suddenly that we were gone before the citizens were aware of our intended departure. We were loaded on the cars together with the 15th [Kentucky Regiment] and away we went. Of course our trip was uninteresting as we went as darkness obscured every object and I slept most of the way. In the morning as old "Sol" sent forth his first rays we found ourselves in the pleasant town of Athens, Limestone Co. where we were informed the rebels were concentrating for the purpose of attacking us.

There we found the 8th Brigade and with our regiment we considered ourselves sufficiently strong to resist any attack.

Five dead bodies were brought in during the forenoon and we soon learned that the rebels retreated (according to their custom) as soon as they captured a company of our men (Co. E, 37th Indiana) after killing those above referred to.

We attended worship in the forenoon on yesterday and were addressed by the Chaplain of the 37th Indiana Reg. It was the funeral sermon [for] the five men buried the day before.

While yet the service was incomplete we were startled by the shrill notes of the bugle which we knew too well meant a march, but as soon as we found out that we were destined to this place we were well pleased as our tents had not been removed.

I was much pleased with the country between here and Athens and it will undoubtedly be very wealthy after awhile, when the forests are felled and their places supplied by fruitful fields.

One thing I perceive-that the planters are raising less cotton and more corn this year than ever before and I presumed they were admonished by the scarcity of provisions at this time.

We arrived here on yesterday eve and found everything as quiet as usual. On last night I was detailed for guard and as the night was very pretty I enjoyed it. The almost perfectly serene night was enlivened by the unceasing carols, chirrups, screams, and warbles of the mockingbirds. I have not heretofore referred to this splendid bird nor can I give you a very distinct description of it. The color is like that of the catbird of Ky., only the wings have a white spot on each, not unlike shoulder straps. The bird is as large as the dove with longer tail feathers and in mocking it does it to perfection. At one time a blue jay, then the plaintive notes of the whippoorwill, then the robin. Next the shrill notes of the hawk and so on through the category of feathered minstrels. I observe they do all their singing between sunset and sunrise and it is in the silent hours of the night when one can appreciate their notes.

Today I visited the famous Calhoun Garden of this city, reputed the best collection of rare plants in the U.S. and costing in the aggregate more than a quarter of a million of dollars. It is certainly one of the attractions of Huntsville and is well worth the visit. The beds are all tastefully laid off and bordered with box plant, a little evergreen shrub growing to the height of six or eight inches, and the walks are bordered with an evergreen which I judge to be a species of bay tree, and some with cedar which looks quite homely in this spot of beauty.

The roses I admired most and there were more species than I had an idea could be collected.

I do wish darling Minie that you could see this garden. I know your sensitive mind would sympathize with the surrounding objects and it would furnish you an agreeable hour. Or that I could stroll together with you and hear the sweet accents of your voice. What a pleasure this would afford me. Oh I want this hateful war to terminate that I can come to my long absent Minie and enjoy the long severed relations that we once enjoyed before this wicked war was.

I am in the enjoyment of the very best health and I am sure when I return to you dearest I will have a restored health, for I have been strengthened in adversity and now when good weather has set in no ills seem to betide me. I am gratified with the progress of events and I have no doubt that the war will be over, at least as far as fighting is concerned, by the 4th of July or even before that.

The weather now is very warm so that we have to suspend drilling generally but I am not sorry for that.

We have drilled so much that we consider ourselves veterans in practice and adepts in experience. (I should have said veterans in experience and adepts in practice.)

Minie my mind is dull and I cannot write anything like a letter as I should. This I suppose is owing to loss of sleep on last night and the warmth today. I will just say darling that I desire your kind prayers for my continued health and safety and to hear that you are still striving to gain the Eternal reward of righteousness in heaven.

Let nothing keep you from a studied obedience to your good and kind parents. Be cheerful and kind to your brothers and sisters and in all things comport yourself as becomes a child of God and the example of Christian virtue.

It cheers me dear to think that while I am to do battle for my country that you are at home having willingly sacrificed your hopes and aspirations for the future, for the good of our flag. I am persuaded that we will be rewarded.

Sweet peace will soon be restored and then I can rejoin you never to be parted except by death. Write soon. I am your affectionate Husband, Harrie

Direct in care of Co. D
21st Regiment O.V.
Mitchel's Division
via Nashville, Tenn.

Camp Taylor
Huntsville, Alabama
May 22nd, 1862

My sweet wife,

As I conjectured in my last letter, at this writing finds me once more restored to health and good spirits. I lost the pleasure of going on an expedition with my company by being unwell. They went to Fayetteville, Tenn. to break up some thieving bands of rebel plunderers and have not returned yet and of course cannot say what their success has been. I would like to have gone there as I hoped to meet with the 21st Ky. regiment which was there at latest accounts. But it may have gone away.

My good spirits arises from the fact that I look upon a suspension of hostilities as a certainty and a speedy restoration of peace a matter of course. I expect to eat my 4th July dinner with you yet my dear and won't we be happy.

Oh will it not be a happy day when the herald of peace will proclaim the success of our arms and invite us, who have been shut out from the refinement of society, to our distant homes.

As the vindication of my country's honor how I shall rejoice to press the soil of Kentucky once more. But sweeter still will be the joy when I shall embrace you sweet Minie who have suffered the pangs of separation so long and trusted to the whims of fate. I thank God for his mercies to me & to you. Your fond and loving heart has not been made to bleed with sorrow while others have and soon in His mercy I believe I will be restored to you. Surely there is a Just God who rules the destinies of nations & though at first the rod of chastisement was laid heavily upon us but after we had drunk the dregs of a weak governmental policy we aroused, and by Almighty assistance stand out, an example of power. Our banners are inscribed with our achievements and our hearts are strong with the one feeling "that in the right success attends the brave."

Our baggage train will without a doubt come through today and then I expect one of those sweet messages of love from you dear Minie, that so delight me.

I cannot complain. I have received letters with tolerable regularity while there are some here who have not heard from their families since we came here.

The weather is warm and pleasant and the nights are just right for our kind of houses. I discover that although we live "out of doors" that gnats and musketoes [sic] do not molest us in the least at night. Why this is I do not pretend to say unless there is yet a streak of sympathy in these pestiverous creatures and they think a soldier has trouble enough without submitting to their unwelcome attentions.

P.M. Joy! Joy! Joy!

A mail has come and as I expected I received a sweet message from you, but joy seems ever to be mixed with sorrow in this world. Accompanying [sic] your letter is one from Mr. Potts giving an account of the sad misfortune he met with. But we must be thankful that it was not worse and as no bones were broken I sincerely hope that he is entirely well before this time. I cannot find suitable expressions of thankfulness for all the kindness I have received at his hands and from his family. Let all please accept my sincere thanks for my being so kindly remembered at home. Sweet home! To be thus remembered repays one though he must march over parched deserts or wade through seas of fire.

Oft in the stilly night when all is quiet (except the mockingbird-the Nightingale of the south) I think of home and to know that there is a reciprocal feeling, or that at home wishes are in unison with my own, makes me feel that the soldier's lot is not so hard as it might be. And this is the connecting link that binds us to society and makes our arms strong, and hearts brave, to encounter every obstacle.

Your letter dearest was written on the 25th & 28th of April and mailed May 3rd. Mr. Potts' written and mailed May 13th and I learn by his letter that you have been visiting your relations in Fayette. I hope you have had a pleasant time in your visit as you have been wanting to go there for some time.

I have only one source of annoyance and that is the unceasing impertinence of abolition scemers [sic] to keep these unhappy difficulties from coming to a close. They cannot wait for the close of war before they begin to plunder or to secure the spoil. I trust alone to the discretion of the President and hope he will still keep back these treasonable tricksters. By so doing he will be the savior of his country & by yielding he will be as one of [the] worst traitors.

I heard it rumored that Gen. Hunter had liberated the slaves of S. Carolina, Georgia & Florida. If he has and the president sanctions it I am ready to give up. It seems that there are always some blockheads who are undoing all that the rest does and if this is to be the way I cannot risk my life in sustaining it.

I trust in God that this is not so and that I am needlessly alarmed. In what I say above, there are many who will do the same. Some say the three fourths of the regiment including the Colonel &c.

I could fight even better if I had the Abolition traitors together with the secesh, for then I would be assured that there are none behind to aggravate for us to remedy.

Excuse me darling for thus alluding to politics as I know it is an unpopular subject to you.

I have hitherto not told you of our camp at this place. It is a lot on which is an Academy and finely shaded, with large trees, just at the outskirts of town and with everything convenient except wood, which we get by railroad. Adjoining the rear is a wheat field already assuming the golden hue of harvest which reminds us that the true mission of man is not war, for here is other work for him to do. Gladly would I yield the paraphernalia of war and assume the garb of peace, but these unhappy difficulties must be settled if possible so that we may enjoy life in security.

But I ask again to be pardoned my dearest, because I am spinning out this letter without adding anything of special interest. Well, the fact is, here we are from day to day & nothing occurs but sameness and camp rumors and these latter it is useless to report as they are tracable [sic] to no reliable foundation and generally amount to nothing. We are doing nothing here now but holding this post which is considered of great importance.

But to conclude, be careful of yourself in every way. Expose yourself to no unnecessary danger. Be a good and candid Christian. Love and obey your good & kind parents. Esteem your brothers & sisters and merit their love. I return a kiss for Ninnie and wish it was a real instead of a paper kiss.

My kindest wishes to Mr. & Mrs. Potts & family.

My first offerings to you my dear Minie. Oh that I could see you & be with you. Write every week, both your letters gave me sincere pleasure.

Address Mitchell's Division via Nashville, Tenn.

Your ever true and faithful, Husband Harrie

Athens Alabama
May 27th 1862

My very dear wife,

I again embrace a leisure moment to write to you though it is only a few days since I wrote before. Just as we were about leaving Huntsville on yesterday, a mail came in and as usual I was one of the lucky ones, as I received your letter of the 12th inst dated at Lexington. Your letters are always so welcome to me- but this last though kind, was so formal, that I have reflected much upon its contents. In the first place you complain of being so very sleepy that you would not remain awake, so as to write any more than it took you to write the short letter you sent, but your promise to write again in a few days which will answer the purpose very well, next you say "that you do not receive letters near so frequent as you used to" and you do not like that way of doing." In this you do me great injustice as I write once in every five or six days, and if you do not get the letters it is in the fault of the mail or rebels in hindering it and not mine. Oh Minie do not let the bright joys that surround you lead your sweet young heart from that spirit of goodness and encouraging kindness in which you have always heretofore written. But I am not unaware that loss of sleep stultifies the intellect and renders thought very contracted, and indeed makes one very uncharitable - I have experienced all this myself my dear, and with this thought I will forget the foregoing and look for a bright, joyous, sweet letter in a few days, and also that miniature which you were kind enough to have taken for me.

We left Huntsville on yesterday at noon and came here via the railroad and as the distance is only 35 miles we arrived here before night.

We will remain here for some time as we are detailed to garrison this town. There is one other regiment here (the 18th Ohio).

In a former letter I spoke of the country between this town and Huntsville, and I will not say anything more just now, except that for this year corn is king instead of cotton. Field after field met our vision and many of these were plantations in themselves.

To give you an idea of the greatness of these fields I will only say that they were of all dimensions, from seven hundred acres down to the half acre lot.

Well I do not wish to assist in the consumption of this huge monopoly- but hope when the time comes for garnering it, I will have forever laid aside the entanglements of strife and equality mixing in the grand moving mass of peace... and having in my heart "peace and good will for all men." But before this will be accomplished I must see what is to be done. The mad effort of self destruction must be stopped. Brother must be reconciled to Brother and father to son. States must be brought back to their allegiance, and armed bands must be broken up or exterminated and then and not before will be restored the unity we are now contending for.

Flag of the free hearts hope and home,
By angel hands to valor given
Thy stars have kit the welkin dome
And all thy hues were born in heaven
Forever float that standard sheet!
Where breathes the foe, but falls before us!
With freedom's soil beneath our feet,
And freedom's banner streaming o'er us.

Oh I am happy to state that the president in repudiating Gen. Hunter's Confiscation act has given unfeigned joy here throughout the army. Yes we have a president one who is not a mere instrument in the hands of others to shape as they would but one who rises above all weakness and stands out in grand relief. A hero - statesman and patriot.

With this grand foundation of republican Government, my darling we cannot fail and in the scathing hour of conflict the finger of God will write victory upon our banners and success upon our shields. With a mild policy such as we have had, he that contends against us must do so at his peril, and his persistence will insure his certain destruction.

Since I wrote last sweet Minie Company D has returned and with the exception of a long march very little was accomplished. They chased the rebels from Winchester Tenn but they retreated to the mountains where it was impossible to follow them with safety or with any promise of success. Capt. Ewing has been exchanged so he is again commander of company D. I attended worship on last Sunday and listened to one of those sweet discourses that makes one think of home and of those we love. The sermon was delivered by Mr. Gaddis chaplain of the second Ohio regt.

These sweet sermons are characteristics of the man for he always preaches that kind. We have no chaplain now.

The mail agent for this division of the army informed us that we might expect the mail now three times a week. So that we will not be so irregular in reception and sending of letters as heretofore. We owe a great deal to Mr. Gaddis for his untiring efforts in getting regularity of passage for mails. Heretofore we could only send or get mail when a train with a heavy guard accompanied it. And it always required 8 days for a train to go from Huntsville to Columbia Tenn. and return.

Athens is a rural town. The houses being built are large lots and very few are connected with another. Trees and shrubbery surround the houses nearly hiding them from view. So that when viewed from a distance it has as much the appearance of a forest as a town. Save that here and there spires rise above the surrounding foliage.

This was an eminently loyal town and only bowed to rebellion under pressing circumstances. Here the stars & stripes waved after the state seceded. And now the flag is restored. We hope never to be lowered again.

The town is about as large as Nicholasville but covers a larger area of ground.

Well dear Minie you will not be much interested in this letter I know. But I think I am doing very well. You must recollect that what is news to me is old to you and it will not answer for me to tell anything that comes by newspapers. The newspapers in the mails are mostly plundered as I do not get many so far only three packages of papers have reached me of all you sent. And they were so long on the way that the newsboy had issued them long before. If we get our mails according to promise we will get the Journal three days after publication and the Nashville Union two days after its issue.

Please sweet Minie do not receive my complaints in the first part of my letter in a spirit of unkindness. As I regret now that I did not pass it over entirely without saying anything about it. Believing that you will forgive me I can sleep sweetly and rest in the assurance of your perfect love. I am well as usual and I sincerely hope that you and all the rest enjoy the same inestimable blessing. I cannot help thinking about the sad misfortune which happened to Mr. Potts and from your last letter I am led to think that the injury was much more severe, than I inferred from his letter. May the all wise giver of all things, who can heal the mind and body speedily restore the wounded limbs to perfect wholeness. In conclusion dear Sweet Minie cast your care upon your savior and live in obedience to his just laws.

Obey your parents and God will bless you. Be kind to your brothers and sisters, remember me to all especially to Mr. & Mrs. Potts & family who are with me in my prayers. My first offering to and for you darling.

Remember me in prayers daily. Write often-don't forget dearest
Direct to Co. D 21st Reg O.V. Mitchell's Division Via Nashville. Tenn. I am your true and faithful husband
Harrie

Fort Ewing Tenn
June 5th 1862

My very sweet wife,

I received your sweet letter postmarked April 24th on the 2nd inst- and would have written on the same day, had I not been busy at work on the fort. But I will relate more by particularizing. We broke up our camp at Huntsville on the 27th ult and went to Athens to relieve Gen. Turchin's brigade which was detailed for other duty. There we remained till Sunday when Cos. D and H were ordered to this place about 12 miles north of Athens and one mile north of the Alabama line. Here is where the Railroad crosses the Elk River and the bridge was burned sometime ago. The object of our being here is to guard the Mechanics while they are reconstructing the bridge. Our whole force does not exceed two hundred effective men. And as a matter of safety we have entrenched our camp and rendered it strong against any attack. By reference to the enclosed plan you will glean an understanding of our position and defenses. Being detached from the main body of the army we fare much better than usual.

Here we can get milk gratuitously and honey at one dollar per gallon. Vegetables are abundant. Yesterday I had an extra dinner of clams. They look like oysters only larger and taste a little more like a fresh fish. I shall pay my respect to clams often if we stay here- and we have the promise of doing so till the war ends or till a guard is unnecessary. We occasionally catch fine fish in the river, upon which we feast with the utmost avidity.

Yesterday we met with a sad accident in the loss of one of our company. He was drowned while bathing. He was a good soldier and his loss will be keenly felt. This will be a warning to all inexpert swimmers not to venture beyond their depth. His body has not been found yet but we expect to do so during the day. I am very glad that Mr. Potts is improving and I hope before this time he is entirely well. This painful accident has caused me to wish often that I was at home that I might render my services.

I am waiting very patiently for my pretty little wife's picture. And if you can get Minnie's taken at the same time I will be so glad. Minie dear I am not quite so far from you now as when I was at Huntsville and may be I will gradually go towards you instead of getting further away. We have heard of the retreat of the Rebels at Corinth and it is rumored that Gen. McClellan has gained a great victory at or near Richmond. Which if true will go very far towards ending the war in that section of country. We have been used uniformly kind since we have been here - but this morning an overseer refused to permit two Negroes to come and search for the body of the young man that was drowned so we had to press them. Dear Minie this is a lovely spot but I hope we will be so far removed from the evils of the army that we will see none of them. If so I am more than satisfied in my loneliness.

News is scarce but occasionally a paper finds its way to this out of the way corner of creation. I cannot think of anything else to write. Excuse my briefness dearest and write very soon. Remember your obligations to God and to your good parents and repay them with your entire obedience and compliance to their wishes.

Address me as I have given you directions in my last letters. Be sure to say Mitchel's division or my letters may be sent to Corinth. Remember with my kindest wishes to Mr. & Mrs. Potts & family. Hoping to hear from you very soon I remain till death your faithful and affectionate Husband, Harrie

Fort Ewing Tenn.
June 11th 1862

My very sweet wife,

Yesterday I received your most welcome letter under date of June 1st. I intended to have written on yesterday morning but I was invited to go out on a scout, so I postponed writing till today. On last Sunday I was selected to go to Pulaski, a distance of 16 miles, to repair the telegraph which was obstructed in some way.

We found the wires down about six miles north of this place. But expecting them cut we went out after repairing the damage [until] we came to Pulaski [where] we found all right. Here it was that Capt. Ewing was taken prisoner by Morgan. We started back about an hour before sundown and slept in a cotton house during the night and arrived in camp about seven o'clock next morning.

Next day I went again and without anything of importance occurring we returned to camp about Meridian. At two o'clock I was detailed by Capt Ewing to guard the Colonel while he visited the various posts under his orders. We went per R-Road as far as Decatur. And then for the first time I saw the Tennessee River. It is a splendid stream and at that point about as wide as the Ohio at Cincinnati. A splendid bridge once spanned the river here but was destroyed by order of Gen Mitchel when our troops were withdrawn from Decatur.

Yesterday we were complimented by a visit from Major Gen Mitchel and Staff. He is a plain blunt man with a noble caste of countenance which heralds him as hero. Fort Ewing is to become an important place - it is to be used as a Depot for supplies for this division. Supplies are to be hauled here and stored and then shipped according to requisition. There are some rumors that we will leave this and go south of the Tennessee River in a few days. I hope this is not so as I will have to go hence with regret. We are progressing finely with the bridge and in two days more we can have about half the distance across the river completed but the other half will require much more labor as it will be in the river. And the trestles will be much higher. In three weeks from this time I judge the work will be done.

We are having very warm weather here now. Yet for the last three days there have been breezes which were quite refreshing - Harvest is about over, the greater part of the wheat being cut before the 5th of this month. We have had an abundance of rain here and even more that was necessary for the crops. Oats is a failure here. I do not know whether it is because of much rain or some other cause. The oats died before heading out. Corn looks well generally but is not half worked. Wheat was rather poor.

Well sweet Minie I reckon you must come here to help me pick you some Blackberries. They are very plentiful and are just beginning to get right for use, i.e., ripe.

I am confident that you never saw the like for peaches. Every bush is full and every fence row and hedge and thicket and orchard and park abounds in peach trees.

So you see we will not suffer from any lack of fruit. Or indeed from vegetables of any kind for there is a super abundance. Young potatoes were being used when we came here in the first of June but I reckon you have them all by this time.

Well my sweet one. I do not know what more to write as this is rather a dull place for news. And we are seldom visited by official dispatches.

We have a Telegraph office here and we hear of all movements of the army. And I am convinced that this suicidal war cannot last long. Every one here seems to be clamorous for peace and if this party will make themselves heard we can have peace and union at one and the same time. I am perfectly delighted with you dearest for all your encouragement to me and your assurances of fidelity to your good parents and God our common creator and benefactor.

Brave the breaks of fortune get short time. My sweet lovely Minie and soon I will come to you. But we must be submissive to the will of God and in his own good time we will be reunited. But I want to see you so much. Please send me yourself in a letter can't you? Bring Minnie along. Why did Geo. Fain come home? Give him my respects. He has the proper grip in him.

My respects to Capt. Overstreet. I wish him success in getting up his home guard. And I trust they will be useful. Yes you need a guard more now than ever. This is the death struggle of rebellion and once over it will never rise again. My love to Mr. & Mrs. Potts & family. My first offering to you lovely Minie. All write soon. I am affectionately and devotedly your husband, Harrie

Fort Ewing
Giles Co. Tenn
June 19th 1862

My very sweet wife,

Under the shady boughs of a friendly tree I find myself seated to indite a letter to you. Not in answer to any I have received since I last wrote which I am sorry for. But to try to interest you sweet one into whose pleasure and happiness every throb of my heart shall be and is centered and for whom I am very willing to meet the frowns of adverse circumstances knowing that the bright sun of better days will soon clear away the thunder mutterings which now surround us and then will be ushered in the bright Halcyon days never to be forgotten but always to be remembered.

One little sentence in your last letter which has come to my mind daily and I almost feel as though you were present and with the inspiration of Heaven on your brow, and the courage of Joan of Arc in your heart, and the willingness and obedience of Ruth filling your soul. Repeating to me this sentence, "The country needs your services." Search all the history of Earth, snatch from its choicest temples the sayings and maxims of its sages which are in records of gold and diamond, yet in all you will not find one so purely disinterested, so modestly patriotic as this.

Oh Minie I am doubly proud of you. For this sacrifice, which I hope will not be long, may God bless you sweet one for this encouragement. Yes the country needs my services as well as that of a thousand of other able bodied men. Soon will be the struggle between light and dark-ness. Between right and wrong. May God protect the right. Every man must now take the field as it were and show where he stands. All the friends of the Union must now stand firm and show a determined front for one or two or possibly three months more and then all will be over and our country free. Now let us draw the grand union psalms of these United States in battle array and oppose it to the loitering nuisance of Jeff Davis and Company. You will see the loved ones of home clinging to those about to go forth to meet the spoiler of our names and the desecrator of our emblems. But as the moment of separation comes amid tears of regret and vows of constance and affection one rises above all Earthly weakness and says "Go. The country needs your services." Pass it along the battle line of life and everywhere it is bound to receive the plaudits of the brave and generous.

You are worthy of it all dearest. With the heroic endurance of one beyond your years by far you have waited the issue of this cruel war. Well dearest the end seems not far. We have penetrated the regions of the rebels, their armies have fled before us, and now they are contracted to a comparatively small boundary with our heroic legions at the gates of the capital. This is the grand issue and the end will inevitably be soon after. If we are successful I would like to serve my country in another capacity now for at least two reasons. I would like to be in Kentucky now to help to drive the miserable robbers and murderers from the state as I hold them in such utter detestation and then I would near to you to protect you if necessity required.

I hope Capt. Overstreet will be able to get up a good company of Guards and train them as mounted as well as infantry soldiers. I wish him every success.

Since I wrote last I have been on several scouts. Thus relieving the otherwise tedium of camp life! True we have here a daily passenger and freight train running to this place and many visitors yet to be contented I must not be confined in the triangular piece of ground called Fort Ewing. One day Capt. Ewing came to me and told me he wished me to go some six or seven miles to get a mysterious gun he had heard of. I was to go secretly and not tell anyone where I was going or what for. I had the permission of selecting any number of men I wished or deemed necessary for the undertaking. I started at Meridian and as I had considerable difficulty in finding the place it was late when I reached the house. I demanded the gun which was given up with no other objections than a few silent tears by the old lady who said her husband had brought it from Virginia many years before. I found the gun to be what is called a Bowie rifle altogether 43 inches in length but very effective. The gun was at this time owned by the son of the old lady, and his (the son's) wife boasted that the gun had been used by a lady in firing upon our soldiers. This was Capt. Ewing's reason for seizing and retaining the gun. But the secrecy was that he may keep it as a trophy.

We have found and taken possession of about a dozen of horses which the rebel cavalry have left in passing through this vicinity at various times. This and for general information is the object of our scouting expeditions. What do you think dearest we get the Journal, that able exponent of what is noble, honest, and patriotic the next day after its publication? The railroad from Nashville to this place needs but about 20 miles of being repaired and then we will get the Louisville papers within twenty-four hours of their publication and the Nashville on the same day. This will certainly be very gratifying to us all.

The weather for several weeks past has been uniformly dry with a slight shower or two on the two nights preceding this. Of course, the ground is dry but not parched or suffering. Today is cool and very pleasant. A few days ago, we were visited by a squad of the first Kentucky Cavalry. It was a part of Capt Hackley's company from Garrard County. I knew one or two and they seemed like brothers almost.

Morrean Bruner promised to call and see me if he could in a few days. Telford is at Columbia Tenn. I have had a good mess of [illegible} and plum pie. Peaches will begin to ripen before long and there are so many of them that all will get enough.

I know of nothing more that will be of interest to you except to inform you of my very good health & spirits.

Live in perfect obedience to God and to your good parents. And be prudent to all. Kind to your brothers & sisters. For kindness begets kindness and brings happiness to all. Your country's cause is my cause. Left up your heart in prayer to God for its speedy success. Write soon. Write often. Write as you have done.

God bless you dear Minie and may his love and holy protection ever be thrown around you. Give my love and regards to Mr. & Mrs. Potts & family. My first offerings of love to you dearest Minie be sure to direct In care of Capt Ewing Co. D 21st Reg. 0. V. Mitchel's Division Via Nashville Tenn.

Hoping to hear from you very soon I am ever and faithfully your affectionate husband, Harrie

Fort Ewing
Giles Co. Tenn.
June 25, 1862

My very dear little wife,

I seat myself again to the pleasant pastime of speaking with you through the medium of the U.S. Mail though I do not expect to finish a letter today as I will wait a few days in hopes of hearing from you before I close this letter.

It is now more than two weeks since I heard from you and uncertainty is becoming painful to me. I cannot conjecture what can be the matter, as we are getting a daily mail here now, and are only two days travel from Louisville. Surely I am at a loss to know the cause of my not receiving letters from you. I received one on last Saturday from brother Mike and heard from Joe and Will. They were all well. Your little namesake is represented as being well and of being quite mischievous. Of course, she does not take after her namesake in that respect.

The weather for the last three weeks has been uniformly dry, but today we have had a fine shower and indications are that we will have more rain during the day & night.

I had a fine dinner of blackberry dumpling and pie on yesterday served up with sweetened milk. It was fully as good an apple dumpling.

For three days since I wrote last I was employed in bringing a ferryboat from Elkton 15 miles via the river to this place. One night I stayed with a citizen and slept in the first regular bed since I left home. You can readily imagine dear Minie that I relished such a luxury after being deprived of it so long.

While I was absent for the boat Morrean Bruner was here to see me. I was very much disappointed in not seeing him. There was a large Union meeting in Pulaski on last Saturday and a citizen who was there told me that the meeting was unanimous for returning to the Union. It is now easily to be seen that the seceded states will come quietly back as soon as the citizens understand the hopelessness of the rebellion. The forces of Gen. Buell are now passing through our lines on their way to East Tennessee. Soon those brave exiles from that part of the state will be able to embrace the loved ones at home.

Long they have been separated but now as they come back they bring peace and the old flag with them. Tennessee is nearly as quiet as Kentucky now.

Dear Minie news is so scarce now that I do not know what to write so that I can interest you. I still enjoy most excellent health and I trust to be able to outride the ills of the campaign and come safely to you again.

Tell me of everything that happens of any interest in the neighborhood and how the folks are getting along. I know that Kentucky bears the tyrannical impress of war, and when I think how she has suffered I can only say noble Kentucky! How freely you have contributed your sons, your treasure & your all for the sake of the Union. In ratio to her population (white) Kentucky has furnished more soldiers than any state in the union. She has won herself a name in History that will stand forever.

Excuse me my dear I must stop writing for this time. Remember me most kindly to Mr. & Mrs. Potts and all the rest of the family. Remember me sweet Minie in your prayers to the giver of every blessing and may God throw around you the safeguard of his protecting mercy. Dearest I bid you goodbye for the present. Respectfully & very affectionately Your Harrie

Fort Ewing
June 28, 1862

Sweet Minie,

Last night I came to camp after being in the saddle all day, and I was cheered by receiving your most welcome letter of the 19th inst. I have little of anything to relate to you today. My scout was very long on yesterday, and the object was as formerly to get abandoned cavalry horses and arms.

One family I found that thought our object was evil and that we would molest the defenseless but before we left they felt so much assured of perfect safety that we were invited to call whenever we passed by that place. Another was exceedingly bitter against us, but before we left they all had to acknowledge our politeness towards them, and I believe that if the son was at home they would advise him to stay at home. I am often led to pity the ignorance of the people when they seem to think that our mission is anything else than to restore the union.

Here all the people are crying up peace, peace, peace. Would to heaven they had peace and if they had the courage to come out bold and decided for the union they could have peace in a short time. I am very well today as usual. Remember me most kindly to your good parents and the rest of the family. I hope Mr. Potts & Middie got a good mess of squirrels for you all. I am most glad to hear of his complete recovery from his painful injuries.

Address as before to Mitchel's division via Nashville Tenn.

I dreamt last night of our earlier days,
Ere I sighted for sword and feather-
When we walked on the hill, in the moon's pale rays
Hand in hand - hand in hand together.

I thought you gave me again that kiss,
More sweet than the perfume of spring,
When I pressed on your finger love's pure golden pledge
The bridal ring - the bridal ring.

I dreamt I heard, them, the trumpet sound,

And at once was forced to sever,
That I fell on the hearth with my last death wound,
Lost to thee - lost to thee forever.

I thought that you gave me again that kiss
Impearled like a flower in spring,
'Neath its warmth I awoke, on this dear hand to present
The bridal ring - the bridal ring.

Fort Ewing Tenn.
July 7th 1862

My very dear wife,

Another week has passed and I again seat myself to write you a letter. I have deferred writing a day or two in order that I might receive a letter from you, as I should have one before this time. But casting this aside as unworthy of thought, I will make the attempt to write you a letter and I am sorry that my stock of intelligence is so scarce this morning that I will fail to interest you I know. As usual I am well, and in good spirits.

The 4th passed off quietly and without any interest. The citizens did not come into camp to bid us Godspeed so we had to go to them. In the country we met with a kind reception as is generally the case, and took dinner with an old Virginia farmer who has two sons in Indianapolis, prisoners of war. These young men were taken out on the last levy made in this state, which was in short a force, or conscription. The parents are anxious for their sons' return, as they have always manifested themselves for the Union. The force at this place has been increased by two companies of the 23rd Ky and the 3rd Regiment of Ky Cavalry, so our force here now amounts to 14 companies, a larger force than is necessary.

The country around is very healthy as yet but the citizens say that the unhealthy month is yet to come. The weather is not warm, no warmer than in Ky I think. We are having an abundance of ripe apples and pears but as yet no peaches have made their appearance in camp. We are expecting to get orders to leave here to rejoin our regiment, and as Gen Mitchel has gone to Washington rumor says our division is to follow him.

We will be sorry to lose him. We have the report here that Richmond has fallen but we can hear from there on this evening. I hope it is so. Dearest I disappointed you by not spending the Fourth of July with you but I am doing all I can to get a leave of absence in order that I may visit you. Dearest I cannot think of anything more to write and you must please excuse the formality in which this is written. You know how to direct your letters. I hope to hear from you soon - very soon. I love to read your sweet letters. My love to Mr. & Mrs. Potts to whom I owe my kindest remembrance. My first offering to you my darling. Remember me in your prayers. My respect to your brothers & sisters.Kiss Minnie for me. Forever your faithful and Affectionate Husband, Harrie

Fort Ewing
Giles Co. Tenn.
July 13th, 1862

My charming wife,

Once more I seat myself to write to you and as I have not received a letter for three weeks or more, I hope to get one before I close this. I am in most excellent health, and sincerely hope that you all may be in the enjoyment of the same blessing. This is Sunday morning and as usual we are feasting on the good things brought to us from the country. Let me see - there is green com, beans, peaches, apple pies, pears, milk and in fact a little of everything calculated to tempt the appetite.

I presume some of these delicacies are in advance of Kentucky but shortly you will no doubt have an abundance of all.

I cannot think why I have not been getting letters for so long. I am getting discouraged in consequence. You cannot imagine how a loving confiding letter inspires the heart doating on sympathy, and love while a disappointment discourages and then there is nothing to inspire a confidence or to raise the drooping spirits.

From the Journal of the 10th inst I quote this in reference to Gen. Mitchel.

"There seems unhappily to be no room for doubt that the course of this officer in North Alabama has been marked by conduct not only injurious to the government, but disgraceful to humanity. We are assured of this fact on authority we do not and cannot doubt. The fact is thoroughly attested we believe it and believing it we publish it. We proclaim it with emphasis. Gen Mitchell and a portion of his command have perpetuated in North Alabama deeds of cruelty and of guilt, the bare narration of which makes the heart sick &c."

Truth is mighty and will prevail. I want the guilty to be punished and the innocent to go clear. The town of Athens was sacked by the 8th Brigade commanded by acting General Turchin of Illinois, composed of 19th & 24th Illinois 37 Indiana and the 18th Ohio. The town of Decatur was sacked by the 11th Ohio under the command of General Lytle. These are the depredations referred to and I am confident that they were done without the consent of Gen. Mitchel and the great fault was his failure to arrest and cashier the depredators. Thank God, I am clear of these atrocities, as I was not near either place when they were in a manner destroyed. Mitchel is a stern man and resorts to stern means but in these two instances there is not a shadow to justify his acts.

There is a splendid house in Huntsville where some ladies made sport of some of his troops and in twenty-four hours the house was changed into a hospital by his order.

I can say it with pride that the 21st Reg stands high in Athens and we stood high in Huntsville. There the citizens petitioned Gen Mitchel to allow us to remain and send another regiment to Athens. But so it is, the good one regiment does is undone by another. The mail has come and I do not get any letter. Can you be sick, God forbid! Do write to me. Be good. Be obedient to your parents, to your God, and kind to all. Remember me in your prayers to God. Remember me to your good and kind parents. Write sweet one for heaven's sake. Forever your affectionate, Harry

To my dear's miniature
Though silent, you are very sweet,
As I gaze upon thy pleasant face,
I sigh from day to day to meet-
The one, whose life I love to trace.

Oh beauteous one you seem to smile,
As when you won my fondest love,
'Tis like an angel's stay awhile-
There flits her wings to heaven above,

In lovely innocence you appear,
As when you last bid me adieu,
Your life to me has been so dear,
That happiness comes but from you.

Your lips so Sweet seem about to speak,
But silent still you prove to be;
Your youthful beauty looks so meek,
'Tis this that seems so dear to me.

Those eyes so bright and pleasant too,
The same I loved to gaze upon,
From heart to heart they spoke most true-
The love we love - now realized.

Fort Ewing
Giles Co. Tenn.
July 17, 1862

My sweet wife,

On day before yesterday I received a brief note from you post-marked June 11th and which had been somewhere misplaced. But thanks to goodness it came to hand, and with it the sweet miniature enclosed. I agree with you that the effect is too much shaded, but the expression is yours, and as I look upon the silent miniature it seems as though I am looking upon my living wife. Oh dear Minie what sweet memories that picture enkindled in my recollection. I almost felt as though I was transplanted from the scenes of war to that of peace. While you sweetest of mortals was with me to smile upon me and bless me with your sweet presence.

Now my sweet darling I do not feel so lonely as when I wrote the last letter. I ask your pardon for what I am going to say, which is, do write once a week to me. I am only asking you to devote an hour or two each week to my interest, or that I may know you are well. The last letter I had from you was dated July 2nd, the one before that one June 21st so you see I repine after my weekly messages of love and affection. I say not this complainingly but I request it and so because merely that you may not forget our agreement of writing at least once a week. These are the only conversations we have, and let them be as frequent as possible. They will render us both happier and more contented, at my lengthy absence.

Well my Minie I am compelled to say that news is still as scarce as ever, and l thought I would have to write you a long letter because you made me so happy by sending your miniature, but now I admit that though I may write this sheet full it will amount to but little else than words or sentences.

I received a letter from Brother Mike on the same day I received your letter and he said that I should give their love to Minie. Besides he does give me most excellent advice how I ought to live, and winds up by hoping the war will soon come to an end. Brothers Joe and Will are still at Annapolis, Maryland and in good health.

You request me to send you a muscle shell ring that you may have it for a keepsake. This I do with a great deal of pleasure, and hope the one I send you will please you. I should have preferred to send you a white one but the one I have got is too large, so I send the red one. Well sweet one I know of nothing more to write so excuse me. I trust to hear of your obedience to God and to your good kind parents. Exercise a degree of kindness around you that you may elicit the esteem of all. Especially your parents, brothers and sisters. Once more I request dearest one write me once a week. I am not asking much and by so doing you will please your Harry. I am all your own, and I live in your sweet affection and esteem. Won't you do so Sweet Minie.

Tell me that you will.

Sweet Minie how I love you. Oh that I could be with you, if it were only for one short hour. Pray for me dearest.

Direct as before I am forever your Affectionate and loving, Harrie

There is nothing doing at present. Genl Buell's army is still lying between this place and Huntsville, waiting for something decisive to be done at Richmond. The rebel raids of bridge burning and mail robbing have discommoded us considerably as at present our whole army is on half rations. This does not affect us in the least, as you can get all the provisions we want in the country around.

We have had a good fall of rain last night and this morning which will make a good crop of corn in this locality.

I am sorry that the guerrillas cannot be effectually driven out of Kentucky. Almost every day I hear of some depredation committed by them, and I do not see any effectual means for wiping them out. They ought to be hung up like so many dogs. Would to heaven I could be in Kentucky to help to drive these desperadoes from the state. But time and tide will change soon and then these foul miscreants must expect to reap as they have sown when retributive justice will pour out of her wrath upon their defenseless heads, they will beg in vain for mercy.

I am in the enjoyment of most excellent health, and I weigh more than I ever did before. The shell from which this ring was made was taken from Elk River, where we are now encamped.

Remember me very kindly to Mr. & Mrs. Potts and all the family. I would like to see all very much. Kiss our little Minnie for me, and I should like to see Kate. Though no one can be prettier or smarter than little Minnie. You once said that Kate looked like you dear Minie then all I have to say is she is very pretty. But I will see them before very long and tell them Good bye.

Oh yes excuse me. Kiss little Kate too for me for I am getting behind sadly quick & Minie I must be several million of kisses behind.

How many say you, Harrie

Fort Ewing
August 1st 1862

My darling little wife,

I embrace a moment of leisure time to write you a brief note to let you know that I am in the enjoyment of good health and oh how sincerely I hope that this letter may find you in the enjoyment of the same blessing.

I have undertaken to write to you at this time not because I have any- thing of interest to write, but in order that I might fulfill my part of our agreement to write at least once a week. Since my last brief there has nothing of interest transpired unless warm weather and big rains is interesting. Oh yesterday while I was on guard, I was exposed to the hardest storm of wind and rain that I had the misfortune to be in during my life, but this morning I feel all right, notwithstanding I slept on two rails laid parallel with an interval of about a foot. Sweet Minie you would laugh if you could see our picket beds or bivouacs. And you good souls at home that took such care that our beds and rooms were properly aired lest we should take cold, what would you think of our sleeping on the ground and only waking when our beds were flooded with water and I recollect frequently of scraping the snow away and then spread my blanket and enjoy a good night's rest.

Well my sweet Minie the bridge is nearly done at this place, and the cars will run over on Sunday or Monday next. The bridge is over six hundred feet in length, and considering the height which is about fifty feet from the bottom of the river, the work has progressed finely.

I am glad of the near-accomplishment of the work for there is a good understanding between the citizens and our company and we will fare very well if allowed to remain.

I have been going to the country twice a week for the purpose of supplying ourselves with butter and eggs, and for uprightness and kindness I think these people have never been surpassed. This has been my experience and come what will I will ever bear in memory the kindness of these people.

I am truly sorry that Allie has met with the misfortune you speak of and hope he will soon entirely recover. You say I ought to come home now. I promise you to be unceasing in my efforts to either get a discharge, or a furlough or a transfer. The last I can most readily get, and if I see that there is no chance of the other I will accept that and be transferred to a Kentucky regiment.

Something seems to tell me that I will see you before another month so cheer up sweet love and hope for the best, but be not too sanguine for we may meet with disappointment.

One thing we must remember an all wise creator presides over us and our destinies will be shaped by our course of conduct towards him. Oh may God direct us to the performance of what is right.

Nothing new is now transpiring except a few little skirmishes & they seem to decide to a great degree against us and I am led to adopt the re- mark, "that I believe God is on our side but Satan is doing us much injury just now." The fight at Mount Sterling is an encouraging item in Kentucky and I hope by such knocks we will soon hear of Ky being freed from guerilla bands as well as their sympathizers.

The slowness of the operations discourages and humiliates me and I am almost led to doubt the ultimate success of our army. If we cannot act now when will we be stronger and if we will be stronger two months hence it is but reasonable to suppose that our foes will be also. I am confident of the acquisition of all except the gulf states and then to keep them in subjection will exhaust the power of the government and there will end the glorious constellations of states unless a uniform system can be agreed upon.

I confess that this is the dark side of the picture and a brighter future may dawn upon our once happy country, but it looks like a game of chance and success may alight upon either side. I hope we may be the happy recipients of fortunes favor.

Tell me sweet angel that you are still mindful of the highest duties of our being - viz obedient to the just commands of God, allowing your prayers day and night to ascend to him and oh Minie our prayers should be for erring man.

Also, I hope that you have a proper regard for your good kind parents to whom we are so greatly debtors, and I hope before long to be able to repay them back for all their kindness.

Blessed Minie you have blessed me with a great deal of happiness and you shall not much longer remain without your Harrie. I have determined it and I now wait for the opportunity to release me from the army forever if possible.

How glad I will be to clasp you my loved one again in my arms. Me thinks I would then gladly meet the assassins of our people if need be to die in defense of the state of my adoption.

I read the wrongs done to her citizens with burning cheeks and it seems strange to me that the citizens do not rise en masse and exterminate those vile seducers of the honor of Ky.

Write me soon darling and give me your ideas as well as the news. I received your last letter a few days ago which was postmarked July 23 and I much pleased in the perusal except that which related to Allie, and of the valiant guards running when they thought that Morgan was coming. They must acquire more nerve or they will be poor soldiers and will not do to hitch to.

Fifty men posted in the rocks about Boon's Knob would make an impassable barrier to almost any force, especially for Cavalry.

I have written enough dearest. My kindest regards to Mr. & Mrs. Potts and the family. Write very soon. Your affectionate, Harrie

Epilogue

Henry's last letter to his "darling sweet wife" is dated August 1, 1862. In that letter he wrote, "You say I ought to come home now. I promise you to be unceasing in my efforts to either get a discharge, or a furlough or a transfer. The last I can most readily get, and if I see that there is no chance of the other I will accept that and be transferred to a Kentucky regiment. Something seems to tell me that I will see you before another month."

Henry must have been notified later that same day that a transfer to a Kentucky regiment had been approved because his service record reflects a transfer date of August 1, 1862. Doubtless he would have left immediately, traveling by railroad via the Tennessee & Alabama railroad to Nashville and the Louisville & Nashville railroad to Nicholasville, a trip that would not have taken more than several days.

According to his autobiography Henry was permitted to return to Jessamine County to enlist in the 9th Kentucky Cavalry. Shortly after he arrived in Nicholasville, he was captured, and paroled, by Confederate cavalry who had made an "irruption into Kentucky." He claimed that he never had official notification of an exchange, so "didn't again engage in active duty in the army." This decision was to adversely affect him, and Minie, later in life.

Henry worked for a time in a mill at Hickman Bridge, Kentucky, and later at a store in the vicinity. In March 1865 he moved to Indiana and taught school in North Vernon and Hardinsburg, where he connected with the Methodist Episcopal Southeast Conference and began preaching in various churches in that area. He returned to Kentucky in September, 1868, where he continued "teaching and preaching" in Kirksville until 1874, when he became a full-time preacher in the Methodist Episcopal Kentucky Conference, serving congregations in Mackville, Chaplin, Texas, and Bradfordsville, Kentucky. In 1882, he was asked to go to Cape Girardeau, Missouri to revive a church there. In 1 891, he moved to West Plains, Missouri, and then to Poplar Bluff, Missouri in 1895, where, in 1899, he was placed in charge of the Bellevue Collegiate Institute, affiliated with the Methodist Episcopal Church, and in 1900, headed the Missouri Children's Home Society.

Henry Ackerman Smith died on November 1, 1907 in Poplar Bluff, and his "Dear sweet Minie" joined him on November 6, 1931. They are buried side-by-side in the City Cemetery there. Henry and Minie had eight children - five daughters and three sons. Their first-born, William Henry, was born July 19, 1863 while Minie was prostrated by typhoid fever and lived only twenty-one days. Their other children were:

- Eugene Herbert, born March 25, 1865, in Garrard County, Kentucky.
- Jessamine, born September 14, 1867, in Jennings County, Indiana.
- May, born September 2, 1869, in Kirksville, Kentucky.
- Blanche, born September 17, 1871, in Kirksville, Kentucky.
- Maggie Zue, born August 13, 1875, in Mackville, Kentucky.
- Mattie Ruby, born September 4, 1877, in Chaplin, Kentucky, and who died November 6, 1878.

- Roy Hiner, born January 30, 1880, in Texas, Washington County, Kentucky.

Henry applied for an Invalid Pension on February 9, 1903, at the age of 66. In his application he claimed permanent disability from "disease of urinary organs, nasal catarrh affecting nasal passages, auditory organ of right ear, (causing) gradual deafness, rupture of right side, and old age." On March 25, 1903, after investigating his military record the War Department reported:

The name Henry (or Harry) A. Smith has not been found on the rolls, on file in this office, of any company of the 9th Kentucky Cavalry Volunteers, nor has anything been found of record to show this man was a prisoner of war. His final record cannot be determined from the evidence before this Department. No record of his discharge from service has been found.

In a subsequent affidavit written in response to a request dated May 18, 1903 from the Bureau of Pensions Commissioner for further information, Henry wrote the following:

I failed to reach the 9th Kentucky Cavalry owing to the fact of my capture, and as I never received any notification of exchange while the regiment was in service, I never had any assignments.

I was on my way to where I was informed the regiment was on duty, (south of Richmond, Kentucky), when I was captured by a detachment of Morgan's cavalry about the time of the battle near Richmond, Kentucky, and the next day I was guarded by one of Morgan's command, named Creath Robinson, who took me to Lexington, Kentucky, where I was paroled and allowed to return to my home. I was taken into custody at the turnpike crossing of the Kentucky River between Nicholasville and Danville, Kentucky. The Provost Marshal who was my paroling officer was Colonel Gracie, who afterwards was Gen.

Gracie of Alabama, and who belonged to Kirby Smith's Column. I continued to reside and work in Jessamine County, Kentucky, in that part of the county which became Camp Nelson, and was personally known to General Fry who was for long time commander of the post. My transfer and parole papers were lost in a desk carried away by a Tennessee company stationed for a time at Camp Nelson."

I never applied for, nor received a final discharge from the Ninth (9) Kentucky Cavalry.

Sincerely and fraternally, yours
Henry A. Smith

The War Department, obviously disbelieving Henry's statement, replied on July 29,1903, that "Nothing has been found of record to warrant a change in the statement from this office, herewith, dated March 25,1903, relative to the case of Henry A. Smith, Company D, 21st Ohio Infantry, transferred to the 9th Kentucky Cavalry Volunteers." This letter further stated, "If this man was in fact captured and paroled by the enemy at or near Richmond, Kentucky, in August or September, 1862 as alleged, he became a deserter by failing to place himself under military control after having been declared duly exchanged in order from the War Department dated November 19, 1862." The Bureau of Pensions disapproved Henry's application.

There was no question that Morgan's cavalry was in the area at the time, and had, in fact, camped in Nicholasville the night of September 3, proceeding to Lexington the next morning.

There was also no question that two battalions of the 9th Kentucky Cavalry had been ordered to Richmond on August 30, only to find that Union forces were falling back, forcing the 9th Kentucky to pass around the town and join the retreat to Lexington, then to Louisville.

It is questionable, given the state of disarray of the Union forces in Kentucky at the time, that Henry would have been notified of the existence of General Order No. 191. Camp Nelson, at the time, was primarily a rendezvous point without a command structure, so who would have notified him?

Henry can certainly be faulted for not being aggressive in seeking to determine his status, vis-a-vis parole and exchange, and it is likely that the Pension Bureau took note of this fact. In so doing, however, they ignored the fact that Henry had volunteered early in the war and had served with distinction for some 11 months. To deny him a pension seems harsh, especially so when others who served as little as 90 days were given them.

In December, 1907, U.S. Representative J. J. Russell of Missouri, wrote to the Pension Department on behalf of Minie, and asked them to review Henry' s file to see if there was any way to remove the charge of desertion from his record, thus allowing a widow's pension based on his record with the 21st Ohio Infantry. He wrote:

Since his death his widow, who is very poor and deserving, is anxious to try to secure a pension, and it seems that in order to do so it would be necessary to have the charge of desertion removed from his record, and would be glad to know from you what the chances seem to be.

I have a long statement of his case, made to me by Mr. Smith in his lifetime, which, if true, would show that he was not at fault, and his widow naturally feels that she is justly entitled to a pension.

There is a cryptic "OK" scrawled across the first paragraph above, and a word that seems to read, "removed" below it, but there is no letter response in the file and no record of Minie receiving a pension.

Conclusion

Henry's letters to Minie chronicle a transformation from a young, newlywed teacher, to a soldier proud of his accomplishments and proud of his flag and the

Union it stood for. Like many of the young men who volunteered early on he foresaw a short war, and a short separation from his "dear Minie," but became disillusioned as time passed with, seemingly, little progress. In his last letter to Minie he had gotten to the point where he would "almost doubt the ultimate success of our army." His transfer, and subsequent capture and parole by Confederate cavalry, were events that, most likely, he did not regret.

Author's Note: The letters of Henry Ackennan Smith published here were obtained by the author from the holdings of the Western Historical Manuscripts Collection, 23 Ellis Library, University of Missouri - Columbia, Columbia, MO 65201-5149. Reference information is: Smith, Henry Ackerman (1837-1907), Papers, 1861-1907, (C431), 2 Rolls (Microfilm), Roll 1: Letters to his wife; Roll 2: Autobiography.

CAPTAIN DAVID H. TODD: "A BROTHER OF MR. LINCOLN'S WIFE"

By Norman M. Shapiro

The following notice appeared in the Madison County, Alabama, newspaper, *The Weekly Huntsville Advocate,* of August 4, 1871:

DIED,
At his residence in this place, on Sunday night 30th July, 1871, of consumption, Capt. DAVID H. TODD, formerly of Kentucky, but for the last six years a resident of Huntsville, in his 40th year. He served in the Mexican war, was engaged in a revolution in Chile, and visited Japan, &c., and was a Captain in the Confederate army.

David Todd, Mary Todd Lincoln's Half Brother
Source: Katherine Helm, *The True Story of Mary, Wife of Lincoln* (NY: Harper and Brothes, 1928)

The notice omitted an interesting fact that impacted much of his short life: David Todd was Mary Todd Lincoln's half-brother and Abraham Lincoln's brother-in-law. The omission was not surprising; Alabama was still under post-war military occupation and much wartime bitterness remained. Although it has been said that David Todd tried to hide the Lincoln "connection," the documented information that we have seems to indicate otherwise.

I "discovered" David Todd in the preparation of an earlier paper on the history of the Confederate battle flag that is in the collection of Huntsville's Burritt Museum. The flag, and a number of other relics, were donated to the Huntsville-Madison County Historical Society in the Civil War Centennial Year 1961 by a step-granddaughter of David Todd. The items were subsequently placed in the holdings of the Burritt Museum. The few words of the death notice that described his life were certainly intriguing and I have attempted to learn more. I found, however, only a few personal writings and have had to rely primarily on information provided in his Combined Military Service Records (CSRs) and in references to Mary Todd Lincoln.

David Humphreys Todd was born March 30, 1832 in Lexington, Kentucky, the ninth of Robert Smith Todd's fourteen living children of two marriages. Two children died in infancy. His half-sister, Mary Ann, was fourteen when he was born and she married Abraham Lincoln when he was ten. The Todd family was comfortably situated and the children of both families had the "usual advantages" of the time. During the war years, six siblings supported the Union; eight supported the Confederacy and their actions plagued Mary for most of her married life. Southerners scorned her as a traitor to her birth, and citizens loyal to the Union suspected her of treason. David and the other brothers are only slightly and often incorrectly mentioned in the several Mary Todd Lincoln biographies. Jean Baker's *Mary Todd Lincoln: A*

Biography, for example, states, "Mary Lincoln did not know David well. The second of Betsey's sons, he had run away from home as a boy and was notorious in family annals for the Chilean flag tattooed on his arm. Posted to the West, David was mortally wounded at Vicksburg in 1863." Another account states, "David would die later from wounds received at Vicksburg." And still another "David, a Confederate soldier, was shot through the lungs at the Siege of Vicksburg and died after the surrender." Katherine Helm, daughter of David's sister, Emilie Todd Helm, published in 1928 her mother's recollections of Mary Lincoln. On page 15 she writes, "David, died from the effect of wounds received at Vicksburg" and in a note on page 193, "David Todd, never recovered from wound received at Vicksburg. Though reported 'dying,' he survived, an invalid, for a few years after the war was over." One would think that Emilie (1836-1930) and Katherine (1857-1937) would have been well acquainted with the circumstances of David Todd's death; however, I have found no evidence that David was even wounded at Vicksburg although it is certainly possible that he may have received a superficial wound. We will see later that he was indeed under fire at Vicksburg, but in one of his CSRs is an application to be examined for disability retirement, dated January 6, 1865, from Hospital, Marion, Alabama, in which he states the cause of disability is "Phthisis Pulmonulis [sic], i.e. 'wasting away of lungs', caused by exposure & from which I have suffered for the past two years with frequent attacks of Hoemaptysis [sic] i.e. 'expectoration of blood or bloody mucus.' I have been absent from my command unable to perform duty for the past few months." And as noted above, some eight years after Vicksburg it was stated in his death notice that he died of consumption.

"Running away from home as a boy" may well describe David Todd's Mexican War service. He enlisted on September 15, 1847, in Captain Robinson's Company

Mary Todd's sister Elodie (Jane B.),
Who Married Colonel N. H. R. Dawson
of Selma, Alabama
Source: William C. Davis, *Breckenridge: Statesman, Soldier, Symbol*
(Baton Rouge, LA: Louisiana State University Press, 1974)

(later Company C), Third Regiment (Thomson's) Kentucky Volunteers at Lexington, Kentucky, at the age of 15. His service dates are documented in the company muster rolls obtained from the National Archives and Records Administration. Two new Kentucky regiments, the Third and Fourth, were mustered into service on October 4, 1847, at Louisville. John C. Breckinridge who was James Buchanan's vice president (1857-1861) was a major in the Third Regiment and the unit's war record is described in his biography. The regiment trained until the end of October and then boarded transport at New Orleans for Vera Cruz, where it arrived on November 18. After more training they made their way to Mexico City, arriving on December 18,1847. They did no fighting, Mexico City having been taken by Winfield Scott on September 18. They remained in Mexico City until May, when the Treaty of Guadalupe-Hidalgo was ratified by Congress (the treaty had been signed on February 2). The regiment then marched back to Vera Cruz and set out for New Orleans on June 29 and finally reached Louisville on July 16, 1848. Private David H. Todd was mustered out July 21, 1848. His age was listed on the muster-out roll as 19. His widow, Susan S. Todd, later received a Mexican War Widow's Service Pension of $8.00 per month, commencing in 1887 until her death in 1894.

Documentation for David Todd's "Chilean episode" and foreign travels has not been found. The Department of State has issued transports to citizens traveling abroad since 1789. With two exceptions, which do not apply here, there was no statutory requirement that American citizens have a passport for travel abroad until 1941. A search of the Indexes to Passport Applications at the National Archives and Records Administration revealed no applications for David Humphreys Todd. The information in his death notice must certainly have been provided by his widow and the incidents occurred between his Mexican War service and his Civil War service. Jean Baker writes that after their father's death in 1849, the boys (i.e., the three half-brothers, Sam, David and Aleck) moved to New Orleans, where a maternal uncle owned a prosperous sugar plantation. They are all listed, however, in the 1850 United States Census of Franklin County, Kentucky, in the household of their mother. The listing, which was enumerated September 3, 1850, is as follows:

- Elizabeth L. Todd 50 [years of age]
- Samuel B. Todd 20
- David H. Todd 18
- Martha Todd 17
- Emmily T. Todd 13
- Alexander H. Todd 11
- Jane B. Todd 10
- Catherine B. Todd 8

The oldest surviving child of this "second" family of Robert Smith Todd, Margaret Todd, had married in 1846.

At the beginning of the Civil War, Katherine Helm writes that Sam and David Todd were in business in New Orleans, Louisiana, and sisters Martha and Elodie Todd were living in Selma, Alabama. Martha had married Clement B. White in 1852 and Elodie was engaged to Nathaniel Henry Rhodes Dawson of Selma, whom she married in 1865. Dawson was a Captain in the Fourth Alabama Infantry Regiment and he and Elodie carried on an extensive correspondence during the war. While many of Elodie's letters were "cross-hatched" or otherwise illegible, three of them were found that mentioned brother David and were quite illuminating. They will be shown later.

David Todd's military record is for the most part delineated in three CSR's: First Lieutenant in Lieutenant W. B. Ochiltree's Detachment of Recruits (Detachment of Regulars); First Lieutenant in the First Kentucky Infantry; and Captain, Company A, 21st Louisiana Infantry. Ochiltree's Detachment was one of the many organizations that were considered to have been raised directly or otherwise formed by the Confederate government and therefore not identified with any one state. They comprised organizations of all sizes and designations including companies, battalions, regiments etc. Ochiltree's Detachment was apparently an administrative convenience created to handle a singular appointment. The jacket envelope of the unit also indicates, "Formerly Lieut. Todd's Detachment of Recruits" and contains his initial appointment as a First Lieutenant of Infantry in the Confederate States Army, dated April 27, I 861, accepted April 30, 1861, and delivered at Baton Rouge, Louisiana.

The Adjutant & Inspector General's Office of the Confederate States Army issued Special Order Number 40/3, dated May 1, 1861 detailing First Lieutenant David H. Todd. The particulars of the detail were not given; however, it was evidently to Richmond, Virginia, as there is a pay voucher in the detachment envelope for the period 27 April 1861 to 31 May 1861 issued by Major Larkin Smith, Quartermaster, at Richmond for $101.99 ($90.00 per month) and accepted 14 June 1861. Also, in one of the letters "E.T. to N.H.R.D." (from the *Dawson Papers)* dated Summerfield (Alabama). June 27th 1861, Elodie writes, "My Bro David wrote from Richmond that he expected to leave in a day or two for Staunton & has been appointed one of Genl Holmes' aides." This appointment was obviously not effected inasmuch as Special Orders No. 85, dated July 1, 1861 at Richmond orders First Lieutenant David H. Todd, Infantry, and two other officers to "report for duty to General [John H.] Winder, in this city." Brigadier General Winder had been appointed Inspector General of the Richmond area prison camps on June 22, 1861. This led to the following hand-written posting which was found in the Detachment envelope:

Richmond
July 4, 1861

Lt. Todd will proceed to the prison corner of Main & 26th Streets & relieve Lt. Archer. Should Lt. Archer be absent, he will take possession of the premises & receive from Lt. Archer all orders etc. when he shall have seen him.

Jn H Winder, Brig Gen

While the rationale for this appointment is unknown, it would be difficult to believe that David Todd would have desired or sought such an assignment. In the Introduction to *Civil War Prisons* William B. Hesseltine writes, "The Civil War left behind it a long list of controversies - yet no controversy ever evoked such emotions as the mutual recrimination between Northern and Southern partisans over the treatment of prisoners of war. Hardly had the war begun when the first prisoners alleged that their captors mistreated them." The recriminations continued throughout the war and, "To the end of their lives ex-prisoners wrote books or letters-to-the-editor, told their stories to country-store gatherings, appeared before congressional committees, or addressed conventions of veterans to recount their adversaries and to point accusing fingers at their cruel and conspiratorial enemy." As Ernest B. Ferguson commented, "Todd may have drawn special criticism because of who he was, but in the long run his name barely made the list of Civil War villains, far below that of his orderly sergeant that summer, a Swiss-born Louisiana physician named Henry Wirz. [later the notorious commandant of Andersonville prison.]" Further investigation has indicated that Todd did indeed receive special attention as his "special relationship" is mentioned in almost every one of the accusations that will be described later.

The prison at the comer of Main and 26th Streets to which Lieu- tenant Todd was assigned was formerly the tobacco factory of George D. Harwood. It was also called Harwood's Hospital and/or General Hospital No. 24, and later called Moore's Hospital and North Carolina Hospital. It was one of many Civil War prisons in Richmond; Blakey lists fourteen, twelve of them former tobacco factories. Michael D. Gorman lists even more buildings that were used variously as prisons and/or hospitals. This led to much confusion in the reporting of prison history as well as prison incidents. For example, there was a General Hospital No. 22 (also called Howard's Hospital) located on Main Street between 25th and 26th Streets which is identified by Wait as both the former tobacco factory of George D. Howard and the former tobacco factory of J. W. Atkinson. The 1860 Federal Census for Richmond lists a George D. Harwood as a tobacco factory proprietor, but no George D. Howard. In the Ochiltree Detachment envelope, however, there is a requisition and receipt for twenty cords of wood for Howard's Jail, dated 2 August 1861, and signed by "D.H. Todd, 1Lt., CSA, in chge Prison."

The accusations of mistreatment had their origin here a few days after the first Union prisoners arrived in Richmond after "First Manassas." This first big battle of the war was fought on July 21, 1861, and Richmond was not prepared to receive shortly thereafter the approximately 1,000 Union prisoners and 1,500 Confederate wounded. There was no official agreement on parole of prisoners at this stage of the war. Abraham Lincoln's position was that that the South was in rebellion and secession was illegal. He refused to recognize the southern captives as prisoners of war and this influenced the treatment of captives on both sides. Some of the first prisoners were confined in Ligon's (or Liggon's) prison, also known as General Hospital No. 23, and in Harwood's prison. The opening paragraphs of an early and colorful report of prison life in Richmond, which may have influenced later accounts, appear below. It was published in the New York *Sunday Mercury* on June I, 1862, by William H. Kellogg, of Company K, 38th Infantry, New York State Militia. Mr. Kellogg was a journalist.

> "Now that our forces are so near Richmond, a few incidents in the prison life in the tobacco manufactories might be interesting to the reader in search of truth. After the Battle of Bull Run, on the 21st of July, 1861, among those captured I was marched to Manassas Junction, where we remained in the drizzling rain, which fell all night. Owing to the extreme fatigue of the body attending on the heat of the day, forced marching, and the battlefield, I slept peaceably and sound, and for a moment on awakening the next morning, it was almost impossible for me to decide where I was, but gradually a vivid sense of my position forced itself upon me, and I realized I was a prisoner. All day on the 22nd, following the battle, we remained standing in the slowly-falling rain, wetting us to the skin. Around us stood guards, close together, and beyond them a gaping multitude of idle gazers, looking at the '*Yan*kees' - evidently, from the way they eyed us, supposing us to be some curious animal, and remarking: 'Why, they look just like our folks!' 'Lord, they're white folks just like we are.' And asking us: 'What made you come down here for?' All day long we were kept in this position, nothing given us to eat, and must I say it? - water could not be attained, unless, thanks to God for the falling rain of that day, when caught in an India-rubber blanket, poured into a tin-cup. And bitter, brackish, sickish to the taste as was this water, 'twas like

nectar to the half-famished men who, many of them, had not tasted a drop of water since the previous bloody day. About 5 o'clock P.M., however, some hard biscuit and rancid bacon were divided among us, and we were marched to the railroad depot, and placed in baggage and freight cars, *en route* for Richmond. Here Fortune was propitious, for the rain dripping from the tops of the cars presented a rich harvest of pure water to the thirsty men. It was a perfect godsend. It was hard in the extreme to see the avidity with which the poor fellows sought to catch the falling drops, as their thirst was doubly increased by the salt meat just served out. About six o'clock the next afternoon, we arrived in Richmond, and, well guarded, were marched through the streets, hooted, hissed and blackguarded in a manner I could hardly have believed would have occurred in a city belonging to a civilized nation. But seeing what I have of them has changed my mind considerably. About dark, we reached one of the vile tobacco factories destined to receive us, and from whose doors many of the brave boys who entered them were never more to pass, until in a pine coffin, conveyed in a rickety cart, they should fill a grave in some distant portion of the [N]egro burying- ground of the capital city of Virginia. Is it too much to ask one passing thought to those who thus died and still fill the humble tenement? In the building with myself were five hundred and thirty-eight souls - two hundred on one floor, and three hundred and thirty-eight on the floor above, these floors being some one hundred by thirty feet. Here, for some three or four weeks - if I may be allowed the expression - we were left to rot; and ere that time, vermin had made their appearance, and, notwithstanding all endeavors to the contrary, 'reigned supreme.' It was a fine specimen of close packing, at night, when we turned in, and it would have been difficult to one not accustomed to moving among a crowd to have made their way through the room without stepping on some part of the human mass that strewed the floor. Even in the day it was difficult navigation.

<u>**Lieutenant [David] Todd.**</u> of Kentucky, C. S. A., notorious for his cruelty, was in charge of us. Much has already been said of his treatment of our suffering prisoners of his war. An incident, however, which I do not think has been in print, occurring at this time, and in which he was chief actor, will better prove his cruel treatment than any other I could mention.

One morning, in passing through one of the crowded rooms, stopped by the crowd who obstructed his passage, he bade them give way; they not obeying his order as quickly as he wished, he drew his sword, and making a step toward one of the nearest of the crowd, who belonged to the First Minnesota Regiment, passed it through the lower portion of the leg, and in withdrawing it he literally cut the piece of flesh to the bone. Remarking coolly, as he passed on: 'Take care of the man and clear the road.' This act was on par with his other cruelties while in charge. By his orders our prisoners were fired on in the windows, and no

> less than five wounded and three killed. Another day we were re- fused water for more than six hours in the day for the mere crime of spilling some on the floor; and frequently our meals were not served until late in the day. Some four weeks after our arrival, the wounded from Bull Run arrived in Richmond, and some placed in the general hospital, and the remainder - by far the largest portion - conveyed in our prison, Hanwood's [Harwood's] Tobacco Factory, on Main, corner of Twenty-sixth street, it being the most convenient of access and best adapted to hospital purposes."

****

Many of the charges concerning David Todd's cruelty toward Union prisoners first appeared in a small volume published in 1893 by William H. Jeffrey comprising "Journals Kept by Union Prisoners of War with the Name, Rank, Company, Regiment and State of the Four Thousand Who Were Confined There" and are extracted here:

> "During the afternoon of August 5th Lieutenant Todd, who, by the way was a half-brother of President Lincoln's wife, and at that time in the immediate charge of the prisoners, ordered all servants belonging to the different messes out of the quarters. It was supposed to be for the reason that through them some of the officers had obtained ardent spirits and because of a disturbance created that morning by one Lyman H. Stone, a surgeon of the United States Army, who was arrested at Manassas and taken to Richmond on the 29th of July. Dr. Stone was a highly educated gentleman, unaccustomed to excessive

> indulgence in liquor, but it was supposed that the excitement of the battle and the circumstances of his arrest caused him to drink too freely. He started out soon after dinner, overturning the tables, dishes and all, and finally laid hold of one of the officers so roughly that it was evident that he was in a high state of frenzy. At last the turmoil became so great that Lieutenant Todd, rushing into the room with great fury, and seeing Dr. Stone clinched with one of the officers, drew his pistol and demanded that the disturbance should cease. It was stopped and Dr. Stone was taken out of the prison to a brick building in the rear and put in irons. There was, of course, nothing wrong in what Lieutenant Todd did in this instance, but the outrages subsequently committed by him upon the prisoners under his charge were spoken of by all in the severest of terms."

The testimony of a Corporal Merrill on this point is as follows: Lieutenant Todd was singularly vicious and brutal in his treatment of the prisoners, and seldom entered the prison without grossly insulting some of them. He invariably entered with a drawn sword in his hand. His voice and manner, as he addressed the prisoners, always indicated a desire to commit some cruel wrong. Upon one occasion he struck an invalid soldier in the face with the flat side of his sword, simply because he did not obey the order to fall in for roll-call with sufficient alacrity. At another time one of the guards, in the presence and with the sanction of Lieutenant Todd, struck a prisoner upon the head with the butt-end of his musket."

Isaac N. Jennings of the First Connecticut Volunteers reported:

> "I can mention no bright spot in Richmond Prison life as I know of none, except the enjoyment derived from social communion with ourselves....A curious case of family unpleasantness was that the brother-in-law of President Lincoln was in charge of us. I never saw any one more bitter in his hatred of 'Yanks.' He seemed bound to make his reputation, which, as he said, '*might be injured by his relationship to Old Abe,* by abusing the prisoners."

According to J. Lane Fitts of Company B, Second New Hampshire Volunteers:

> "In the evening of the fourth day after the battle of Manassas, or the first Bull Run, we arrived in Richmond. We were marched from the rail- road station to one of the tobacco houses in the lower part of the city, near the James River and the Canal. There were over fifty of us members of the 2nd New Hampshire Volunteers, including the wounded, who were put in another building nearby. We were in charge of the notorious Wirz, known in prison at that time as the 'Dutch Sergeant.' The officer next to him was Lieutenant Todd, a brother of Abraham Lincoln's wife. Lieutenant Todd, when upon the street near our windows one day, overheard some conversation that did not suit him. He drew his sword and rushing upstairs, stabbed the first man he came across, wounding him so that he had to be removed to the hospital. 'Every d--------d

> Yankee,' he said, 'ought to be served the same way.' A favorite expression of his was, 'I would like to cut 'Old Abe's heart out.'"

And from another member of Company B, Second New Hampshire Volunteers, we learn:

> "The officer who had chief charge of us was Lieut. Todd, a brother to Abraham Lincoln's wife. Once when a Yankee prisoner had died and the guards took the body down to headquarters, they thoughtlessly laid it on the doorstep while they rang the bell for the Lieutenant. This so exasperated him that he kicked the body out into the street, where it laid over night. With this man in command, and the notorious Wirz, who was afterwards hanged, to execute his orders, the reader can judge something of the treatment we received. We afterwards heard he was killed in battle, and were not sorry to hear it, although he deserved hanging as richly as did Wirz."

Additional, similar descriptions of Lieutenant Todd's "cruelty" can be found on the Internet and are said to have taken place at Richmond's Libby Prison, formerly the warehouse of L. Libby & Sons, Ship Chandlers. Richmond's most famous prison, "Libby" was probably second only to Andersonville in the lexicon of notorious Confederate prisons. It was not, however, used as a prison until the summer of 1862 when David Todd was engaged in the fighting at Vicksburg.

The other two legible letter excerpts from his sister, Elodie to her fiancée, Nathaniel Dawson exemplify the additional perils associated with David Todd's odious assignment.

"E.T. to N. H. R. D.
23 July 1861, Selma, Alabama

I see from today's paper Mrs. Lincoln is indignant at my Bro David's being in the Confederate Service and declares 'that by no words or act of hers should he escape punishment for his treason against her husband's government should he fall into their hands.' I do not believe she ever said it & if she did & meant it, she is no longer a sister of mine, nor deserved to be called a woman of nobleness or truth & God grant my noble and brave hearted brother will never fall into their hands and have to suffer death twice over, and he could do nothing which would make one prouder of him than he is doing now fighting for his country. What would she do to me, do you suppose? I have so much to answer for."

"E.T. to N. H. R. D.
15 September 1861, Selma, Alabama

I supposed you had seen an account of my Brother's arrest in the Richmond papers. He was arrested for having some of the dead Yankee prisoners who had been dead a day or two in prison coffined and sent to the Q'Master's department as his commander told him 'to be commented & gazed upon as a spectacle for the public' by standing there before his, the Q'Masters's door. I believe upon investigating the matter it was found he (the Quartermaster) had been in neglect of his

> duty & not my brother. At any rate, I hope he will not be called upon to play jailer any more."

His sister's hopes were realized when First Lieutenant David H. Todd was assigned to duty with the First Regiment of Kentucky Infantry on September 19, 1861 by Special Order No. 336, Headquarters, Army of the Potomac. He reported to the regimental commander, Colonel Thomas H. Taylor, when the regiment returned to camp near Centreville, Virginia, on September 27, 1861. The First Kentucky was formed about July or August 1861, by consolidation of several smaller units. Camping around Manassas during the late summer of 1861, the regiment saw little action for the next three months beyond guard duty and skirmishes with the enemy. On 20 December, however, the regiment joined with the 6th South Carolina, 11th Virginia, 10th Alabama, Cutt's battery of artillery, and 150 cavalry under Brigadier General J.E.B. Stuart on a foraging expedition in the northern Virginia countryside. This substantial force encountered an even larger Union force near the small community of Dranesville about 20 miles from Centerville. After a stirring fight of several hours, the Confederates withdrew to Centreville, the First Kentucky having lost one killed, twenty-three wounded and two missing. The regiment went into winter camp near Centreville on Christmas Day, 1861 and performed sentry duty for the next three months. For most of this period (September 1861 - February 1862), David Todd was assigned to Field and Staff of the regiment, but the muster roll shows that he was on leave in New Orleans for 30 days during December-January and it is unknown if he participated in the fight described above. A copy of the following letter was in the 21st Louisiana CSR:

"Head Qtrs 1st Ky. Regt.
Major Copeland
Comnd. 1st Ky. Regt.

Having no duties to perform in this Regt. and nothing to which I can be assigned and having an opportunity of obtaining a position in our Army at New Orleans where I can render needed services I request a transfer from this Regiment to Maj Genl Lovell's Command in New Orleans.

Yours Respect.
D.H. Todd 1st Lt. Inf. C.S.A."

This was followed in a few days by "Special Order Number 36/13, dated Feb. 13, 1862 Subject: Relieved & Assigned, Todd, D. H. 1st Lt. 1st Regt. Ky. Vols."

The next document in his CSR was dated May 9, 1862, Company D, where he, "Signs Certificate as Inspector and Mustering Officer," Muster Role of Miles Legion, Louisiana Volunteers (also known as 32nd Regiment Infantry). This was followed by similar documents for: "Co. F, Miles Legion, La. Vols.," dated May 17, 1862; "Co. E, 30th Regt., La. Inf.," dated May 18, 1862; and "Co. B, Stockdale's [Battalion]., Miss. Cav.," dated May 14, 1862 to May 27, 1862. There are also two pay vouchers: the first, for the month of April, dated 30 April and received at Richmond, Virginia, and the second, for the month of May, dated 31 May and received at Tangipahoa, Louisiana. His activities during the undocumented periods are unknown, however, three letters from the Emile Todd Helm Papers describe the death of his brother, Samuel B. Todd, at Shiloh, (6 - 7 April 1862), and suggest that David went to Tennessee to recover Sam's body in late April. (Two of the letters from his brother's fellow soldiers were previously unpublished and are shown in the appendix to this article.) David's letter to his sister Emile, which follows, is one of only two writings in his own hand (other than material requisitions and signatures) that were found in his documentation.

"New Orleans, 15 April '62

Dear Sister,

It is my sad task to transmit the unwelcome news that our poor Brother Sam is no more. The report has been here for several days but I could not believe it as no one had seen him either dead or even wounded. I thought he might be a prisoner. Today his wounded Captain informs me with certainty of his decease. He was shot through the body in the first charge of the Crescent Regiment from this City on Monday, 7th April & lingered until Tuesday morning 8th inst. & was surrounded by kind friends & attentive surgeons who bore him off & attended his wants. I will procure his body as soon as Genl Beauregard will allow, Dr. Stille having kindly marked the spot he was buried on. I cannot describe the grief of his widow & with sorrow write these few lines.

I remain aff
Your Bro.
D. H. Todd"

Special Order No. 87, dated June 17, 1862 and signed, by Brigadier General. M. L. Smith, Dept. of Mississippi and East Louisiana assigned First Lieutenant. D. H. Todd to the 22nd Regiment of Louisiana Volunteers. Six days later, on June 23, 1862, he signed a requisition as "Captain, Co. A, 22nd Regt." for 20 pair shoes, 10 pair pants, 10 pair drawers, 10 shirts and 10 pair shoes, "my men having worn out their clothing in 12 months service." The official or effective date of his promotion is unknown. His service with this regiment continued until the end of the war. The regiment, which had actually trained as heavy artillery, had other designations and so did the company which was sometimes consolidated with other units to form an artillery battery detachment.

The military situation in the Department of Mississippi and East Louisiana in the spring of 1862 was dominated by strategies concerning control of the Mississippi River. The Union wanted such control in order to split the Confederacy and restore free commerce to the politically important Northwest. The river cities New Orleans, Vicksburg and Memphis were critical to this control and in April 1862 a Union fleet under Flag Officer David G. Farragut began operations against New Orleans. The city was captured on May 1, 1862, Baton Rouge fell on May 8 and Farragut arrived at Vicksburg on May 18 to demand its surrender. The demand to surrender was emphatically refused and after a few days of ineffectual shelling, Farragut sailed back to New Orleans. He returned to Vicksburg on June 25th and passed the city's defensive batteries on June 28th with tremendous shelling on both sides. It was at this critical stage in the defense of Vicksburg that Captain David Todd joined the action which is described in Bergeron's history of the 22nd Louisiana Infantry:

> "At Vicksburg, Company A, now under Captain David H. Todd, a brother- in-law to President Abraham Lincoln, was placed in

> Battery No. 8, which consisted of two 42-pounder smoothbores and two 32-pounder rifles on navy carriages. This battery was located near the Marine Hospital, about a half mile below the city and about fifty or sixty feet above the river, and was also known as the Marine Hospital Battery. Just where Company C was stationed is unknown, but it may have helped Company A at the Marine Hospital Battery.
>
> Todd's battery was fired on occasionally by Federal gunboats from May 27 until June 21, but his men did not return the fire because General Smith had ordered his batteries not to do so unless the enemy came into close range (note: Todd did not join the unit until about June 25). The situation changed on June 28 when Farragut's fleet ran the Vicksburg batteries in attempt to knock them out. The Marine Hospital Battery was fired upon by each vessel as it passed and received special attention from the U.S.S. *Hartford.* Farragut's flagship forced Todd's men to abandon their guns and seek protection in their bombproofs. Once the *Hartford* got underway again, the men returned to their stations and 'renewed their fire with precision.'"

As Edwin Bearss records,

> "Todd's gunners next engaged gunboats from the mortar fleet and the U.S.S. *Brooklyn.* The resulting momentary confusion among the enemy vessels gave Todd's men relatively stationary targets. Seizing their temporary advantage, they hit and disabled two of the

> gunboats with 32-pounder shells. The rest of the vessels withdrew rather than risk running the gauntlet of Confederate fire. During the day the Confederate guns had been silenced intermittently but none had been disabled. Farragut had learned that only a land assault would reduce the South- ern citadel."

The remainder of the operations were rather uneventful for Todd's men and the Union fleet withdrew on July 27. Highly praising his battery commanders and their men for their excellent defense of Vicksburg, General Smith noted that:

> "For more than seventy-five days and nights have these batteries been continuously manned and ready for action at a moment's notice; during much of this time the roar of cannon has been unceasing, and there have been portions of it during which the noise of falling shot and the explosion of shells have been such as might make the stoutest [sic] heart quail, yet none faltered; the blazing sun, the fatiguing night-watch, the storm of battle, all were alike cheerfully endured, and whenever called upon heavy and telling blows were dealt upon our foes in return."

This last was from Brigadier General M. L. Smith's report on the operations at Vicksburg, May 18 - July 27, 1862. General Smith also wrote: "It will thus be seen that the enemy were in front of Vicksburg sixty-seven days, during which the combined efforts of two powerful fleets have been foiled, and the accompanying land force, from 4,000 to 5,000 held at bay. The number of shot and shell thrown by the fleet is unknown; it had been estimated as high as 25,000 and put as low as 20,000."

The number, however, is unimportant, and mentioned only to illustrate the fact that the loss to a land battery when attacked by one afloat is comparatively small. The casualties from the enemy's firing were 7 killed and 15 wounded; in the town 2 only are reported. The enemy fired at least ten shots to our one, and their number of killed and wounded can, from information, be safely put down at five times as great.

The companies of the regiment remained at Vicksburg through the summer and into the fall and then moved into the defensive perimeter of the city to counter General Grant's converging assault. Grant planned this operation early in November 1862 after his appointment as Commander, Department of Tennessee, on October 16. To this end, Sherman led an expedition down the river from Memphis to attack the city from the north, while Grant himself advanced overland from the east. Confederate cavalry under Van Dorn and Forrest cut Grant's line of communications, forcing him to retreat, and Sherman was repulsed in the battle of Chickasaw Bluffs.

In January 1863, Grant concentrated his army across the river from Vicksburg. After several unsuccessful attempts to gain an approach to the seemingly impregnable city (February - March 1863), Grant in April began a brilliant move to capture the city from the south. He moved south and crossed the river on Commodore Porter's fleet which had passed the Vicksburg batteries on the night of April 16-17. Joined by Sherman on May 7, he marched northeast and then turned west at Jackson. After defeating the Confederates at Champion's Hill and Big Black River Bridge, he eventually began the six-week siege of Vicksburg which culminated in the surrender on July 4, 1863.

In his history of the 22nd Louisiana Infantry, Bergeron writes (and in so doing compounds the inaccuracies of David Todd's demise), "the men of the 21st (the regimental designation had been changed in January, 1862) all became prisoners. During the siege the regiment's casualties had totaled 2 officers and 14 men killed, 7 officers and 43 men wounded, and one deserter. One of the wounded officers was Captain David H. Todd, who died in 1866 as a result of his injury."

At Vicksburg, on July 8, 1863, Todd gave his parole under oath as "Captain, Co. A, 21st Regt. Louisiana Vols., C. S. A." The regiment, now a part of Brigadier General Louis Hebert's Brigade, moved to Demopolis, Alabama, during the last days of July or the first part of August to await exchange. On September 2, 1863, the 21st moved to a better organized parole camp near Enterprise, Mississippi. David Todd spent much of this period on leave in Selma, Alabama, presumably with his sister, Elodie. As Bergeron concludes his history of the regiment:

> "On December 26 the regiment was partially exchanged, and within several days it was armed and equipped. Lieutenant General Leonidas Polk ordered on January 16, 1864, that the remnants of the 3rd, 17th, 21st, 22nd, 26th, 27th, 29th and 31st Louisiana regiments remaining east of the Mississippi be consolidated into one regiment. Consolidation accomplished by January 26, the new unit was designated the 22nd Louisiana Consolidated Infantry, or 22nd Heavy Artillery, with 780 men....During its Civil War career, the 22nd (21st) Louisiana Infantry had proven itself to be one of the finest heavy artillery units in the

> Confederate army despite the fact that its men's disparate professional backgrounds had not prepared them for this aspect of military service....Punishing blows were dealt to Federal gunboats and ironclads at Vicksburg and twice at Snyder's Bluff. So highly esteemed was the 22nd that it was assigned the task of defending the largest and most important fort on the Confederate line behind Vicksburg, a feat it performed exceptionally well. When the men were mustered into the new 22nd Consolidated Infantry, it could truly be said of them that they had borne themselves 'with distinguished gallantry.'"

The records of David Todd's remaining Civil War service are incomplete, perhaps because he was on "detached" service for much of the time. The service began with another undesirable assignment outlined in a Special Order issued at "Headquarters - Demopolis, Ala," dated February 23, 1864:

> "Capt. D. Todd P.A.C.S. will proceed at once, with a detail of Two Officers and Ten Men to Selma Ala. and report to Capt. J. C. Graham A.Q.M. [Assistant Quartermaster] to assist in impressing horses for the Artillery of this Army. Quartermaster will furnish the necessary transportation. By Command of Lieut. Genl. Polk, Sd. Actg. Chf. Of Artillery"

This was followed by a receipt for $180.00 for his personal expenses from the February 24 - March 9, 1864; a receipt for $87.60, dated February 22, 1864 from Selma Arsenal for "1 Officers Saddle, 1 Breast Strap and 1 Gripper, for his own use;" and two "Requisitions for Forage," also at Selma, dated May 17 and June 1, 1864. These requisitions were signed, "D. H. Todd, Capt. 21st La Rgt., Act (or Asst) Chf. Artillery, Lorings Div." All but two of the remaining papers pertain to another degrading situation he encountered in his assignment as Impressing Officer.

The incident, described in the following letters, occurred while he was performing his duties as Impressing Officer in the town of Claiborne, Monroe County, Alabama, in April 1864:

"Meadow Bank, near Claiborne, Alabama
April 21, 1864

To the Honorable James A. Seddon
Secretary of War of the Confederate States

We have had & yet have at Claiborne, a captain D. H. Todd calling himself impressing officer acting under authority of Maj. A. M. Paxton, assistant Quarter Master, and against whom I prefer the annexed charges which I am prepared to establish. He has come here with the annunciation that he is the Brother in Law of Mr. Lincoln. I address this communication to you & hope to have early action in the matter. I am Respectfully

Your Obdt Servant
Robert G. Scott

1st I charge Cap. D. H. Todd with duplicity & deception in the discharge of his official duties as impressing officer of the Confederate States in the county of Monroe, acting as he represents under (authority) of Major A. M. Paxton, assistant Quarter Master.

2nd I charge him with insulting and striking in his office a citizen of the county of Monroe & otherwise maltreating him; that citizen being in the office attempting to transact business with the said Todd, & while the said officer was surrounded by his soldiers.

3rd I charge him with giving a false certificate in reference to impressed property.

4th I charge him with taking and holding property as condemned for the Confederate States & as regularly appraised for the Confederate Government that he never previous to such appraisement offered to purchase at any price.

5th I charge him with receiving a gift made to him individually of a horse from one with whom he had just transacted business in reference to the impressment of horses for the Confederate States.

Robert G. Scott April 21, 1864"

Mr. Scott wrote a second letter, dated April 27, 1864 to General Polk with the same five charges, but with a different introductory paragraph:

"To Lt General L. Polk

Sir,

A Captain D. H. Todd calling himself impressing officer acting under authority of Major A. M. Paxton, has been here, & against whom I prefer the annexed charges & which I am prepared to establish. I am an entire stranger to you, but refer you the Honorable Mr. Lyon, member of Congress from the District in which Demopolis is, & to the Honorable Willis P. Bocock of the county of Marengo. I ask the arrest of D. H. Todd, if really a Confederate officer, & his trial. Be pleased to give me an early reply.

I am
Your obedient Servant
Robert G. Scott"

The letter did make its way to the Secretary of War, received his endorsement, and was sent by the Adjutant & Inspector General on May 28, 1864, to Major A. M. Paxton who was in charge of "Impressing Animals in Alabama" and directed him to investigate the charges. It was noted on the correspondence that, "The writer is a responsible citizen of Alabama." Indeed he was; as noted by Thomas Owen in his *History of Alabama and Dictionary of Alabama Biography:*

> "Scott, Robert Gormain, lawyer, was born December 22, 1791, at Savannah, Ga., and died 1870 at Claiborne, Monroe County....He graduated at the University of Georgia and at William and Mary, Williamsburg, Va. where he practiced law before settling in Richmond, Va. He was a member of the Virginia legislature and afterward was elected a member of the council of state. He was a noted criminal lawyer and had a large practice outside of Virginia. He was a captain of cavalry in the War of 1812, a

Democrat in politics and consul to Rio de Janeiro, Brazil, under President Polk. At the age of seventy-five, he went to Mobile and volunteered to defend the city during the war of secession."

Major Paxton apparently replied to Mr. Scott on June 8, 1864 and Scott wrote to him on June 17, 1864:

"Meadow Bank Near Claiborne, Alabama
June 17, 1864

Major A. M. Paxton Sir,
Your letter of the 8th inst was received by me on the 14th just as I was about to leave home & I now hasten on my return to answer it: It has now been nearly two months since I preferred charges against a certain D. H. Todd acting as impressing officer; & hearing nothing officially of them...I had concluded that the charges were deemed of too little importance by those high in authority for any notice from them. By your communication however, I am notified that they have been referred to you for investigation, & you inform me that the charges are in some respect indefinite, & you ask of me to be more specific. Before proceeding to comply with this request I have to enquire of you, if I make these charges specific & distinct, in what manner is the 'investigation' to be made by you? - Shall I be heard in that investigation, & be permitted by proof to establish the charges I have made? - Will the proof be an oath, & be subject to cross examination? - Will the

investigation be open or secret? - I ask to be informed on these points, as I learn the man accused has been busy in procuring certificates & endeavoring to forestall the enquiry into his conduct. I have nothing to conceal in this matter & I have in advance frankly to say that if the 'investigation' is to [be] conducted before you upon such materials & secretly I would scorn to have part in it & I would not value it as worth a pepper corn. Give me a prompt reply to this, & I will according to what you inform me shape my future action in this matter.

Very Respectfully Robert G. Scott"

The "certificates" that Mr. Scott mentioned are apparently the three letters supporting Captain Todd that were in the CSR. One of the letters is completely illegible and the other two were written by Samuel Forwood of Gosport, Clarke County, Alabama:

"Gosport, Clarke Co. Ala
To Capt. David H. Todd

Dear Sir,

You having informed me on yesterday that Col. R. G. Scott had preferred charges against you in regard to the performance of your duties as an 'Impressing Officer' in impressing Horses whilst at Claiborne. One of the charges made by Col. Scott you informed me was that I had bribed you by giving you one of my Horses. I take occasion to say here it is an emphatically a foul and slanderous falsehood.

In this statement I will mention the facts as they occurred in reference to my Presenting you a Horse. After you had examined my Horses and refused them saying they were not suitable for artillery service, I afterwards insisted on your taking one of them as I wished to do something for the Government and said to you as an evidence of the fact, that I would present you with one, the largest Horse of them. You asked me if I meant it as a present to yourself. My reply was you were not a Government Officer. You answered in the affirmative. I then said I will present him to you; you replied that you could not accept of him, unless I would make you a Deed of Gift to him. I told you to write one out for your own benefit & use which was done and I signed it. On these terms you accepted it and mentioned previously you could not on any other terms, saying you might be accused of Impressing Horses for the Government and then appropriating them to your own use. I think I have recited the substance of the Horse case. Mr. Seymour and two other men were present and I am satisfied they will endorse the same.

I will further take occasion to state that I never saw you in my life only short time the day before when I went to Claiborne to see you to get you to come over to my House to get my Horses. You informed me that I must bring them the next morning which I did and the result was what I have stated in the foregoing. Sir I had, and still have, a better opinion of you than to have offered you a Horse to bribe you even had there been the remotest occasion to have done it. And will say even though I am 65 years of age I would spit in any man's face that would ask one of me.

I will further add injustice to you, as I think, no man could have given more satisfaction by doing impartial Justice than yourself, so far as came under my own knowledge.

There are men who ranted and bellowed for the war before it commenced thinking it would be over before breakfast. But now call upon them to fight, or assist by giving a part of their substance to carry it on, you will find them the most cold & complaining beings in the Confederacy. They are mad with everybody who will call upon them to help, or to fight. They will do neither if not forced. I say force them.

Respectfully Yrs.

S. Forwood"

****

"Gosport May 21st 1864

Capt. D. H. Todd
Selma, Ala

Dear Sir,

I wrote out a statement of facts in the Horse Present case, or as is insinuated by old Col. R. G. Scott, the Horse Bribery case. I put the letter on board the Steamer Rindin? myself today. I met the Col. on board of her and took him to one side and told him I understood he had preferred charges against you and that one of them was that I had bribed you by presenting you with a Horse. He denounced it as false. He took out the paper preferring charges against you and read them. He has several charges, and the Horse amongst this list. He says that he does not mean in the charge that you were bribed but that it was improper conduct in you to have received the Horse being Government Impressing Officer. It matters not to me in what light he places on it. So that he denied to me of saying it was a Bribe given by me to you. I read him the most of my letter, all of it, as far as the Horse matter was concerned, and sealed it in his presence. He asked if I was going to send it to you without explaining what he said. I then opened it again and got the slip of Paper enclosed from the Clk. of the Boat and wrote what you will find on it. The Boat was about leaving. I did not have time to say more, consequently write now to explain fully.

Now I will give you what he says. He said he was a going to persist in the preferring of the charges to the death. My own opinion of them is they are simple and silly and founded in malice, and if proposed ought not to be noticed by any sensible Board of men. I also think what he has said about the Horse, if he sends up any such charge, though he avers to me was not a charge of bribery against me (as in my presence he dared not to make such a charge against me) that by the insinuating manner in which he has written it out it was intended to bear that light against you and common sense would say if you were guilty I participated in it and must be equally so. You are at liberty to use my letter as you please. I have had no connivance and have no secrets to conceal.

Mr. Jas. R. Bettis, Frank Nichols & Mr. Seymour will all endorse what I said in reference to the statement in regard to presenting you the horse.

It is a ponderous document of nonsense. I wrote to Lorenzo James, stating the facts you wished him to give about the Fuss. Right here I will say to you what Col. Scott said to me shortly after it happened. He said he was raising his stick to strike you but you struck too quick for him and knocked him down and persons present separated you. Otherwise he would have hurt you before he would have been done with you.

Respectfully Yrs.
S.Forwood

I have no stamps to pay Postage. being out, will send this on the morning Boat."

David Todd replied to the charges preferred against him by Robert G. Scott in a letter to Major A. M. Paxton dated September 27, 1864:

"Selma, Ala, Sept 27, 1864

To Major A. M. Paxton
Chf Inspr Field Transpn
Brandon, Miss

Sir

I am today in receipt of a Copy of the charges preferred against me by R. G Scott a citizen of Monroe County Ala. To these charges I give a most distinct and positive denial and state they are malicious, false & unfounded, as well as absurd and ridiculous.

Previous to my entering Monroe County, and while on duty under your orders in the adjoining county of Wilcox, I notified the citizens of Monroe Co that I would attend at Claiborne, and Monroeville on certain days for the purpose of impressing artillery horses for the army then at Demopolis under Lt Genl Polk.

This R. G. Scott took great pains as I learned on my arrival in Monroe Co, to create a bad feeling amongst the Citizens of his County, not only against the duties I had to perform (already sufficiently disagreeable) but also against me personally, as being the Brother-in-Law of Mr. Lincoln, President of the U.S. This fact caused me some trouble and created a bad impression, which it required sometime to remove.

In the pursuance of my duties, I have always strictly adhered to the Law and the instructions furnished me: Giving notices of desire to purchase and in cases of impressment furnishing certificates on forms furnished for that purpose from the Quarter Master's Department.

It is true that a scuffle took place in my office at Claiborne, but caused in the endeavor to protect myself from assault made by this same R. G. Scott upon me (he being a very old man and feeble). When he entered my office, he commenced a furious tirade of abuse because I had impressed from his wife (he owning no property) a pair of carriage horses. He accused me of making a false certificate, of being a liar and used every term of abuse an angry man could. I told him I wished he had twenty years less upon his head; that his age protected him from my just resentment. Finally, he raised his cane to strike me, when I attempted to take from him the cane and in the scuffle for it, he fell to the floor. I did not strike him, though he well deserved a good beating from me. I append statement made by an intimate friend of Col Scott & a statement made by other citizens of Monroe County who were present at the time of the difficulty, which shows distinctly the forbearance I exercised.

As to the 5th charge - I accepted a horse from Col S. Forwood - a stranger to me. This gift from, so far from being a stain, I consider a great complement to me. Few officers on such duty can expect to make friends amongst the citizens however courteous and impartial.

I have good reason to believe I left behind me many friends and but one enemy in Monroe County that I know of, although I am conscious I performed my duty.

I could readily produce the evidence of my clerk and two other soldiers present at the time of the difficulty, said men being in the escort of Genl Hood, but think the evidence of citizens sufficient to prove the charges malicious, and having their origin in the brain of an irritable, arbitrary and avaricious dotard.

I am, very Respectfully
Your Obdt Servt

David H. Todd
Capt. 21 La Regt"

There was no official document giving the final disposition of this case in the CSRs or in the Record Group 109 Letters at the National Archives. There was, however, this letter from Major G. W. Holt, Office of the Adjutant and Inspector General:

"Meridian, Sept 6, 1864
Capt. D. H. Todd

Capt.

Your communication was received yesterday and in answer to your question I will inform you that I think you need not trouble yourself about the matter any longer. The letters you sent to me relieved you from all censure in the case, and the charges were deemed absurd. The reason the papers have not been returned to you is because they were referred to Maj. Paxton and he has not as yet returned them. Hoping this will prove satisfactory.

I am Capt.
Your Obd Svt
GW Holt, Maj A IG"

The remaining documents of interest in the CSRs were David Todd's application for disability retirement from the hospital at Marion, Alabama, dated January 6, 1865, which was mentioned earlier and his parole after the surrender given at Meridian, Mississippi, and dated May 15, 1865.

His illness probably accounts for the lack of documentation in his records for the last eight months of the war.

The circumstances of David Todd's marriage on April 4, 1865, in Marion, Alabama, to the young widow, Susan Turner Williamson, of Huntsville, Alabama, were told (so far as they were known) in my earlier article concerning him. They moved to Huntsville in late April 1865, and took up residence in the Turner home at the corner of Franklin and Gates. David apparently joined his father-in-law, Daniel B. Turner, in his mercantile business which had its beginnings in the early 1820s. A daughter, Elise, was born to the couple on January 22, 1866. In order to regain the rights of full citizenship, David Todd applied in May 1867 for a pardon under President Andrew Johnson's amnesty proclamation of May 29, 1865. Johnson's proclamation supplemented President Lincoln's proclamation of December 8, 1863, which declared a general amnesty for most persons, but required applications for special pardons for seven classes of persons such as Confederate officials and Confederate military officers above the rank of colonel. Under Johnson's proclamation, 14 classes of persons were excluded from the general amnesty. The pardons of the 95 Madison County, Alabama residents in these categories are discussed in an earlier article by the author. David Todd's request for pardon and the recommendation by his cousin, J.B.S. Todd, are shown below:

"Huntsville, May 15, 1867

His Excellency
Andrew Johnson
President
Washington DC

Mr. President

Having taken an active part in the late war on the side of the South & having since the surrender of all the Southern armies taken at Nashville Tenn the oath described under the 'Amnesty Proclamation' I would respectfully request that you grant me dispensation from the penalties of being worth more than $20,000 & having been a soldier in the Mexican war, taken an oath to support the Constitution of the United States, both exceptions being disqualifications to vote or have anything but an existence or privilege of living in my home with a keen patriotic feeling. I fought in 1846-47 and with the same idea of duty in the last war to the best of my ability & can again shoulder my gun in the defense of what is my country. Prior years have satisfied me as to what is my country and to that is my allegiance due.

Respectfully &
Your Servant
David H. Todd"

****

"Washington, D. C.
June 22nd 1867

The President:

I have the honor to enclose the application of David H. Todd of Huntsville, Alabama, for a release and pardon of the laws and penalties incurred in consequence of participation in the late rebellion, and to respectfully recommend and request that Executive clemency be extended to him. His letter is frank and explicit and the promise it contains explicit and positive. Knowing him from his boyhood I have every confidence in his plighted word. I also appeal to your Excellency's clemency in his behalf on my own account - twenty years of active service in the army of the Unites States and my services in the army during the late rebellion in defense of the Union, I promise myself, will induce you to favor this application.

I am very Respectfully
Your Obt Servt
J.B.S. Todd
Dakota Ty"

General J. B. S. Todd states that David Todd's letter is "frank and explicit" and it is certainly that and quite different from any of the other Madison County applications. Its tone is what one might expect from a "soldier of fortune" or, at least, a professional soldier and David Todd's career, to that point, is even suggestive of the former. This characterization together with the ever present factor of his special relationship could account for the problems he encountered during his Richmond prison assignment. He probably thought his responses, the accounts of which may have been exaggerated, were required to maintain order and, so far as is known, no official charges of cruelty were ever filed against him by either the Federal or the

Confederate government. It will be noted that even the frivolous charges of Robert G. Scott were investigated expeditiously.

As yet, there is no other information available concerning David Todd's remaining years. He died on July 30, 1871 and was probably buried near his father-in-law, Daniel B. Turner, in Plot 4-6-5 of Huntsville's Maple Hill Cemetery, but their stones have not survived. Turner died in January 1867. So let us think a little more kindly of Captain David H. Todd as we view the item below, which is a copy of his funeral notice in the Emile Todd Helm Papers:

FUNERAL NOTICE
The friends and acquaintances of the
Late CAPTAIN DAVID H. TODD and family, are
invited to attend his funeral at the Church of the Nativity, this
afternoon at
5 ° o'clock.
HUNTSVILLE, ALABAMA August 1, 1871

APPENDIX

"Camp near Corinth (Tennessee) April 21, 1862

Capt. D. Todd:

Dear Sir - I have just received your letter requesting particulars concerning the death of your brother, Sam'l B. Todd. He was my particular friend and I lament his loss as I would that of my own brother. We fought side-by-side unhurt through the battle of the 61 and slept together that night in one of the enemy's tents. At about ten o'clock next day, when our regiment was making a charge upon the enemy, he fell, pierced through the lower part of the abdomen by what I suppose to have been a Minie ball, from the nature of the wound. As soon as possible afterwards, Lieut. Field, myself and two other men, carried him out of range in a blanket, procured an ambulance and sent him to the hospital. Our regiment was ordered to another part of the field, and I found it impossible to get an opportunity of seeing him afterwards I understand that one of our men, named George French, who was wounded and returned to the city, stated before he left that your brother was put into one of our wagons, died on the way in to Corinth, and was buried by the side of the road. French can be found at French's Auction Store, Poydras St. See Directory. If this be true, I don't think that the men who were present, or who drove the wagon, belong to this regiment, as I have been unable to find any one who knows anything about it. If true, however, it would be easy to recover the body.

I have written to his widow, giving her the particulars of this unhappy affair, and should I obtain any further information I will communicate with you both.

Respectfully yours,

G. W. Stoddard"

"Corinth (Tennessee) 22 April '62

Friend Dave,

Yours of the 18th at hand, I regret sincerely that even at this late date you should not be in possession of the facts concerning the death of your Brother. It certainly has been from no fault of mine, as I have made a special request of each member of the company who has returned (and there has been some 10 or 12) to see that your brother's family were made acquainted with all the particulars in our possession. I thought they might do this much as a large portion of our time, immediately after our return from Shiloh, was absorbed in getting their furloughs, discharges, etc.

Well to the facts: from the time I first met you brother at Camp Crescent to the time I last saw him, can heartily testify that he conducted himself in every respect as becomes a first class soldier. On Sunday he fought with us the whole day. On Monday morning we were under fire for a considerable length of time without being able to reply. The Washington Artillery was placed in battery, a very advanced position - we supported them under the most murderous fire you ever had any idea of. The Yankees advanced steadily, the whiz of the minie balls increased at a fearful rate. I heard the artillery boys calling on their mates for 'Cannister,' the Yankees were within 70 or 80 yards and becoming very visible. The artillery lumbered to the rear, one piece, of which one after another all the horses were shot down, by that delay lost our Regt some 3 or 4 gun shots - we were ordered to advance - done so - fired 3 or 4 rounds and drove the Yankees back and as we were in a very exposed position and the Yankees entirely under cover, we were ordered to fall back to a Ravine. It was in falling back that your brother was shot. I was not aware of his being absent when we formed in the Ravine, we had been there but a short time, however, when I saw him coming down the hill apparently wounded. Stoddard, myself and 2 or 3 others immediately ran to him. Bosworth unstrapped his blanket from his saddle and we put him in and carried him to the ambulance. He was shot by a minie ball, which I believe passed entirely through his body. I noticed the wound only in front in the lower part of the abdomen, from which the intestines protruded. We left him in the ambulance & cautioned the driver particularly about driving carefully. He seemed to think his wound mortal and the last remark in answer to mine saying 'I hoped it was not serious' was 'Ah. Lieut., I believe they have got me this time.' The ambulance drove off and that was the last time I ever saw him. Private Geo. B. French (now in the City) says he saw him afterwards in the ambulance and talked with him and afterwards saw the driver of the same ambulance who told him that his friend (meaning your brother) had died and they had buried him. This is all the information I have about his death. You had better call on French. I gave three or four little things from his effects to your brother (who called on me) and to your brother-in-law - have forgotten the names of both - the remainder I sent to his wife - there was very little, but you know how soon a soldier gets rid of all surplus weight.

I made the following mention of him in my report to the Colonel:

'On the 7th, the first charge, Private Samuel B. Todd was mortally wounded (I may be permitted to observe that he is a brother-in-law of Abraham Lincoln, Pres. of the Northern Republic). Both here and in the engagement on the previous day, he displayed remarkable coolness, bravery and courage. His loss will be a source of deep regret to his fellow soldiers. Always pleasant and ready to do his duty, either in the trenches with a spade or on the field of battle, he died as he had lived, a true Knight worthy to be remembered hereafter.

You must excuse not only the composition but the lack of legibility as I am flat on my back in the Crescent Hospital.

Yours,
Seth R. Field Lt. Cmdg.
Co.A
Cres.Reg.'"

THE BIRNEY BROTHERS OF HUNTSVILLE, ALABAMA

Raised as unionists and abolitionists,
These brothers took their convictions to war

By David L. Lady

Although William and David Birney were born in Madison County, both served as United States Army generals during the American Civil War. Older brother William was born in Huntsville in 1819, and David on a plantation outside of Huntsville in 1825.

The boys were the sons of James G. Birney, a rich Kentucky planter, newspaper publisher, and Presidential candidate. James came to Alabama to practice law and to farm. He was very successful and served as mayor of Huntsville from 1829-1830. As he grew into middle age, his evolving religious beliefs caused him to adopt an anti-slavery attitude. James became one of the most notable of Southern abolitionists and he became a southern agent for the American Colonization Society in 1832. Within a year he resigned, disillusioned with the Society's scheme of gradual emancipation based on ideas of racial inferiority. In 1833 the family returned to Kentucky where James emancipated their slaves, and then moved to Ohio and Pennsylvania. James' views on emancipation continued to evolve, as he came to espouse first gradual and then immediate emancipation of all slaves in the United States.

Convinced of the importance of united action by all opponents of slavery, he moved to Cincinnati in 1836, and established the newspaper *Philanthropist*, one of the first anti-slavery papers in the Midwest. The growth of Birney's influence in the anti-slavery movement is evident in his correspondence and pamphleteering, as well as in his many public lectures. He resigned as editor of *The Philanthropist* in

1837 and moved to New York to become the corresponding secretary of the American Anti-Slavery Society. Birney saw the need for a new political party whose sole purpose was to promote the abolition of slavery, and with his leadership, the Liberty Party was founded in 1840. As its presidential candidate in 1840 and 1844, Birney argued that neither the Bible nor the Constitution supported slavery.

Birney retired from public life after the election of 1844, although he continued to write occasional articles for the anti-slavery press. James' beliefs and examples inspired both his sons to become politically active in the Republican Party, which was founded in the 1850s, and espoused several of the anti-slavery policies of the Liberty Party. With the election of Abraham Lincoln to the Presidency and the secession crisis, both William and David entered the Union Army and became the most distinguished of Huntsville's four generals in blue.

WILLIAM BIRNEY

A scholar who enlisted black regiments and led them to battle

William Birney

Following the family's move north, William was educated at four colleges including Yale, became fluent in thirteen languages, and first worked as a lawyer. Moving to Europe, he was a professor of literature in England and France. William returned to United States in 1853, and worked as newspaper publisher of *The Daily Register* in Pennsylvania.

In 1861 he entered the 1st New Jersey (NJ) Infantry as a Captain, and led his company at the First Battle of Bull Run. He was later appointed to be Major of the 4th NJ Infantry, but quickly became their Colonel, leading the regiment at Chancellorsville. Many suspected that he owed his promotion to political influence for "as a combat soldier, he was a fine linguist."

After Chancellorsville, William was reassigned to the Union forces garrisoning Baltimore, Maryland, a loyal slave state. The Union Army encouraged slave owners to free their slaves in order to enlist them into regiments of United States Colored Troops (USCT). When slave holders proved reluctant to release their male slaves in order to enlist, William Birney put his abolitionist beliefs into action by actively recruiting African-Americans, whether enslaved by "loyal" or "secesh" owners. On July 24, 1863, three weeks after the Battle of Gettysburg, he was among the Union officers who freed the inmates of a slave trader's jail on Pratt Street near the Baltimore harbor. They found a grisly scene. The slaves were confined in sweltering cells or in the bricked-in yard of "Camliu's slave-pen," where "no tree or shrub grows" and "the mid-day sun pours down its scorching rays," Birney wrote. Among those imprisoned was a 4-month-old born in the jail and a 24-month-old who had spent all but the first month of his life behind bars. "In this place I found 26 men, 1 boy, 29 women and 3 infants," Col. Birney wrote to his commanding officer. "Sixteen of the men were shackled and one had his legs chained together by ingeniously contrived locks connected by chains suspended to his waist." The liberation of the slave jails marked the end of Baltimore's slave trade.

Benefiting from influential friends in the Lincoln administration and the Congress, William Birney was in 1863 appointed Colonel of the 22d United States Colored Troops (USCT), and was soon appointed Brigadier General and made one of three superintendents employed in enlisting escaped slaves into Federal regiments; in less than a year he had enlisted seven USCT regiments.

Among these regiments was the Fourth USCT, initially part of the garrison of Baltimore, Maryland. On 20 July, 1863, two companies of the 4th USCT (Companies 'A' and 'B,' which had been in uniform for only five days), represented the United States Army at a garrison flag presentation ceremony.

General Birney made the presentation speech. The following excerpt indicates his strong feelings for free blacks enlisting in the US Army:

> "The flag they present you today, is in token of their loyalty. Their hearts are true. Whoever else may be swayed from duty, the black remains firm. Pluck him from the very core of rebeldom and he is a true man. You may trust him. All his aspirations are for the success of the right, the triumph of the nation. For him the success of traitors is his own degradation, the dishonor of his family, the doom of his race to perpetual infamy."

In 1864 he led a brigade of USCT to the Department of the South, becoming the commanding general of the Federal District of Florida. Later he and his brigade went with the Tenth Army Corps to Virginia as part of the Army of the James. He led his brigade without much distinction in the battles around Bermuda Hundred and north of the James River during the siege of Petersburg. In December, 1864 his brigade was assigned to the 2d Division of the all-USCT Twenty-Fifth Army Corps and he soon was appointed to command a division. In 1865 General Birney ran afoul of his Corps and later Army Commander, Major General Edward Ord, who considered him a mediocre commander and a poor disciplinarian, and had initially opposed to employing USCT regiments in combat.

William Birney's division was included in the detachment of the Army of the James that was moved south of the Appomattox River by General Ord to strengthen the final assault of Petersburg. Following the fall of Petersburg and Richmond, Ord led these units in pursuit of the Army of Northern Virginia.

On April 7th, 1865 (two days before Lee's surrender), General Birney was relieved of duty by General Ord and sent to take command of the army depot at City Point, Virginia. Ord stated that he wanted the black units under his best commanders for the final fight with the Army of Northern Virginia. The two brigades of Birney's former division were each assigned to other Federal divisions and the both fought the next day as part of the battle-line which repulsed the Army of Northern Virginia's final attack of the war at Appomattox Court House. Although General Birney wrote political sponsors protesting the injustice of his relief, no action was taken to restore him to another command. With the end of the war he resigned his volunteer commission and left the military.

William Birney was brevetted Major General in the post-war mass brevet-promotion of deserving officers (Brevets were honorary promotions in recognition of good service, there being no military awards for distinguished service at this time). He resided in Florida and later Washington DC after the war, where he served as a US Attorney for the District of Columbia. Although he remained proud of his service to abolitionism and the Union, and published a very popular biography of his father, he no longer actively supported African-American causes. He died in 1907 at his home in Forest Glen, Maryland.

DAVID BIRNEY

A Political General, but also a Fighter

Younger brother David was educated in Massachusetts and then practiced law in Philadelphia. Like his father he was prominent in the abolitionist movement and the pre-war Republican Party.

In 1861 he raised the 23d Pennsylvania (PA) Infantry Regiment, largely at his own expense. Initially appointed as Lieutenant Colonel, 23d PA, he was promoted to Colonel in August, 1861. Although a non-professional, he was promoted to Brigadier General in 1862. As a "political general," he was

avid Birney (1825-1864)

much resented within the Army of the Potomac for his support of the Republican Party, the abolitionist movement, and for being critical of Army commander Major General George McClellan. Serving as regimental and later brigade commander with the Army of the Potomac's Third Corps, Birney was befriended by Generals Phil Kearney and Joe Hooker, who were also harsh critics of General McClellan.

Birney's aggressive seeking of political support for promotion made him very unpopular with his fellow officers despite his proven competence. Theodore Lyman, a Federal staff officer, described him in this way:

> "He was a pale, Puritanical figure, with a demeanor of unmoveable coldness; only he would smile politely when you spoke to him. He was spare in person, with a thin face, light-blue eyes, and sandy hair. As a General he took very good care of his Staff and saw they got due promotion. He was a man, too, who looked out for his own interests sharply and knew the mainspring of military advancement. His unpopularity among some persons arose partly from his own promotion, which, however he deserved, and partly from his cold covert manner."

David Birney was noted as a good disciplinarian and trainer of soldiers and as a competent, even brilliant, fighting commander. He was also arrogant and contentious, following his own counsel and disdaining contrary opinions and even lawful orders. Accused by his own corps commander of disobeying orders at The Battle of Fair Oaks, a Court Martial found him not guilty due to testimony of his brigade commander. He was also accused of failing to support MG Meade's assault on Jackson's Second Confederate Army Corps during the Battle of Fredericksburg, but was never charged with dereliction or disobedience.

Birney was promoted to Major General in May, 1863 for displaying fine leadership at Chancellorsville where his division had suffered the heaviest casualties in the Army. He was by now regarded as one of the best of the Federal division commanders, and as the Army of the Potomac marched toward Gettysburg, David Birney was identified as a potential army corps commander should there be casualties among the higher ranking officers.

Major General Birney at Gettysburg

On the morning of the second day of the Battle of Gettysburg, Major General Dan Sickles, commanding the Federal Third Army Corps, ordered his divisions forward from Cemetery Ridge to occupy the Peach Orchard. General Humphreys' Second Division was formed in line of battle along the Emmitsburg Road, and General Birney was forced to stretch his First Division's line over too much territory in order to occupy the ground between Devil's Den and the Peach Orchard. When General Longstreet's Confederates attacked in the afternoon, Birney had great difficulty defending his position; he had no second line of troops or forces in reserve, and could not launch strong counterattacks or reinforce his line. Late in the day General Sickles was seriously wounded and carried from the battlefield. Birney as senior division commander became the temporary corps commander, but his line of battle was already pierced by the Confederate attack at the Peach Orchard and his men were withdrawing toward Cemetery Ridge. Birney's attempt to reform his men along a line from the Emmitsburg Road toward Little Round Top was undone by the rapid advance of

Barksdale's Brigade and other Confederate forces, and the entire Third Corps was driven toward Cemetery Ridge, suffering very heavy casualties along the way.

David Birney was himself wounded the afternoon of 2 July, but returned to lead the Third Corps after receiving first aid. He was extremely distraught by the defeat of the Third Corps, stating that he wished that he had been shot and killed like his horse. Later that evening his spirits revived and he reorganized his Corps to support the battle line along Cemetery Ridge. During General Meade's council of war that evening, General Birney was one of the officers who voted to stay on the defensive. His men were placed to help resist Pickett's Charge the next day, but were not called on to engage the Confederates.

In 1864, during General Grant's march toward Richmond, David Birney commanded a division in the Army of the Potomac's Second Corps. He led his men with distinction during the Battles of The Wilderness, Spotsylvania, Cold Harbor, and the assaults on Petersburg. In the autumn that year, General Grant appointed him to permanent command of the Tenth Corps of the Army of the James, then serving in the siege works opposite Richmond. This Corps included a division of USCT, for Birney was one of the few senior generals in the Army of the Potomac who did not object to commanding African-Americans in battle. Birney's last fight was an offensive north of the James River, along the Darbytown Road (6-7 October); he led his Tenth Corps from the front although suffering from malaria. By 7 October, General Birney's health collapsed and he became bedridden and delirious. He was rushed by train to his home in Philadelphia in order to convalesce. State elections were occurring at that time, and Birney had himself carried to the polls where he voted a straight Republican ticket. He lingered until October 19th 1864, in his delirium shouting orders and encouraging his men.

His final words were "Keep your eyes on that flag, boys!"

52703297R00177

Made in the USA
Lexington, KY
18 September 2019